CW01262832

Palgrave Pioneers in Criminology

Series Editors
David Polizzi, Indiana State University, Terre Haute, IN, USA
James Hardie-Bick, School of Law, Politics & Sociology, University of Sussex, Brighton, UK

Palgrave Pioneers in Criminology examines the theorists and their work that has shaped the discussions and debates in the interdisciplinary, growing field of Criminology, focussing particularly on Critical Criminology. The pioneers range from established to newer academics in Criminology and beyond from other disciplines including Sociology, Psychology, Philosophy and Law. Each book in the series offers an overview of a pioneer and their contribution to the field of Criminology, from the perspective of one author or multiple contributors. The series charts the historical development of key theories and brings discussions up to the present day to consider the past, present and future relevance of these theories for society. This series presents in-depth, engaging, new discussions about this field and the directions that it will continue to grow in.

More information about this series at
http://www.palgrave.com/gp/series/15996

Tony Jefferson

Stuart Hall, Conjunctural Analysis and Cultural Criminology

A Missed Moment

palgrave
macmillan

Tony Jefferson
School of Social, Political and Global Studies
Keele University
Newcastle-under-Lyme, UK

Palgrave Pioneers in Criminology
ISBN 978-3-030-74730-5   ISBN 978-3-030-74731-2   (eBook)
https://doi.org/10.1007/978-3-030-74731-2

© The Editor(s) (if applicable) and The Author(s), under exclusive license to Springer Nature Switzerland AG 2021
This work is subject to copyright. All rights are solely and exclusively licensed by the Publisher, whether the whole or part of the material is concerned, specifically the rights of translation, reprinting, reuse of illustrations, recitation, broadcasting, reproduction on microfilms or in any other physical way, and transmission or information storage and retrieval, electronic adaptation, computer software, or by similar or dissimilar methodology now known or hereafter developed.
The use of general descriptive names, registered names, trademarks, service marks, etc. in this publication does not imply, even in the absence of a specific statement, that such names are exempt from the relevant protective laws and regulations and therefore free for general use.
The publisher, the authors and the editors are safe to assume that the advice and information in this book are believed to be true and accurate at the date of publication. Neither the publisher nor the authors or the editors give a warranty, expressed or implied, with respect to the material contained herein or for any errors or omissions that may have been made. The publisher remains neutral with regard to jurisdictional claims in published maps and institutional affiliations.

This Palgrave Macmillan imprint is published by the registered company Springer Nature Switzerland AG
The registered company address is: Gewerbestrasse 11, 6330 Cham, Switzerland

Photo of Stuart Hall

'The challenge of modernity is to live without illusions and without becoming disillusioned'
—Antonio Gramsci

'Where I am, I don't know, I'll never know, in the silence you don't know, you must go on, I can't go on, I'll go on'
—Samuel Beckett

'…when/ you're falling behind in this/ big blue world/ Oh you got to/ Hold on, hold on/ You got to hold on'
—Tom Waits

The proceeds from the sale of this book will go to the Stuart Hall Foundation

Preface

It all started with Stuart's funeral. I couldn't make it because I was going to be in India. I felt bad, but the thought of postponing a trip that had been long in the planning and difficult to organise, and going through the whole process anew at a later date, felt like a step too far. Instead, I rationalised my decision (Stuart would understand; he'd say 'make the trip') and spent the time when the funeral would have been taking place quietly thinking of him in a hotel room in Jaipur, having just completed a six-hour drive from Delhi. Not the same as being at the funeral, of course, but the thought was there.

Then there were the Obituary notices. Masses of them. From all over the world. By those who knew him well and those who had never met him. It was an extraordinary outpouring of love, affection and gratitude. Again, I went awol, even though I had known him for over 40 years, as teacher, mentor and collaborator, but also as a close friend. As with the missed funeral, I rationalised my decision: nobody asked me (although in the internet age nobody needs another's permission). There were, however, deeper reasons for not writing something then. First, I had been out of cultural studies for a long time and felt that

I could not do proper justice to his intellectual accomplishments. For those, like Stuart, for whom such accomplishments have been central to their lives, these necessarily constitute a significant element in their obituaries. At the same time, I felt unable to write about him just as friend. Partly because, for the reason just mentioned, his accomplishments could not be simply sidelined. Partly because, borrowing Wordsworth's notion of poetry as 'emotions recollected in tranquillity', I never felt tranquil enough to recollect, and then write about, the emotions I was feeling around his death. But perhaps mostly because friendship is so difficult to write about. 'Happy families are all alike', as Tolstoy memorably said, which explains the story teller's preference for the unhappy family, because, as Tolstoy continued, 'every unhappy family is unhappy in its own way'. Good friendships are similarly 'all alike' in their indefinable combination of mutual affection, trust, recognition, ease and pleasure in each other's company. How to write interestingly about the many different occasions when we 'did' friendship, since these were, in essence, 'all alike'?

Finally, there was his memorial the year after the funeral. It was a big gathering of family and friends. There were allocated speaking slots and a time for memories from the floor. Contributing thus entailed a long walk to the microphone, the discipline to be brief and to the point, and the ability to say something revealing or amusing or, preferably, both (to an audience replete with intellectual heavyweights). That was the moment I was going to rectify my absence from his funeral and my failure to write an obituary notice by sharing an anecdote; my moment, finally, to acknowledge publicly something of what Stuart meant to me. But maybe my anecdote wasn't revealing or amusing enough? Maybe it said more about me than Stuart? Maybe the occasion was too august for such a minor intervention? Or maybe, I rationalised, other people needed to tell their stories more than I needed to tell mine. And so the moment passed, again.

Then, several years later and out of the blue, came the invitation to write a book about someone who had been a 'major figure' in criminology, and that someone could be Stuart. Being cautious, long retired and still feeling I knew too little of Stuart's later intellectual work, I hesitated. But not for long. Deep down I knew this was it; the moment when I could rectify my previous 'missed moments'. My 'now or never' moment. The moment to bear witness, albeit indirectly, to the important role Stuart played in my life. This, then, is the 'long' story of how I came to write this book about Stuart. However, this is also a book about cultural criminology. And, although my own trajectory from cultural studies had not taken me into the cultural criminology 'camp' but to psychosocial criminology, I nonetheless began to feel that if anyone was going to write a book such as this, it might as well be me. I had had a long apprenticeship in cultural studies, including working with Stuart on the crucial 'crossover' texts, *Resistance through Rituals* and *Policing the Crisis*, and also a long career in criminology. There were few better placed to attempt such a book, which is, in the end, a book that asks a simple question: Is the meaning of 'culture' in cultural criminology the same as the meaning of 'culture' in Stuart's version of cultural studies; and if not, why not? The cryptic answer is 'conjunctural analysis'; the longer one requires you to read the book.

I have given myself the liberty here of speaking of 'Stuart', the name by which I always knew him. In the main text, however, he becomes, on the advice of one of my trusted readers, 'Hall'. Although difficult at first, this was the right decision since it is Hall's work, not him as a person, which is the subject matter of this book.

Sheffield, UK   Tony Jefferson

Acknowledgements

Acknowledgements are never easy because we all stand on the shoulders of giants (even the giants). However, confining myself, in the book's spirit, to my more conjunctural debts, this book would never have been started but for the invitation, out of the blue, by Anthony Amatrudo, to write a short book on one of a number of persons from a list he supplied, for a series called 'Pioneers in Criminology'. Stuart Hall was one of the names supplied. My decision to accept was helped by the fact that after a long time thinking more about criminology than cultural studies, I was invited to talk at two cultural studies conferences in 2014, just months after Stuart died, one at Birmingham University marking the 50th anniversary of the Birmingham Centre for Contemporary Cultural Studies, the other at Goldsmiths, University of London exploring Stuart's legacy. These got me thinking again about cultural studies. So, a big thank you to the conference organisers, Kieran Connell and Matthew Hilton (Birmingham) and Julian Henriques, David Morley and Van Goblot (Goldsmiths) for the invites. Also to *Theory, Culture and Society* for the serendipitously well-timed invitation to review Stuart's posthumously published Memoir *Familiar Stranger* (2017, Hall with

Schwarz) and, at my suggestion, *Stuart Hall Selected Political writings* (2017, edited by Davison, Featherstone and Schwarz). After these dips back into cultural studies, I was feeling re-familiarised with the field and in a position to say 'yes' when the book invitation followed.

As it happened, this coincided with a moment of frenzied publishing of Stuart's work, some of it never before published lectures. These books proved invaluable to me, not just in making available in one place material that was otherwise widely dispersed or previously unavailable, but also in providing informed and thoughtful introductory route maps through the material. In no particular order, then, my thanks go: to Jennifer Daryl Slack and Larry Grossberg (2016) for rescuing Stuart's highly influential US lecture notes from the 'gnawing criticism of the mice' in *Cultural Studies 1983,* which they also edited and introduced; to Kobena Mercer for his similar rescue job on Stuart's 1994 W. E. B. Dubois lectures at Harvard in 1994, published in 2017 as *The Fateful Triangle*; and to David Morley, whose two-volume selection of Stuart Hall's *Essential Essays* were certainly that to me: published in 2019, my copies are as well-thumbed and annotated as any in my possession. Also essential was Nic Beech's monumental attempt at a complete biography of Hall's work in any and every medium, including all translations: this was my 'bible' for tracking down difficult to find material. Rob Waters' invitation to present a paper at the Birmingham University Conference 2019 to mark the opening there of the Stuart Hall Archive gave me an opportunity to try out some of the ideas informing the book.

Unusually for me, this book is singly authored. However, I regard it as a collective effort. My team of readers, serendipitously assembled but between them with considerable expertise and long experience in cultural studies, criminology, sociology, psychology and psychoanalysis, has been indispensable. They helped me when my belief in the enterprise was flagging; they rescued me from blind alleys; they suggested things I might read; they supplied things I should read; they helped me think through knotty problems; they told me what I didn't know; they unlocked what I didn't know I didn't know; they were kindly in their criticisms and generous in their support. Without them, the loneliness of the long distance writer would have been…lonelier. In short, they helped with everything from broadening my horizons and forestalling my errors to highlighting my 'tics' and shortening my sentences. It helped that these were also my friends, many of whom I have known for a long time (several since our shared postgraduate days at Birmingham) and most of whom I had collaborated with before. Nevertheless, friendship and collegiality never got in the way of the task in hand: ensuring the book was as good as it could be. With that in mind, I wish to reverse something we said, in jest, in the acknowledgements in *Policing the Crisis:* 'all the errors contained in this book are somebody else's fault, and the good bits belong to the authors'. Rather, I wish to say, in earnest, that the good bits in this book were a team effort, and the errors are all mine. In alphabetical order, the team were Dave Brown, Ros Brunt, John Clarke, Lynn Chancer, Dave Gadd, Wendy Hollway, Bob Jeffrey, Brian Roberts and Joe Sim. My heartfelt thanks to you all.

Praise for *Stuart Hall, Conjunctural Analysis and Cultural Criminology*

"This is a book which wears its erudition and intellectual ambition lightly. Yet it is steeped in a knowledge of cultural studies: its histories, quarrels and debates. Examining these, Tony Jefferson shows how they can usefully inform an understanding of the ways 'conjunctures' actually work. The book also places an innovative emphasis on the relevance of psychoanalysis and the arena of the psycho-social as means for developing deeper analyses of the conjunctural."

"The intellectual scope of the book makes it a really original, enlightening and accessible read—not only for criminologists, but for all those interested in any aspect of social and cultural research. Particularly because it demonstrates how to apply a wide range of theoretical arguments to the very specifics of concrete situations. And because it does this through the careful and rigorous use of highly relevant contemporary case studies."

—Rosalind Brunt, *Visiting Research Fellow, Media Studies, Sheffield Hallam University, UK*

"An incisive and perceptive reminder of Stuart Hall's towering intellectual legacy and of the urgent need to resuscitate conjunctural analysis. The benefits of applying it to issues and movements such as Brexit, Black Lives Matter and Trumpism could hardly be more evident or more topical."

—David Brown, *Emeritus Professor, University of New South Wales, Sydney, Australia*

"There is nothing more important right now than to understand the current conjuncture, and Jefferson, whose psychosocial work in cultural studies and criminology remains groundbreaking, is just the person to illuminate the ways race, class, and heteronormativity are yoked together currently and expressed in the Brexit movement and in Trumpism. A first-class cultural analyst, Jefferson goes where few go, concluding with fascinating insights into unconscious processes, defenses, and, in a nonreductive way, an analysis of how, in the current moment, the social world is shaping psychic life and psychic life, in turn, is shaping the social world."

—Lynne Layton, *Harvard Medical School, Boston MA, USA. Author of Toward a Social Psychoanalysis: Culture, Character, and Normative Unconscious Processes*

"Tony Jefferson's much needed intellectual tribute to Stuart Hall brilliantly demonstrates the centrality of conjunctural analysis across all of Hall's work including but not limited to the spectacular cultural and criminological classic *Policing the Crisis*. Most importantly, Jefferson's work succeeds in making the powerful political case that Hall's conjunctural analysis is the opposite of outdated. This method needs rigorous re-application now more than ever to best illuminate, and understand how to respond to, neoliberal capitalist inequalities and the growing psychosocial appeals of populist authoritarianianism."

—Lynn Chancer, *Professor and Executive Officer, PhD Program in Sociology, Graduate Center of the City University of New York*

"Stuart Hall was without question a pioneer in criminology, whilst certainly never a criminologist. But then, he was also a pioneer in media and cultural studies, race, migration and post-colonial scholarship, political theory and so much else. Amongst Hall's most valuable gifts to criminology was that of never being contained by it. Tony Jefferson honours Hall's legacies to critical thought in and beyond criminology by seeking to apply his methods and insights in the present. Jefferson consciously writes in the spirit of what he owes to Hall. And so, he gives us a combative, original, provocative book that ranges far beyond the standard criminological topics to include encounters with Trump and Brexit; the politics of race and nation; populism and the currents of anger in our personal and political lives. Jefferson wants us to attend to the contradictions and particularities of the conjuncture, as Hall so tirelessly did."

—Richard Sparks, *Professor of Criminology, Edinburgh University*

"Stuart Hall and his co-authors, Tony Jefferson prominently among them, gave us *Resistance through Rituals* (1975) and *Policing the Crisis* (1978)—landmark books that deployed cultural, historical and neo-Marxist theory to develop brilliant explanations of youth crime and law and order politics. But criminology has mostly failed to appreciate Hall's break-through analyses or to assimilate the neo-Gramscian concepts he deployed, the most important of which is 'conjunctural analysis'—the structural equivalent of a history of the present. Tony Jefferson's timely new book clearly and accessibly re-introduces Stuart Hall's ideas for a criminological readership and goes on to demonstrate, with flair and imagination, how Hall's concepts can illuminate the complex, disturbing conjuncture that we are living through today."

—David Garland, *Arthur T. Vanderbilt Professor of Law and Professor of Sociology, New York University*

Contents

1 **Introduction and Overview** 1
   Chapter by Chapter Overview 10
   References 15

Part I Stuart Hall and Conjunctural Analysis

2 **Conjunctural Analysis Part One: From Early Political Writings to *Resistance Through Rituals*** 23
   What Is a Conjuncture? 24
   What Is Conjunctural Analysis? 27
   RTR and *PTC*: Different Sides of the Same Conjunctural Coin 32
   References 37

3 **Conjunctural Analysis Part Two: The Case of *Policing the Crisis*** 39
   A Short Detour via Marx 40
   PTC Part I: From Particular 'Mugging' Trials to the Determinations of an Over-Reaction 41

	Part II: From the Reception of Media Messages to the Determinations of Ideologies of Crime and Punishment	43
	Part III: From Moral Panics to the Determinations of a Crisis of Hegemony	44
	Part IV: From the Lives of Black Youths to the Determinations of the Politics of Mugging	46
	Conclusion	53
	References	54

Part II Cultural Criminology, Theorising and Stuart Hall

4 Cultural Criminology Part One: The Problems with a Theory-Driven Methodology — 57
An Overview of the Cultural Criminology Project — 58
City Limits and the Limitations of Theory — 65
'Merton with Energy, Katz with Structure': An Imaginary Synthesis — 71
Summary and Conclusion — 77
References — 79

5 Cultural Criminology Part Two: Ethnography, Carnival and the Need for Critique — 81
A Tale of Two Ethnographies — 83
Comparing the Ethnographies in Their Own Terms — 89
Comparing Ethnographies in Terms of their Relationship to Conjunctural Analysis — 96
Comparing a Conjunctural and a Cultural Criminological Approach to Carnival — 99
Cultural Criminology and Conjunctural Analysis: A Summary Conclusion — 106
References — 108

6	Hall's Theorising: The Importance of a Principled Eclecticism	111
	Principle 1: A Historically Materialist Starting Point and Problematic	113
	Principle 2: A Dialogic Approach to Critique	115
	Principle 3: A Complex Understanding of Social Relations	119
	Summary and Conclusion	134
	References	135

Part III Conjunctural Analysis Today: Brexit, Trump and the Politics of Difference

7	Race, Immigration and the Politics of Difference	139
	New Ethnicities, New Identities	139
	The Multicultural Question and the Politics of Difference	147
	References	154

8	The Brexit Conjuncture Part One: The Referendum Result and How We Got to 9/11	157
	The 2016 Referendum Results	158
	Critiquing a Common Sense Understanding of Brexit	160
	Building a Better Analysis: Getting Started	161
	The Geography and Demography of the Leave Vote	166
	From Phenomenon to Explanation: Beginning the Analysis	170
	Deepening the Analysis: How We Got There	175
	References	182

9	The Brexit Conjuncture Part Two: From 9/11 to the 2016 Referendum	187
	But How Has It Been for the Middle Classes?	188
	From New Labour to the Coalition Government, 2010	192
	From the Coalition Government to 2016	195
	Immigration, Racism and Xenophobia	198

	The Brexit Conjuncture: What Kind of 'Moment'?	205
	References	212
10	**Conclusion: From *Policing the Crisis* to Trump, and Beyond**	215
	The Politics of Populism: Is a Left Populism Possible?	218
	Authoritarian Populism and the Authoritarian State: Complementary Poles	220
	Ideal Types or Conjunctural Analysis: The Importance of Contradictions	223
	After Trump: Climate Change, the Refugee Crisis, Black Lives Matter and the Covid Pandemic	230
	Coming to an End, for the Moment	243
	References	244

Part IV Coda

11	**Hall, Psychoanalysis and the Problem of Populist Anger**	249
	Why Is It Difficult to Think About Anger in Relation to the Conjuncture?	250
	Why Did Hall Find Psychoanalysis and the Psychosocial Difficult to Work with?	252
	Why Have Psychoanalytic Attempts at a General Theory Been 'Largely Unsuccessful'?	254
	How Might Psychoanalysis Focusing 'on Its Own Object' Provide a Way Forward?	258
	So, Where Does All This Leave Us, Politically?	264
	References	267

Index   269

About the Author

Tony Jefferson was a Postgraduate Student at the Centre for Contemporary Cultural Studies, Birmingham University during the 1970s where he worked with Stuart Hall and others to produce *Resistance through Rituals* (1976/2006) and *Policing the Crisis* (1978/2013). Thereafter, he has taught at the universities of Sheffield and Keele and researched and published widely on policing, masculinity, race and crime, fear of crime and racial violence. He has held Visiting Professorships in Denmark, Sweden, Australia and the USA. His books include *Controlling the Constable* (1984) and *Interpreting Policework* (1987) (both with Roger Grimshaw), *The Case Against Paramilitary Policing* (1990), *Doing Qualitative Research Differently* (2000/2013) (with Wendy Hollway) and *Psychosocial Criminology* (2007) (with David Gadd). He is currently an Emeritus Professor in Criminology at Keele University.

Abbreviations

BLM	Black Lives Matter
BNP	British National Party
CCCS	Centre for Contemporary Cultural Studies
EDL	English Defence League
ISAs	Ideological State Apparatuses
MT	*Marxism Today*
NDC	National Deviancy Conference
OU	Open University
PTC	*Policing the Crisis*
RTR	*Resistance through Rituals*
SPS	*State, Power, Socialism*
TNC	*The New Criminology*
TPOM	*The Problem of Method*
UKIP	United Kingdom Independence Party
WPCS	*Working Papers in Cultural Studies*

These will appear in full in their first usage in each chapter in which they appear but only in abbreviated format for each subsequent usage.

The list does not include abbreviations like UK, USA, EU, etc. which are so commonplace as to be self-explanatory.

Emphases within quotes. These will only be acknowledged when they have been added. Otherwise, all quotes containing emphases are as they appear in the original.

1

Introduction and Overview

For those interested in the ideas of Stuart Hall, there are now four biographies,[1] at least four edited volumes[2] and ten special issues of journals[3] specifically devoted to his ideas, the first volume of his long awaited autobiography,[4] several new collections of his writings,[5] including previously unpublished lectures,[6] and two films by John Akomfrah,[7] that can be

---

[1] Rojek (2003), Procter (2004), Davis (2004), and Scott (2017).
[2] Morley and Chen, eds. (1996), Gilroy et al., eds. (2000), Meeks, ed. (2007), and Henriques et al., eds. (2017).
[3] *Journal of Communication Inquiry* 10 (2), 1986; *Matrizes* 10 (3), 2016; *Inter-Asia Cultural Studies* 18 (2), 2017; *South Atlantic Quarterly* 115 (4), 2016; *Discourse* 36 (2), 2015; *International Journal of Cultural Studies* 19 (1), 2016; *Social Text Journal Online*, 2014; *Critical Studies in Media Communications* 33 (5), 2016; *Howard Journal of Communication* 27 (2), 2016; and *New Formations* 96/97, 2019.
[4] Hall with Schwarz (2017).
[5] Hall (2017a) and Morley, ed. (2019a, b).
[6] Hall (2016) and Hall (2017b).
[7] *The Unfinished Conversation* (2012) and *The Stuart Hall Project* (2013).

© The Author(s), under exclusive license to Springer Nature Switzerland AG 2021
T. Jefferson, *Stuart Hall, Conjunctural Analysis and Cultural Criminology*, Palgrave Pioneers in Criminology,
https://doi.org/10.1007/978-3-030-74731-2_1

consulted. So, why another volume? Why now? And, why should criminologists be interested? Over the course of eleven chapters, this book will attempt to answer these questions.

For those unfamiliar with Hall's life, I start with a brief sketch to help situate elements of the argument to come.[8] Born into the brown middle classes in Jamaica in 1932, he grew up during the struggle for independence and came to England on a Rhodes scholarship to study English Literature at Oxford in 1951. The doctoral study of Henry James that followed was interrupted by the 1956 invasions, of Egypt by an Anglo-French-Israeli alliance, and of Hungary by the Soviet Union. These seismic events led to Hall abandoning his doctorate for politics, becoming a founder member of the new left, editor of *Universities Left Review* and then *New Left Review*, and a committed Campaigner for Nuclear Disarmament. Supporting himself by supply teaching at a South London secondary modern school, his co-written *The Popular Arts* (Hall and Whannel 1964) led to a research fellowship at the newly started Centre for Contemporary Cultural Studies (CCCS) at Birmingham University, the Centre which was to create a new transdisciplinary field, namely, cultural studies. Hall went on to become its inspirational Director during its 1970s heyday and to produce a slew of writings many of which were to become classics of cultural studies. After Birmingham came his Open University (OU) years where he was the key thinker, writer and teacher-broadcaster of numerous, exciting, new OU Social Sciences courses, many of which introduced recently developed cultural studies ideas to a mass, undergraduate audience. He also began to explore questions of identity through a series of highly influential essays.

Being a committed intellectual also entailed working outside as well as inside the academy. Outside the University he was the intellectual force behind the transformation of *Marxism Today* (*MT*) from a Communist Party journal to the most significant British political journal of the

---

[8] Many short introductions to his life can be found among the obituary notices that followed his death in February 2014. The best source of these is the Stuart Hall Foundation website's 'Obituaries, Reminiscences and Commentaries' established after his death and is open to be added to. Of many moving and eloquent appraisals, Eley (2015) is probably the most comprehensive, single overview.

1980s. He also gave generously of his time in all manner of political and public settings.[9] After the demise of *MT*, he became one of the founder-editors of a new journal, *Soundings*, to which he contributed until his death in 2014. During this same, largely post-retirement, period, Hall began to champion the black arts movement, by helping to create a new arts centre, Rivington Place in Shoreditch, and through chairing two attached organisations, namely, the Institute of International Visual Arts (InIVA) and the Association of Black Photographers (Autograph). In many ways, this return to the arts, informed by the politics of culture, ethnicity and identity, constituted a fitting endpoint to an immensely productive, influential and wide-ranging political/intellectual life.

When he died, in 2014, the outpourings of grief, love and respect came from all over the globe. Variously, though remarkably consistently, these addressed: his extraordinary range of talents—as orator, writer, broadcaster, teacher, mentor, collaborator and enabler; the breadth of his knowledge, subtlety of his thinking and prolificacy of his contributions across many intellectual disciplines and fields; the depth and steadfastness of his political commitment to a juster, fairer world; and the graceful, humorous charm that constantly underpinned his generosity towards struggling student and political opponent alike. The occasional appearance of 'the Godfather of multiculturalism' label was perhaps to be expected, although it was not one Hall himself liked because multiculturalism carried such a variety of contested meanings (Hall 2000: 210–11), most of which he opposed. However, the idea that he 'was mourned like some kind of Nelson Mandela of cultural studies' (Fornäs 2014), or was described as an academic version of Usain Bolt (by Annie Paul quoted in Niaah 2014), or 'the "Che Guevara" of the academic field' (Zhang 2017), or 'the Du Bois of Britain' (by Henry Louis Gates Jr quoted in Yardley 2014; Londis 2017), neatly encapsulate, respectively, the love bordering on veneration that he generated, his peerless talent, his revolutionary spirit and the height of his intellectual standing. In similar summary

---

[9]For example, to a series of unofficial inquiries to investigate police misconduct—*Southall 23 April 1979* and *The Death of Blair Peach* (Unofficial committee of Enquiry 1980a, b); the death of Colin Roach and policing in Hackney 1945–1984 (Hall 1989); and Broadwater Farm—as well as to public inquiries like the Lawrence Inquiry (Hall et al. 1998) and as a member of The Commission on the Future of Multi-Ethnic Britain (Parekh 2000).

vein, I wish to propose that Hall is Gramsci's natural heir. What I mean by that, criminology's failure, for the most part, to appreciate what this entailed, and its contemporary relevance, will provide the spine of the book's argument.

As many of the obituary writers attest, conjunctural analysis—a term often associated with the work of Antonio Gramsci (1971)—was central to Hall's work and to the cultural studies project more generally, certainly as conceived by Hall: 'If there is a *leitmotif* running through his work it is that of conjuncture' (Bennett 2016); 'conjuncture (a Gramscian term of art found on almost every page of his work)' (Bhabha 2015); 'Stuart Hall was perhaps the most consistent practitioner of contextualism. His version…was expressed in his commitment to study the conjuncture' (Grossberg 2015); 'His unit of analysis was the conjuncture' (Henderson 2014). So, one important task will be to examine precisely what is a conjuncture; another, what conjunctural analysis entails. Broadly speaking, this requires a commitment to understanding any historical 'moment' in its full complexity.

The pre-eminent example of conjunctural analysis is widely seen to be *Policing the Crisis* (*PTC*), a text first published by Hall and others in 1978.[10] Of the 137 obituary and memorial notices I read,[11] *PTC* was easily the single most-mentioned text (with 53 mentions) and half of these added a highly complimentary adjective: 'seminal', 'magisterial', 'groundbreaking', 'exemplary'.[12] For some it was Hall's finest achievement, the culmination of the work of the CCCS, 'the most important single product of the CCCS' (Jacques 2014), that remains 'as fresh and

---

[10] As one of the 'others', I should declare an interest at this stage. Since most assume, rightly, that Hall was the intellectual leader of the project they are content to attribute its strengths to him. In talking of *PTC* as Hall's contribution, in the singular, I am following suit. However, as will become clear, I also often use the plural 'we' when talking about the project; which is accurate since it was a collective effort. There is, unfortunately, no simple resolution to this; hence the reader will have to put up with the switches between a singular 'Hall' and a collective 'we'. All direct quotations from the book will be taken from the 2nd edition published in 2013.

[11] I arrived at this figure by counting each notice, whether singly or collectively authored, as one, and similarly counting authors only once even when, as in some cases, they produced two, or even three, notices (usually emphasising similar points).

[12] The only other text that was regularly singled out, often in a similarly complimentary way to *PTC*, was the article 'Encoding and decoding in the television discourse' (Hall 1973/2019a). However, this received only half the mentions (26) of *PTC*.

mighty as ever' (Carrigan 2014). Hall himself, in his last interview, saw it as 'dead-centred to the cultural studies project' and responsible for his approach to politics: 'I...think conjuncturally about politics now' (quoted in Jhally 2016).

With fewer mentions (21), though still more than any other (except 'Encoding and decoding in the television discourse'), the edited volume, *Resistance Through Rituals* (*RTR*) (Hall and Jefferson, eds. 1976)[13] was sometimes paired with *PTC*—'the two most influential full-length books that came out of Birmingham in the 1970s' (Scannell 2016); 'this work [at CCCS]...made a major impact through a succession of original and path breaking books - most notably *Policing the Crisis* and *Resistance through Rituals*' (Murdock 2014). This pairing certainly echoed the similarly conjunctural thinking informing both. So, having spelled out what conjunctural analysis entails, an examination of Hall's relationship to conjunctural analysis follows, showing how his conjunctural cast of mind made him a Gramscian before he had read any Gramsci. This starts with examples from Hall's early political writings, continues with his subsequent article on 'the hippies', itself a precursor to the youth subcultures project that produced *RTR*, and ends with analysing first *RTR* and then *PTC* in terms of their shared conjunctural methodology.

What has this to do with criminology? Only two, by Biko Agozino (2014) and Joe Sim (2014), of the 137 obituary notices were written by criminologists, and no criminology journals produced 'in memoriam' special issues. *PTC* and *RTR* are regarded, historically, as a significant contribution to the development of new deviancy theory or the 'new criminology' of the 1970s, hence a part of criminology's 'canon', but

---

[13] All direct quotations from the book will be taken from the 2nd edition published in 2006.

with little lasting significance beyond that[14]; an inspiration to contemporary cultural criminology but not an analytical model to be replicated and used. (Hence, perhaps, the reason for the lack of obituary notices by criminologists.) For example, of the 25 criminology books and 98 'authors'[15] consulted for references to Stuart Hall, covering the period 1981 to 2017,[16] around three quarters of the authors (72) mention *PTC*, and often (30) with a positive endorsement, like 'seminal', 'major', 'key', etc. Only *RTR*, with 33 mentions, 11 with additional positive comments, came remotely close. After that, only *Drifting into a Law and Order society*, the 1979 Cobden Trust Human Rights Day Lecture (Hall 1980)—which largely drew on the argument in *PTC*—received any significant mentions, namely, 16. However, neither American textbook consulted (Henry and Einstadter, eds. 1998; Hagan 2002) made any mention of Hall.

But herein lies the rub: conjuncture and conjunctural analysis are not how either *PTC* or *RTR* are remembered within criminology. Neither term appears as an index entry in any edition of the well regarded and much used *The Sage Dictionary of Criminology* (McLaughlin and Muncie, eds. 2001/2006/2013), and 'conjunctures' appears only once in

---

[14]There are important exceptions to this statement. However, even with these, questions of theory rather than method predominate. For example, the volume by Coleman et al., eds. (2009) is both a celebration of *PTC* and an attempt by a variety of critical criminologists to explore its contemporary relevance to their particular area of criminological interest, with issues of the state and 'authoritarian populism' prominent. Likewise, in the special section of the Journal *Crime, Media, Culture* (4(1): 2008) devoted to '*PTC*: 30 Years On', only Clarke (2008)—one of *PTC*'s authors—addressed the issue of conjunctural analysis. The same could be said of Murray Lee's (2007) argument that *PTC* is an important precursor of the fear of crime debate: this was a theoretical and not a methodological argument.

[15]'Authors' really means chapters or articles since some were written by more than one author yet were still counted as one.

[16]The choice of criminology texts was a fairly random consultation of books from my shelves. They ranged from authored texts (e.g. Heidensohn 1989; Downes and Rock 1982; Burke 2001; Coleman and Norris 2000) to edited volumes (like Fitzgerald et al., eds. 1981; Maguire et al., eds. 2002; McLaughlin and Newborn, eds. 2010; and Brisman et al., eds. 2017). The two principles informing my choice were that the texts were written as, or were likely to be regarded as, suitable for use as student texts, and that between them they covered the period from 'early' (post *PTC*) to 'late' (almost the present).

the specifically methodological texts I consulted,[17] and that was a reference to a brief and oddly cryptic discussion of the idea by Howard Becker (2000).[18] Where *PTC* is cited to exemplify a research methodology, its conjunctural approach is misrecognised as 'critical reflection' (Hudson 2000). By this Hudson means using theoretical ideas to 'critically reflect' upon existing ideological understandings of a phenomenon; a misunderstanding that omits *PTC*'s empirical starting point and commitment to understand that better, and transforms the exercise into a purely theoretical one. So, we have a situation where *PTC* and *RTR* are widely seen as two of Hall's most significant contributions to cultural studies and criminology, but only in the case of cultural studies is their importance attributed to their conjunctural form of analysis. This disjunction within criminology, between recognising *PTC* and *RTR* as canonical texts but not their conjunctural form of analysis, is the conundrum at the heart of this book and its central justification.

Given the shared interest in culture and the canonical status within criminology of *RTR* and *PTC*, it is surprising that cultural criminology and cultural studies continue to occupy quite different intellectual universes. In the early National Deviancy Conference (NDC) days,[19] the new criminologists and the *PTC* team were very close. Jock Young, Ian Taylor and Stan Cohen, for example, were early, enthusiastic readers of the draft text of *PTC* and when Hall moved to the OU to replace Paul Halmos, he was recruited by NDC friend and colleague, criminologist Mike FitzGerald, subsequently a charismatic OU Dean, to be a

---

[17] Jupp et al., eds. (2000), Gomm et al., eds. (2000), Maxfield and Babbie (2001), and Atkinson et al., eds. (2001).

[18] Basically, Becker (2000: 225–26) argues that a conjunctural approach is consequential on the belief that 'causes are [only] effective when they operate in concert' and is usually 'seen as necessary' when dealing with 'the complexity of real historical cases'. 'Here…rather than the relations between variables in a universe of hypothetical cases', the idea is 'to make historical cases intelligible as instances of the way posited variables operate in concert'. Having converted 'history' into a science of 'variables' and 'causes', Becker concludes with the problem of numbers: '[w]e do not have many rigorous numerical methods for the assessment of this kind of conjunctural influence of variables'. Although conjunctural analysis is concerned with 'the complexity of real historical cases', it is not reducible to quantifiable 'variables' and 'causes', as we shall see in the next chapter.

[19] The NDC was a group of radical criminologists, many with links to activist, campaigning groups, who broke away from traditional criminology and its correctionalist and positivistic approach.

course member of the new 'Issues in Crime and Society' course team that produced the innovative Course Reader, *Crime and Society: Readings in History and Theory* (Fitzgerald et al., eds. 1981). NDC's critical criminology was an umbrella term embracing a broad mix of marxists, anarchists and symbolic interactionists, but with a common enemy: traditional, mainstream criminology. Of course there were many internal disagreements, but also a sense in its 1970s heyday of a shared set of interests, if not a shared approach.[20]

Thatcherism, the collapse of communism, the birth of 'new times', to say nothing of the emergence of feminism, post-colonialism and gay and lesbian studies, challenged the left on every front. Wondering how best to respond, the left fragmented. Old 'lefties' fought *MT's* attempts to understand these 'new times', while some radical criminologists, Jock Young prominently among them, thought the only way to combat the right was to echo their so-called 'realism' and offer a 'left realism' that would also 'take crime seriously'. Because, so the argument went, working-class people were the ones most affected by it. Unfortunately, this set aside many of radical criminology's erstwhile nostrums—now dismissed as 'left idealism'—and effectively mistook working-class common sense about crime for 'good sense'. Others became Foucaultians with discourse and governmentality replacing class struggle and the state as objects of enquiry. Or, they became seduced by the nihilistic brilliance of the postmodern turn with its series of 'end ofs' (grand narratives, history, the social). Identity politics, variously underpinned by feminism, post-colonialism and gay and lesbian studies, constituted yet another sort of challenge to the traditional left.

When Young moved on from left realism to launch cultural criminology, teaming up with the younger Keith Hayward (whose intellectual formation was 'post-marxist'), Mike Presdee and the American anarchist ethnographer, Jeff Ferrell, the resulting project was a strange hybrid: a revitalisation of ethnography with a dose of postmodernism, a smidgeon of unreconstructed marxism, a touch of Merton, and lashings of a

---

[20] Although not a set of interests shared by feminists at that time. For all the NDC's many strengths, feminists tended to feel excluded.

somewhat misunderstood Katzian phenomenology.[21] In short, a chaotic *mélange* for 'late modern' times. As with the earlier NDC project, the enemy was still traditional positivistic and quantitative criminology. The historical backdrop, 'late modernism', was never theoretically interrogated (though endlessly phenomenologically described) and the state remained an undefined entity still to be imagined (Ferrell et al. 2008: 75). The chapters dealing with cultural criminology will build on these ideas to highlight how different is the approach to that of conjunctural analysis. Cultural criminology's failure to think conjuncturally is what makes it a very different project from that of Hall's version of cultural studies, and the poorer for it.

Hall's journey through these seismic changes involved ongoing battles with his marxist critics. Some, especially traditional marxists, thought this period constituted Hall's post-Marxist turn. Though he came close, he never abandoned marxism. He was, like Marx, never a 'Marxist', meaning he was always critical of vulgar, reductive marxism, just as Marx sometimes despaired of what went on in his name. The Marx of *The Eighteenth Brumaire* (Marx 1852/1968)—a masterclass in conjunctural analysis—continued to inspire Hall, as did Gramsci and the continuing importance of the idea of hegemony. But class had now to share a space with other influential 'identities', especially those of gender, race and sexuality. Rejecting the idea that discourse (or meaning) was all there was (even though it was only through discourse that things become knowable), Hall also rejected the idea that difference (as in different identities) was all there was. For a politics to be possible, the idea of an underlying structure—'the limits to political action given by the terrain on which it operates…the existing balance of social forces'—continually changing to be sure, had to be preserved. This was 'marxism without final guarantees' (Hall 1983/1996: 45). And the only way to understand what was going on in any given moment? Conjunctural analysis. This was now understood in terms of articulated relationships and not the symptomatic readings of earlier times when surface appearances might be read as symptoms of the underlying class struggle (which is not to say that class struggle disappears).

---

[21] A reference to Katz (1988).

Hall's attention in this period to questions of race, ethnicity and identity is interrogated as a preamble to a reading of the Brexit conjuncture—a conjuncture in which questions of race and immigration figure prominently. In analysing Brexit, I try to demonstrate the continuing relevance to criminology of Hall's intrinsic mode of thinking. The concluding chapter that follows offers a brief summary answer to the questions posed at the outset before showing how a conjunctural analysis might make sense of the USA in 2020, both the moment of Trump and what his defeat might presage. Finally, a Coda has been added to deal with that which Hall found difficult to incorporate politically, namely, psychoanalysis. This is then used to explore the emotion of anger, which was much in evidence in explanations of Brexit, and how it might be incorporated into conjunctural analysis.

Chapter by Chapter Overview

Chapter 2 starts with an exploration of the meaning of the term 'conjuncture', both its everyday meaning and its take up within Marxist theorising by Althusser and by Gramsci. This entails a consideration of its relationship to the idea of crisis and its difference from the cognate Gramscian term 'organic', and is followed by a summary definition. Examples from Hall's early political writings are then deployed in order to demonstrate what is involved in conjunctural analysis. Although written before Hall consciously adopted the term, these nonetheless show Hall thinking and analysing conjuncturally. The research-based article about 'the hippies' is similarly analysed. Here, Sartre's 'progressive-regressive' methodology was consciously adopted, a methodology that is a form of conjunctural analysis. The chapter ends with an examination of the youth subcultures project that produced *RTR*. Although not conceptualised as such at the time, in retrospect it resembles a successor project to Hall's hippies article. By this point in time, the Gramscian-inspired, conjunctural methodology had become explicit.

Exemplifying conjunctural analysis continues in Chapter 3 with a detailed look at *PTC*. Although similarly conjuncturally focused to *RTR*, it was significantly different in several ways, crucially in being a sustained piece of empirical research designed to understand the harsh sentencing of three juveniles. This concrete starting point, validated by Marx's methodological ruminations, guided the whole project's movement from particular cases to the general crisis of hegemony they signified. The step-by-step outline of the book's four parts demonstrates the constant movement from simple to more complex understandings, as more determinations are uncovered, via critique and re-theorising. Thus, the critique of the common sense understanding of the role of the police, courts and media that revealed an overreaction was replaced with the idea of 'moral panic' in Part I. However, this term proved insufficiently historical when put to the empirical test and so became re-theorised, in Part III, as a symptom of the 'crisis of hegemony' that began in the 1960s. This same methodological strategy is shown to be at work also in understanding the role of social anxiety in the reception of media messages, in Part II of the book, and in the 'politics of mugging' in the somewhat neglected concluding Part IV.

Chapters 4 and 5 demonstrate the very different thinking informing the project of cultural criminology. Since cultural criminology is a broad church covering many topics and approaches, I focus on the key foundational texts that specifically introduce the project as a project and on four exemplary texts produced by the key authors of the foundational texts. Between them these offer several statements of intent covering an array of theoretical and methodological ambitions as well as some concrete examples of the approach-in-action. Chapter 4 starts with a critical overview of the introductory texts and then focuses on Keith Hayward's *City Limits* (2004) and an article by Jock Young (2003), attempting to combine a Mertonian structuralism with a Katzian phenomenology, called 'Merton with energy: Katz with structure'. In both examples, the key difference from a conjunctural approach is shown to be their failure to adopt a specific, concrete starting point, in favour of starting with theory. Neither text lacks ambition or imagination. They are also theoretically sophisticated. However, not being disciplined by historical particularities as must be the case with conjunctural analysis, their theorising is shown to be simply speculative. Although not intentionally, their work, which is similar along many dimensions, seems to be wanting to produce a general theory of 'expressive' crime in late modernity, an ambition, like all attempts at general theorising about something as multifaceted as crime, that is doomed to failure.

Chapter 5 continues the exploration of key texts in cultural criminology. Specifically, it compares and contrasts two pairs of texts, one of each pair from outside cultural criminology and the other by one of cultural criminology's founding figures. The first pair are ethnographies, since ethnography is a key methodology of cultural criminology; the second pair are focused on a core concept within cultural criminology, that of 'carnival'. The general idea is to explore how well each text succeeds in its own terms, how compatible each is with conjunctural analysis, and whether the cultural criminology examples have managed to break new ground. The traditional ethnography used as the comparator for Jeff Ferrell's cultural criminology offering *Tearing Down the Streets* (2001) is Carl Nightingale's *On the Edge* (1993), chosen because it is much admired and widely cited by the cultural criminologists under investigation. Fortuitously, both the texts focused on carnival use Bakhtin as their theoretical starting point, thus enabling a direct comparison between a conjuncturally-focused text, *The Politics and Poetics of Transgression by* Stallybrass and White (1986), and one adopting a cultural criminology approach, *Cultural Criminology and the Carnival of Crime by* Presdee (2000). In both instances, in the ethnography and the carnival comparison, the cultural criminology texts fare less well than their comparator texts, partly because, like with both Hayward and Young in Chapter 4, theory and not the specificity of the particular is in command. There is also an unwillingness to start by critiquing existing approaches as a basis for building better explanations; which means that an unprincipled theoretical eclecticism holds sway. In the next chapter, Hall's very different approach to theorising is the focus.

Chapter 6 is an attempt to show that conjunctural analysis is not opposed to theory per se since it relies upon it. Rather, through a demonstration of Hall's use of theory, which I call principled eclecticism, it attempts to contrast this with the unprincipled, pluralistic eclecticism that was the hallmark of cultural criminology's use of theory as argued in Chapters 4 and 5. Although Hall's relationship to theory was often seen as eclectic, mixing Marxist and post-Marxist ideas, his theorising, as I demonstrate, was always principled, never arbitrary. These principles included a historically materialist and not idealist starting point, the importance of conducting a dialogue even with intellectual opponents, and a commitment to complexity, which meant recognising social relations are underpinned by diverse forms of power, with different origins, trajectories and temporalities. These principles are variously demonstrated using examples from Hall's many efforts at theorising. The 'complexity' principle, for example, is examined using examples from Hall's theorising about the relative autonomy of the superstructures, the turn to discourse, and identity and articulation.

In Chapter 7, I begin to contextualise the conjunctural analysis of Brexit that follows in Chapters 8 and 9. Using Hall's later writings on identity, which address theoretically notions of race, ethnicity, nationalism and immigration while remaining conjuncturally-focused, the idea is to show, as was the case with *PTC* and Thatcherism, how prescient they are of present debates, despite being written before 9/11. Their unifying thread is the importance of what Hall called the 'politics of difference', or how to find a way of 'living with difference', which he thought was the defining problem of the twenty-first century. Starting locally with the shift in British race politics from an essentialist, black anti-racist politics (Identity Politics One), born of the failures of assimilation, to a multicultural politics of 'living with difference' (Identity Politics Two), Hall situates this shift internationally in relation to decolonisation, the ending of the cold war and globalisation. Within this scenario, Brexit can be seen as a 'local' example of this larger, conjunctural picture.

Chapters 8 and 9 attempt to show how conjunctural analysis continues to be relevant by following its methodological protocols in examining Brexit. Chapter 8 starts by identifying the specific elements of the phenomenon in need of explanation, namely, the 2016 UK Referendum result and the series of questions this raised about the media and the voters. It then critiques the broad common sense explanation for the Leave victory before preliminary discussions of the media and expertise and the geography and demography of the Leave vote. The analysis starts with a look at the long-term Eurosceptic voter. This is followed by the identification of a composite white, working-class Leave voter from struggling, ex-industrial areas, which initiates the construction, using a selection of research-based ethnographies, of a historical narrative of class, gender and race relations from the 1970s to 9/11, where the chapter ends. This, as the next chapter shows, is a crucial turning point in the story of the politics of difference. Occasional references to *PTC* are an attempt to show that criminological concerns also attach to Brexit.

Chapter 9 concludes the Brexit story. It starts by offering an explanation of the middle-class Conservative Brexiteers. The historical backdrop to their Leave votes is argued to be the multiple challenges to traditional middle-class authority that encompass an expansion of middle-class occupations, the culture wars going back to the 1960s and the loss of Empire. The historical narrative that ended with 9/11 in Chapter 8 is then continued, first with New Labour up until the coalition government of 2010, and then the subsequent period up until the Referendum. As austerity bites and political alienation grows, immigration, and race become ever more salient. Given this, together with the denial of racism by everyone from politicians to convicted racists, space is devoted to the complex connections among 'immigration, racism and xenophobia' and how all this impacts 'living with difference'. The chapter ends with a summary account of the multiple crises comprising the Brexit conjuncture.

The concluding Chapter 10 starts with a summary answer to the book's opening questions about why another book about Hall might be of interest to criminologists at this point in time. It then makes the case for turning to the American election of 2020, a populist moment of global significance politically, for which a conjunctural analysis is designed. This also adds a comparative dimension to my Brexit analysis. Two contrasting Gramscian-inspired analyses of Trump's populist electoral victory of 2016 provide a theoretical and political framework for the ensuing discussion. This highlights key issues of relevance to conjunctural analysis, namely, the relationship between Hall's notion of 'authoritarian populism' and 'left populism', the role of the state, and what is entailed in theorising the complexity of a conjuncture. Additionally, the Hart (2020) analysis introduces the notion of 'global conjunctural moments', an idea that connects with Hall's international framing of his discussion of the politics of difference. Following these analyses, I offer my own evaluation of Trump's responses to the globally significant challenges of climate change, the refugee crisis, Black Lives Matter and the pandemic, how his multiple failures in these areas may have impacted the election result, and what we might expect 'after Trump'.

Chapter 11 is about the anger commonly associated with the Brexit vote. It exists as a **Coda** and not incorporated into the main text since it implicates a discipline, psychoanalysis, that Hall did not interrogate theoretically in the way he did other disciplines. So, this is an attempt to go beyond Hall and begin to consider the issues raised in attempting to introduce psychoanalysis into conjunctural analysis. The initial problem is evidential: how do we know who were the angry voters? In the absence of this knowledge, incorporating anger into conjunctural analysis apparently becomes impossible. Yet still necessary given its obvious relevance to the Referendum outcome. So, the Coda begins to explore the nature of the difficulties. Hall's one article specifically on psychoanalysis is used as a starting point. An attempt to explain Brexit anger psychosocially, combining psychoanalytic ideas with sociology, is also used to exemplify the theoretical problems. Finally, psychoanalytic ideas from Melanie Klein and Jessica Benjamin are used to show their potential in illuminating the social issues of racism and misogynistic violence, and how these might be incorporated into conjunctural analyses.

References

Agozino, B. 2014. Long live Stuart Hall. *Web Log*, February 10.
Atkinson, P., A. Coffey, S. Delamont, J. Lofland, and L. Lofland (eds.). 2001. *Handbook of Ethnography*. London: Sage.
Becker, H. 2000. Cases, causes, conjunctures, stories and imagery. In Gomm et al., eds. (2000: 223–33).
Bennett, T. 2016. The Stuart Hall conjuncture. *Cultural Studies Review* 22 (1): 282–86.

Bhabha, H. 2015. "The beginning of their real enunciation": Stuart Hall and the work of culture. *Critical Inquiry* 42 (1): 1–30.
Brisman, A., E. Carrabine, and N. South (eds.). 2017. *The Routledge Companion to Criminological Theory and Concepts*. Abingdon, Oxon: Routledge.
Burke, R.H. 2001. *An Introduction to Criminological Theory*. Cullompton, Devon: Willan.
Carrigan, M. 2014. Policing the "benefits crisis": What would Stuart Hall do? *The Sociological Imagination*, February 10.
Clarke, J. 2008. Still policing the crisis? *Crime, Media, Culture* 4 (1): 123–29.
Coleman, C., and C. Norris. 2000. *Introducing Criminology*. Cullompton, Devon: Willan.
Coleman, R., J. Sim, S. Tombs, and D. Whyte (eds.). 2009. *State, Power, Crime*. London: Sage.
Davis, H. 2004. *Understanding Stuart Hall*. London: Sage.
Downes, D., and P. Rock. 1982. *Understanding Deviance: A Guide to the Sociology of Crime and Rule Breaking*. Oxford: Oxford University Press.
Eley, G. 2015. Stuart Hall, 1932–2014. *History Workshop Journal* 79 (1): 303–20.
Fitzgerald, M., G. McLennan, and J. Pawson (eds.). 1981. *Crime and Society: Readings in History and Theory*. London: Routledge & Kegan Paul/Open University Press.
Ferrell, J. 2001. *Tearing Down the Streets: Adventures in Urban Anarchy*. New York: Palgrave.
Ferrell, J., K. Hayward, and J. Young. 2008. *Cultural Criminology: An Invitation*. London: Sage.
Fornäs, J. 2014. Stuart Hall's dialogical interventions. *Inter-Asia Cultural Studies* 15 (2): 186–90.
Gilroy, P., L. Grossberg, and A. McRobbie (eds.). 2000. *Without Guarantees: In Honour of Stuart Hall*. London: Verso.
Gomm, R., M. Hammersley, and P. Foster (eds.). 2000. *Case Study Method: Key Issues, Key Texts*. London: Sage.
Gramsci, A. 1971. *Selections from the Prison Notebooks*, ed. and trans. Q. Hoare and G.N. Smith. London: Lawrence & Wishart.
Grossberg, L. 2015. Learning from Stuart Hall: Following the path with heart. *Cultural Studies* 29 (1): 3–11.
Hagan, F.E. 2002. *Introduction to Criminology: Theories, Methods and Criminal Behavior*, 5th ed. Belmont, CA: Wadsworth/Thomson Learning.

Hall, S. 1973/2019a. Encoding and decoding in the television discourse. In Morley, ed. (2019a: 257–76).
Hall, S. 1980. *Drifting into a Law and Order Society: The 1979 Cobden Trust Human Rights Day Lecture.* London: Cobden Trust.
Hall, S. 1983/1996. The problem of ideology: Marxism without guarantees. In Morley and Chen, eds. (1996: 25–46).
Hall, S. 1989. Foreword. In Independent Committee of Inquiry (1989).
Hall, S. 2000. Conclusion: The multi-cultural question. In Hesse, ed. (2000: 209–41).
Hall, S. 2016. *Cultural Studies 1983: A Theoretical History*, ed. and with an intro. J.D. Slack and L. Grossberg. Durham and London: Duke University Press.
Hall, S. 2017a. *Selected Political Writings: The Great Moving Right Show and Other Essays*, ed. S. Davison, D. Featherstone, M. Rustin and B. Schwarz. London: Lawrence and Wishart.
Hall, S. 2017b. *The Fateful Triangle: Race, Ethnicity, Nation*, ed. K. Mercer with a Foreword by H.L. Gates, Jr. Cambridge, MA: Harvard University Press.
Hall, S., and T. Jefferson (eds.). 1976. *Resistance Through Rituals: Youth Subcultures in Post-War Britain.* London: Hutchinson. 2nd edition published by Routledge with a new Introduction in 2006.
Hall, S. with B. Schwarz. 2017. *Familiar Stranger: A Life Between Two Islands.* London: Allen Lane.
Hall, S., and P. Whannel. 1964. *The Popular Arts.* London: Hutchinson.
Hall, S., C. Critcher, T. Jefferson, J. Clarke, and B. Roberts. 1978. *Policing the Crisis: Mugging, the State and Law and Order.* Houndmills, Basingstoke: Macmillan. 2nd edition published by Palgrave Macmillan with a new Preface and Afterwords in 2013.
Hall, S., G. Lewis, and E. McLaughlin. 1998. Evidence on "Racial Stereotyping in the Police" to *The Lawrence Inquiry.*
Hart, G. 2020. Why did it take so long? Trump-Bannonism in a global conjunctural frame. *Geografiska Annaler: Series B, Human Geography* 102 (3): 239–66. https://doi.org/10.1080/04353684.2020.1780791.
Hayward, K. 2004. *City Limits: Crime, Consumer Culture and the Urban Experience.* London: Glasshouse.
Heidensohn, F. 1989. *Crime and Society.* Houndmills, Basingstoke: Macmillan.
Henderson, L. 2014. In memoriam: Stuart Hall, 1932–2014. *The Massachusetts Review.* Posted February 14, 2014.
Henriques, J., D. Morley, with V. Goblot (eds.). 2017. *Stuart Hall: Conversations, Projects and Legacies.* London: Goldsmith's Press.

Henry, S., and W. Einstadter (eds.). 1998. *The Criminology Theory Reader*. New York: New York University Press.
Hesse, B. (ed.). 2000. *Un/settled Multiculturalisms*. London: Zed Books.
Hudson, B. 2000. Critical reflection as research methodology. In Jupp et al., eds. (2000: 175–92).
Independent Committee of Inquiry. 1989. *Policing in Hackney: 1945–1984*. London: Karia Press/Roach Family Support Committee.
Jacques, M. 2014. A true original. *Inter-Asia Cultural Studies* 15 (2): 174–77.
Jhally, S. 2016. Stuart Hall: The last interview. *Cultural Studies* 30 (2): 332–45.
Jupp, V., P. Davies, and P. Francis (eds.). 2000. *Doing Criminological Research*. London: Sage.
Katz, J. 1988. *Seductions of Crime: Moral and Sensual Attractions in Doing Evil*. New York: Basic Books.
Lee, M. 2007. *Inventing Fear of Crime: Criminology and the Politics of Anxiety*. Cullompton, Devon: Willan.
Londis, J. 2017. Why we need Stuart Hall's imaginative left. *The New Republic*, September 27.
Maguire, M., R. Morgan, and R. Reiner (eds.). 2002. *The Oxford Handbook of Criminology*, 3rd ed. Oxford: Oxford University Press.
Marx, K. 1852/1968. *The Eighteenth Brumaire of Louis Bonaparte*. In Marx and Engels (1968: 94–179).
Marx, K., and F. Engels. 1968. *Selected Works in One Volume*. London: Lawrence and Wishart.
Maxfield, M.G., and E. Babbie. 2001. *Research Methods for Criminal Justice and Criminology*, 3rd ed. Belmont, CA: Wadsworth/Thomson Learning.
McLaughlin, E., and J. Muncie. 2001/2006/2013. *The Sage Dictionary of Criminology*, 1st, 2nd and 3rd eds. London: Sage.
McLaughlin, E., and T. Newburn (eds.). 2010. *The Sage Handbook of Criminological Theory*. London: Sage.
Meeks, B. (ed.). 2007. *Culture, Politics, Race and Diaspora: The Thought of Stuart Hall*. London: Lawrence and Wishart.
Morley, D. (ed.). 2019a. *Stuart Hall Essential Essays Vol. 1: Foundations of Cultural Studies*. Durham and London: Duke University Press.
Morley, D. (ed.). 2019b. *Stuart Hall Essential Essays Vol. 2: Identity and Diaspora*. Durham and London: Duke University Press.
Morley, D., and K.-H. Chen. 1996. *Stuart Hall: Critical Dialogues in Cultural Studies*. London: Routledge.
Murdock, G. 2014. Britain's most distinguished post-war public intellectual and cultural analyst. *MeCCSA Three D* Issue 22, July 15.

Niaah, J. 2014. Stuart Hall, cultural studies and the new (carry/beyond) faculty of interpretation. *Inter-Asia Cultural Studies* 15 (2): 205–13.
Nightingale, C.H. 1993. *On the Edge: A History of Poor Black Children and Their American Dreams*. New York: Basic Books.
Parekh, B. 2000. *Commission on the Future of Multi-Ethnic Britain*. London: Runnymede Trust.
Presdee, M. 2000. *Cultural Criminology and the Carnival of Crime*. London: Routledge.
Procter, J. 2004. *Stuart Hall*. London: Routledge.
Rojek, C. 2003. *Stuart Hall*. Cambridge: Polity.
Scannell, P. 2016. Regenerating Stuart Hall. *Critical Studies in Media Communication* 33 (5): 468–72.
Scott, D. 2017. *Stuart Hall's Voice: Intimations of an Ethics of Receptive Generosity*. Durham and London: Duke University Press.
Sim, J. 2014. For Stuart Hall: Joe Sim remembers his PhD supervisor. *Criminal Justice Matters* 96 (1): 28. Published online 22 May.
Stallybrass, P., and A. White. 1986. *The Politics and Poetics of Transgression*. London: Methuen.
Unofficial Committee of Enquiry. 1980a. *Southall 23 April 1979: The Report of the Unofficial Committee of Enquiry*. London: National Council for Civil Liberties (NCCL).
Unofficial Committee of Enquiry. 1980b. *The Death of Blair Peach: The Supplementary Report of the Unofficial Committee of Enquiry*. London: NCCL.
Yardley, W. 2014. Stuart Hall, trailblazing British scholar of multicultural influences, is dead at 82. *New York Times*, February 17.
Young, J. 2003. Merton with energy, Katz with structure: The sociology of vindictiveness and the criminology of transgression. *Theoretical Criminology* 7 (3): 389–414.
Zhang, L. 2017. How to understand Stuart Hall's "identity" properly? *Inter-Asia Cultural Studies* 18 (2): 188–96.

Part I

Stuart Hall and Conjunctural Analysis

2

Conjunctural Analysis Part One: From Early Political Writings to *Resistance Through Rituals*

This chapter and the next will explore Hall's relationship to conjunctural analysis. As 'conjuncture' is an everyday term that has gained a specialised meaning, I start in the next section by tracing its take-up in Marxist theorising by Althusser and Gramsci, before advancing a summary definition. I then begin to demonstrate what is involved in conjunctural analysis by using examples from Hall's early political writings. These show him thinking and analysing conjuncturally even before he was aware that that was what he was doing. The research-based article about 'the hippies' that followed constituted his first sustained example, using Sartre's 'progressive-regressive' methodology, of conjunctural analysis, though still not named as such. This, I argue, was a precursor to the youth subcultures project, *Resistance Through Rituals (RTR)*, with its explicit, and by this time Gramscian-inspired, conjunctural methodology. And this, in turn, was the other side of the same conjunctural coin that produced what is the focus of the next chapter, namely, *Policing the Crisis (PTC)*.

What Is a Conjuncture?

Conjuncture is a simple idea that has been complicated, over time, by its usage in slightly different ways. *The Shorter Oxford English Dictionary* definition starts with the simple notion of things joined together ('the action of joining together'; 'the act or state of being joined together') but then adds its 'only current sense', namely, 'a meeting of circumstances or events; a juncture, crisis'. This immediately introduces one source of the problem: are all meetings of circumstances or events 'conjunctures' or only crisis-laden meetings? Althusser, whose writings have been one important source of thinking on the issue, tends to use the term in the neutral sense of a meeting of circumstances or events, but in discussing the term in relation to Lenin and the Russian revolution can be seen to be suggesting the importance of crisis to the term. Let me illustrate. The glossary definition in *For Marx*, supplied by his translator, Ben Brewster, but approved by Althusser (1969: 249), unambiguously yokes the term to Marxism, but there is no mention of crisis:

> The central concept of the Marxist science of politics (cf. Lenin's 'current moment'); it denotes the exact balance of forces, state of overdetermination (q.v.) of the contradictions at any given moment to which political tactics must be applied.[1]

Although the definition talks about 'any given moment', not just moments of crisis, throughout the essays, revolutionary conjunctures are often returned to for what might be learned from them. In summarising what this might be in the key essay 'Contradiction and Overdetermination', Althusser starts by reminding us that 'the contradiction between two antagonistic classes' is not enough: 'If this contradiction is to become "active" in the strongest sense, to become a ruptural principle, there must be an accumulation of "circumstances" and "currents" so that whatever their origin and sense…they '*fuse*' into a *ruptural unity*: when they produce the result of the immense majority of the popular masses *grouped*

---

[1] The term 'overdetermination' is borrowed from Freud for whom it refers to the fact that generally symptoms are determined by several things, hence *over*determined. Althusser uses the idea to denote that at any given moment there are several contradictions happening simultaneously.

in an assault on a regime which its ruling classes are *unable to defend*' (ibid.: 99). In other words, revolutions occur when, and only when, an accumulation of contradictions produce a revolutionary rupture. This kind of revolutionary conjuncture is by definition an overdetermined moment of crisis. Unfortunately, the Preface to the 2nd edition of *PTC* mistakes this definition of a particular kind of conjuncture for a general definition of conjuncture (Hall et al. 2013: xv).

The second source of confusion stems from the writings of the Italian Marxist, Gramsci. Writing at a time when classes and class struggle were the fundamental antagonism to be addressed by Marxists, yet forced to write cryptically to avoid the censorship of his fascist captors, he uses a series of contrasting terms to talk about his 'principles of historical methodology': 'structure'/'superstructure'; 'situation'/'conjuncture'; 'organic'/'conjunctural':

> It is the problem of the relations between structure and superstructure which must be accurately posed and resolved if the forces that are active in a particular period are to be correctly analysed, and the relations between them determined…in studying a structure, it is necessary to distinguish organic movements (relatively permanent) from movements which may be termed 'conjunctural' (and which appear as occasional, immediate, almost accidental). Conjunctural phenomena too depend on organic movements to be sure, but they do not have any very far-reaching historical significance. (Gramsci 1971: 177)

In a footnote to the above quote, Gramsci defines the difference between 'situation' and 'conjuncture': 'the conjuncture is the set of immediate and ephemeral characteristics of the economic situation' (ibid.: 177). All these distinctions—structure/superstructure; organic/conjunctural; situation/conjuncture—would appear to be different ways of distinguishing between economic, class-based issues and ideological ones. This reading is borne out when Gramsci goes on to talk of the 'common error' in confusing the organic and the conjunctural:

> A common error in historico-political analysis consists in an inability to find the correct relation between what is organic and what is conjunctural. This leads to presenting causes as immediately operative which

operate indirectly, or to asserting that the immediate causes are the only effective ones. In the first case there is an excess of 'economism', or doctrinaire pedantry; in the second, an excess of 'ideologism'. (ibid.: 178)

Marx's *The Eighteenth Brumaire*, which is an analysis of the period between the overthrow of Louis Philippe in 1848 and Bonaparte's *coup d'etat* in 1851 (Marx 1852/1968), masterfully demonstrates—without ever mentioning them—the difference between Gramsci's terms. On the one hand, it was a detailed account of the political events of the day: a blow by blow examination of what happened: Gramsci's conjunctural phenomena. On the other, it was a brilliant exposition of how these political events were related to the actions of underlying classes and class fractions: Gramsci's 'organic movements'.

However, the distinction between 'organic' and 'conjunctural' has now become confusing. This is because, in today's very different theoretical world, the primacy of the economic or class structure is not a starting assumption as it appears to be in these early formulations. What this means, practically, is that distinguishing the 'organic' from the 'conjunctural' or finding the 'correct' relation between the two, is like looking for a needle in the proverbial haystack. What happens when the terms are retained is that they get used interchangeably, with the same phenomenon sometimes called 'organic' and sometimes 'conjunctural'. Thatcherism is a good example: Was this an 'organic' movement or a 'conjunctural' reshuffling? The truth is that it doesn't really matter. Hall himself has used both terms, on different occasions, when referring to Thatcherism; but that has not undermined the cogency of his analysis. Given this, I want to suggest that their more recent usage is a way of distinguishing 'surface' movements (conjunctural) from 'deeper', less visible ones (organic).

In sum, then, conjuncture refers to what is happening—politically, economically, ideologically, culturally—at any given historical moment. Because moments of crisis have more often been the subject of analysis (a point to which I return below), crisis has sometimes become part of the definition of conjuncture, but this is a mistake. Finally, all historical moments comprise an observable, empirical dimension, that which is taking place before our eyes (the conjunctural); and an invisible, structural dimension, that which is taking place 'behind all our backs' (the organic). Making sense of the historical moment requires that both be given full attention: to avoid a chaotic empiricism in the case of noticing only the conjunctural dimension, or a reductive theoreticism in the case of noticing only, or moving too quickly to, the organic dimension.

What Is Conjunctural Analysis?

As the above makes plain, conjunctural analysis is associated with Marxism and has largely been undertaken for political purposes, to understand the 'exact balance of forces' at any historical moment. Such analyses can be anything from brief political essays responding to a contemporary theme or event, through the somewhat lengthier analysis typified by Marx's *The Eighteenth Brumaire*, to the full-scale research-based analysis exemplified by *PTC*. Later, in the next chapter, I shall be looking in detail at *PTC* as not only the most sustained example of Hall's conjunctural form of analysis, but as what went on to inform his subsequent highly influential essays on Thatcherism. However, I wish to start with his early political essays, both to show that Hall has always thought conjuncturally, that he was 'a Gramscian before he had ever read Gramsci' (Davison et al. 2017: 2), and how the core methodological elements of conjunctural analysis were already in place well before *PTC*.

Some of Hall's early 'new left' political essays were republished in 2017 (Hall 2017). They are wonderfully informed at the level of immediate politics, as with all good political journalism, but they don't rest there. As with all good conjunctural analyses, they probe further, to underlying structural changes that aid understanding. Thus, in what he called his 'first properly political essay' (Hall with Schwarz 2017: 237), his assessment of the Conservative party in the aftermath of the Conservative election victory of 1955 and the subsequent debacle of Suez was situated first in relation to the 'limited revolution' of the new welfare state and then to 'deeper changes in society, with their roots not so much in the welfare state as in the capitalist sector of the economy' (Hall 1957/2017:

20–21). Hall himself regarded it as anticipating 'what would later…become crucial for me: the primacy of conjunctural analysis' (Hall with Schwarz 2017: 237). Moreover, he thought it read 'like an earlier, practical incarnation of…"The Great Moving Right Show"…[or] if not an incarnation, then a kind of anticipation in intellectual sensibility of what was to come in my theorizations…of Thatcherism'. And, in case one forgets the political cost of unsettling orthodoxies, he reminds us that, just as happened with his writings on Thatcherism, 'the severity of the ripostes I received…from the Left, was sharp' (ibid.).

This idea of Hall's 'intellectual sensibility' anticipating his Thatcherism essays (Hall 1988) would seem to be even more in evidence in 'A sense of classlessness', another *Universities and Left Review* essay published the following year (Hall 1958/2017). It starts thus: 'clearly there has been a major shift in the patterns of social life in this country. How deep they go, and whether they alter our older notions of "class" is difficult to tell' (ibid.: 28). This is followed by a long 'endnote' on 'the post-war boom' which concluded thus: 'if what I am arguing is true, if the working class has itself, to some degree, been seduced into playing a complementary role to capitalism, then the changes in social attitudes run deeper than talk about a "temporary period of prosperity" would suggest' (ibid.: 43, n1). As it turned out, he was right: 'changes in social attitudes' did indeed 'run deeper'. So deep, in fact, that the essay could almost be read as a predictive foretaste of Thatcher's later appeal to the working classes. In any event, it is a demonstration that his intellectual sensibility was peculiarly suited to conjunctural analysis.

But it was his essay, 'The Hippies: an American "moment"', published eleven years later (Hall 1968), that began to spell out explicitly the methodological implications of a conjunctural analysis, albeit not yet named as such since it still predated his encounter with Gramsci and Althusser. It was more explicitly research-based than the early political essays. It is rarely anthologised, though it does appear in Gray et al., eds. (2007). However, to my mind it is an overlooked precursor of the *RTR* project, which makes it particularly instructive for my project. In what follows I will be using the original 1968 paper and not the anthologised version because the latter, though easier to locate than the former, has not reproduced the footnotes of the original article which contain, among other things, an extended discussion of the article's methodology.[2]

Hall's introduction of the notion of the 'Hippie *style*' (Hall 1968: 1) clearly anticipated *RTR* substantively. However, it is the methodological issues that concern me here. What a consideration of these makes clear is the influence of Sartre, especially *The Problem of Method (TPOM)* which had not long been published in English (Sartre 1963). Like Gramsci and Althusser, Sartre was attempting to revitalise marxism, in his case by rigorously following up the notion that it is men who make history, not the prior conditions. *TPOM* was the introduction to that monumental two-volume enterprise, *Critique of Dialectical Reason* (Sartre 1960/1976; Aronson 1987) and is an excellent, short introduction to Sartre's Marxism at that period of his life. The appeal of *TPOM* to Hall was its commitment to a form of analysis that proceeded from the uniqueness of 'particular, historical realities' rather than, as traditional Marxism constantly did, attempting to squeeze unique particulars into pre-existing theory and thus produce 'general particularities' (Sartre 1963: 24). Sartre's discussion of Marx's *The Eighteenth Brumaire*—which he thought was an 'excellent article' (ibid.: 124)—demonstrated the point. Marx certainly starts out, Sartre said, with 'synthetic intent', aware 'that facts are never isolated appearances…that they are bound together by internal relations' (ibid.: 25). However, this does not

> render useless the appreciation of the process as a *unique* totality. When, for example, he studies the brief and tragic history of the Republic of 1848, he does not limit himself - as would be done today - to stating that the republican petite bourgeoisie betrayed its ally, the Proletariat. On the contrary, he tries to account for this tragedy in its detail and in the aggregate…In other words, he gives to each event, in addition to its particular signification, the role of being revealing…living Marxism is heuristic…In the work of Marx we never find entities. Totalities (e.g., 'the petite bourgeoisie' of the *18 Brumaire*) are living; they furnish their own definitions within the framework of the research. Otherwise we could not understand

---

[2]The decision to omit the footnotes was probably made because the original article failed to identify where, in the text, the footnotes should go. They appear to have been added after the text's completion. This omission also meant a much-reduced list of references in Gray et al., eds. (2007) since many of these only appeared in the footnotes.

> the importance which Marxists attach (even today) to 'the analysis' of a situation. It goes without saying that this analysis is not enough and that it is the first moment in an effort at synthetic reconstruction. But it is apparent also that the analysis is indispensable to the later reconstruction of the total structures. (ibid.: 25–27)

The notion of '"the analysis" of a situation' followed by 'synthetic reconstruction' is conjunctural analysis *avant la lettre*.

Hall's starting point with the hippies was to see them, not as a 'symptom', but as attempting a 'project' (in Sartre's terms), or 'as meaningful human action' (Hall 1968: n1). This required, first, 'a phenomenological and thematic "reading"' of what being a hippie meant to its participants (ibid.: 1): a reading that produced eleven themes, such as 'mysticism and withdrawal', 'love', 'togetherness', and so on that most will associate with being a hippie. While it is unclear if Hall spent any time with real-life hippies, there was clearly an ethnographic intent here, albeit one achieved largely through an extensive reading of secondary materials. Ethnographic purists may object to this but the 'Preface to the Second Edition' of *PTC* mounts a defence of such secondary ethnography (Hall et al. 2013: xi–xii). This form of ethnography certainly underpinned much of the research for *RTR*.

Having achieved a phenomenological or subjective understanding, the next step was to 'situate' such meanings: to establish their 'context of determinations'. This constituted the 'objective' or '"structuralist" moment' of the analysis (ibid.: n1). This was followed by a direct echo of Sartre's point about the wrong way to 'insert' the subjective into the objective:

> the characteristic way of making this insertion is to evoke a set of 'global' determining factors which are assumed to give the 'objective' meaning of the phenomenon which has been subjectively defined. But I follow Sartre in supposing that this detour is frequently a substitute for explanation, in the sense that the crucial mediations are missing. (ibid.)

Although other authors are mentioned, it was Sartre who best encapsulated the entirety of the methodological protocols, especially with respect to the importance of mediations in *TPOM*.[3] And, in situating his 'phenomenological account within its proper structures and mediations', he was, he said, trying to 'give a brief genetic-historical account of its evolution' (ibid.: 1). 'Genetic-historical' stemmed from Sartre's *TPOM*, though it was actually a concept Sartre took from the Marxist sociologist, Henri Lefebvre. In a long footnote, Sartre praised Lefebvre for what he, Sartre, regarded as 'a simple and faultless method for integrating sociology and history in the perspective of a materialist dialectic'. According to Lefebvre, any social formation comprises both '*a horizontal complexity*' offering 'a multiplicity of aspects which must be described and fixed' (Lefebvre's 'descriptive' stage) and a '"vertical" or "historical complexity"' comprising '"the coexistence of formations of various ages and dates"' (Lefebvre's 'analytico-regressive' stage). These 'two complexities "react upon one another"'. Lefebvre's third stage, the 'historical-genetic' is an "attempt to rediscover the present, but elucidated, understood, explained" (Sartre 1963: 51–52, n8). It was this method 'with its phase of phenomenological description, and its double movement of regression followed by progress' (ibid.: 52, n8) that became Sartre's 'progressive-regressive' method and, broadly, at this point in time, also Hall's.

His phenomenological account (Lefebvre's 'descriptive' stage) having been achieved, the next step of situating this 'within its proper structures and mediations' meant, for Hall, its political context. When he presented a potted history of the growth of what he called 'a "generational underground"' (Hall 1968: 18), from the Beat Generation, through Civil Rights, campus rebellions, ghetto rebellions, black militancy and resistance to the Vietnam war, and finally 'the moment of the Hippies' (ibid.: 19), Hall regarded this as part of their 'historical/genetic evolution'. (In its 'regressive' attempt to place/date the Hippies it feels like Lefebvre's 'analytico-regressive stage'.) Thereafter, he amplified similarities between the Beat Generation and the Hippies and the 'evolving politicization of the underground' (ibid.) before asking what such a placement meant.

---

[3] Hall referenced the book as *The Question of Method*, which was a literal translation of the French title.

(This, in Lefebvre's terms, would be the stage of the 'historical-genetic': 'the present…elucidated, understood, explained'.)

Rather than see them, as many did, as a 'reaction against' the 'overtly political' (ibid.: 21), Hall suggested, against the conventional grain and 'perhaps in spite of themselves' (ibid.) that their 'wider meaning' had been to expand the meaning of political contestation in various ways: through their 'style' (ibid.: 21); by imaginatively expanding the repertoire of revolt; by 'living out…a set of counter values' (ibid.: 22), and by prefiguring 'a new kind of subjectivity' (ibid.: 23). Finally, Hall suggested that they were a reminder of the 'two poles - two "moments" - in the materialization of a revolutionary project…the *expressive* and the *activist*' (ibid.: 25). They would continue 'to appear and disappear' as 'long as the dialectical trajectory of the movement lasts'. They remained 'adaptive to the system', the 'broken refraction of the so-far absent or missing "content" of the emergent revolutionary project' (ibid.: 27). If the 'truth' of any analysis is the extent to which it becomes a new reality (a point about which I have more to say later), Hall's prediction about the 'two poles', the expressive and the activist, continuing to appear and disappear appears accurate—think 'new age' travellers and environmental activists, for example. It certainly appears truer than the conventional, one-sided view of Hippies as retreatist 'drop-outs'.

RTR and *PTC*: Different Sides of the Same Conjunctural Coin

RTR was first published in 1975 as a double issue (7/8) of the old Centre for Contemporary Cultural Studies (CCCS) journal, *Working Papers in Cultural Studies (WPCS)*. Centre sub-groups took it in turns to produce the journal and this was the 'work-in-progress' effort of the Subcultures group, newly formed in 1972. It consisted of those new arrivals whose intended postgraduate dissertations were to be the study of some aspect of 'youth', plus Hall, just promoted to acting CCCS Director (a position that became permanent when Richard Hoggart decided not to return to the Centre at the end of his secondment to UNESCO). In 1973, work began on *PTC*. Though *RTR* and *PTC* were separate projects with different emphases—the former broadly on the meaning of the 'action' of youth subcultures, the latter largely the meaning of the social reaction to a particular, delinquent, youthful activity, namely, 'mugging'—they were undertaken simultaneously and used the same theoretical resources that were developing in the Centre at that time. As I intend to show, they were also both conjunctural analyses. Hall was also a member of the media subgroup, a fact of particular relevance to the work of *PTC*, and led the weekly theory seminar, which fed into all the many subgroups.

Talking about *RTR* is confused somewhat by the fact that the volume *RTR*, though intended as a report about the progress of the work of the Subcultures group, also includes work by Centre members who were never in that group and 'outsiders' who were never Centre members. This is perhaps a useful reminder that the Centre's notion of collectivity was never exclusive: whoever could contribute to the dialogue was welcome. However, it is the theoretical and methodological framing provided by the Subcultures group that will be the focus of what follows, especially the long opening essay (Clarke et al. 1976). Written only a few years after 'The Hippies' paper, big strides had been made. Sartre was still a point of reference but Gramsci had now been read and become a significant influence. Most importantly, class was centre stage as the spectacular 'styles' of British post-war youth subcultures became the point of entry to examine what was the Centre's overriding theoretical problematic: how to understand the relationship between culture and class.

'Subcultures, cultures and class' starts with a critique of the term 'youth culture', a reminder that critique—of political economy (Marx); of dialectical reason (Sartre); etc.—must be the starting point of any form of social analysis. Here, the critique effectively continued the argument of 'a sense of classlessness', but 15 years later. 'Youth' had now become something of a metaphor for these changes, which were often glibly summarised in the trinity of (economic) 'affluence', (political) 'consensus' and (cultural) 'embourgeoisement'. But the new youth subcultures, from the teddy boys to the skinheads, were all plainly working class. What then could their emergence at particular historical moments tell us about the state of play of class relations, and how were their respective subcultural 'styles' implicated. This then was the conjunctural project: reading the phenomenology of style but historically contextualised in relation to the appropriate mediations.

Although the project was centred on working-class youth subcultures, there are eleven pages in the opening essay devoted to the 'Rise of the counter-cultures' (45–56). Interestingly, Hall's 'The hippies' article is not referenced. Yet, this could be read partly as an update for the British context, albeit that the focus was the broader one of 'the counter-culture' and not just the hippie 'sub-culture' within it. In many ways, in line with the 'big strides' mentioned earlier, it was a superior analysis because the mediating context was more developed. Instead of the 'generational underground', there was a lengthy analysis of the new, class-based contradictions impacting the dominant, middle-class 'parent' culture and how this was producing counter-cultural rebels among its off-spring. However, it was the new contradictions affecting the working class— its class problematic—and their manifestations at the level of subcultural styles, that was the central focus of the essay.

Unfortunately, the book's opening essay, in a section called 'Theory 1', made it appear as if theory was 'in command'. In actuality, the starting point was the research into the spectacular 'styles' that were the subject matter of the second section called 'Ethnography'—the teddy boys' draped jackets, the mods' scooters, the skinheads' 'bovver' boots, etc. In other words, the research problem the subcultures group presented itself with, what it wanted to understand better, was how to make sense of the post-war emergence of a series of spectacular, working-class youth subcultures, quite different from what had gone before. That would ultimately require situating them in their appropriate socio-historical contexts, of course, but that would become part of the analytic strategy, and subservient to it, not the entry point. This is an important methodological point about conjunctural analysis: the need for a concrete starting point, about which I shall have more to say in Chapter 3 when I discuss *PTC*. For now, suffice to say that, appearances notwithstanding, the entire theoretical edifice that apparently defined the opening essay was actually in place to make sense of the phenomena of subcultural styles; even though, paradoxically, these styles were only of interest to the extent that they could illuminate the conjuncture.

In trying to make sense of working-class youth subcultural styles, and finding existing work including American subcultural theory lacking in various ways, the group came across Phil Cohen's (1972) seminal account of 'sub-cultural conflict and working class community', about the relationship of youth subcultures to post-war changes taking place in the East End of London, which had recently been published in an earlier issue of *WPCS*. Importantly, this account was based on a project of community activism and thus, although it never sold itself as such, it had an 'ethnographic' component. In other words, its highly sophisticated theorising was trying to make sense of what it saw happening to an observed working-class community at a particular moment in time. Cohen concluded that changes in the local economy and in the neighbourhood, combined with their impact on extended kinship networks—cumulatively their historically specific 'class problematic'— effectively drove a wedge through the respectable working class, offering only the unsettling options of either upward or downward mobility. Youth subcultures reflected these contradictory changes. In Cohen's memorable and oft-quoted words, 'the 'latent function of sub-culture is …to express and resolve, albeit "magically", the contradictions which remain hidden or unresolved in the parent culture' (Cohen 1972: 23). The actual analysis involved working through how each subculture's 'subsystems' ('dress', 'music', 'argot' and 'ritual') were articulated together and how they changed 'from one subcultural moment to another' (ibid.: 23–24)—what Cohen called the 'structural or semiotic' level of analysis (ibid.). The connection back to the historically specific class problematic—his 'historical' level of analysis (ibid.)—followed. In other words, it was attentive to the structural mediations between the subculture as lived reality and the socio-historical moment it crystallised, as with any conjunctural analysis—which is certainly what it was.

However, as with all conjunctural analyses, everything depends on just how Sartre's' problem of mediations' (1963: 35–84) is resolved. Have the relevant mediations been identified? Have *all* the relevant mediations been noted? Since the answer to the latter question is invariably 'no', the better question might be: have a sufficient number of mediations been properly identified such that an approximately accurate or good enough analysis becomes possible. Judged by the absolute criterion of '*all* the relevant mediations', Cohen's analysis inevitably fell short—not least because his own third level of analysis, the 'phenomenological' ('the way the subculture is actually lived out' by its members) was never addressed. We should not be too critical about this for, in the absence of long term, primary ethnographic encounters with actual subcultural participants, lived reality can only be a construction/deduction from other levels of analysis and/or from secondary accounts. It is also, rightly, one of the criticisms of *RTR*. The 'ethnographies' in *RTR* too were, mostly, the more limited secondary ones. As for the question of sufficiency, was it a 'good enough' analysis? The subcultures group felt that despite its many strengths and obvious superiority to all other existing subcultural analyses, it raised a few questions that we might address: in other words, we found what felt to be missing mediations. We also dealt more expansively with Cohen's subsystems (our 'styles'), which was our attempt, however inadequately, also to address the phenomenological level.

Cohen explained that the various youth subcultures were all variations on a theme, the theme being the unsettling changes their working-class parents' culture were living through (their 'class problematic'). This seemed to overlook the specifically generational mediations—school, work (part-time Saturday jobs, etc.), their leisure activities, the police, youth and social workers—which made the experiences of the young different from those of their parents: 'It is at the intersection between the located parent culture and the mediating institutions of the dominant culture that youth subcultures arise' (Clarke et al. 2006: 41). Cohen also failed to address the sequencing of the subcultures and why particular subcultures explored the particular 'options' ('upward' or 'downward' mobility) that they did. So, we attempted to find a tighter fit between 'subcultural style' and historical moment, which, again, entailed more detailed attention to the mediations affecting each style: What were the original significations of the objects used in assembling a given style; how were these re-signified when appropriated for subcultural usage? How well the interim, 'work-in-progress' analyses of *RTR* have withstood the test of time is for others to judge—as many have. This is not the place to address these criticisms, partly because this has been attempted in the new material in the second edition of the text (Hall and Jefferson 2006: vii–xxxii), but mostly because my argument here has been that it is the conjunctural approach that constitutes the continuing importance of the text to criminology. The same is true of *PTC*, to which I now turn.

References

Althusser, L. 1969. *For Marx*, trans. Ben Brewster. Harmondsworth: Penguin.
Aronson, R. 1987. *Sartre's Second Critique*. Chicago: University of Chicago Press.
Clarke, J., S. Hall, T. Jefferson, and B. Roberts. 1976. Subculture, cultures and class. In Hall and Jefferson, eds. (2006: 3–59).
Cohen, P. 1972. Subcultural conflict and working class community. *WPCS* 2: 5–51.
Davison, S., D. Featherstone, and B. Schwarz. 2017. Introduction: redefining the political. In Hall (2017: 1–15).
Gramsci, A. 1971. *Selections from the Prison Notebooks*, ed. and trans. Q. Hoare and G.N. Smith. London: Lawrence & Wishart.
Gray, A., J. Campbell, M. Erickson, S. Hanson, and H. Wood (eds.). 2007. *CCCS Selected Papers*, vol. 2. London: Routledge.
Hall, S. 1957/2017. The new Conservatism and the old. In Hall (2017: 18–27).
Hall, S. 1958/2017. A sense of classlessness. In Hall (2017: 28–46).
Hall, S. 1968. The Hippies: An American moment. *Stencilled Paper* 16. Birmingham: CCCS, University of Birmingham. Republished without footnotes in Gray et al., eds. (2007: 146–67).
Hall, S. 1988. *The Hard Road to Renewal: Thatcherism and the Crisis of the Left*. London: Verso.
Hall, S. 2017. *Selected Political Writings: The Great Moving Right Show and Other Essays*, ed. S. Davison, D. Featherstone, M. Rustin, and B. Schwarz. London: Lawrence and Wishart.
Hall, S., and T. Jefferson (eds.). 2006. *Resistance Through Rituals: Youth Subcultures in Post-war Britain*, 2nd ed. London: Routledge.
Hall, S. with B. Schwarz. 2017. *Familiar Stranger: A Life Between Two Islands*. London: Allen Lane.
Hall, S., C. Critcher, T. Jefferson, J. Clarke, and B. Roberts. 2013. *Policing the Crisis: Mugging, the State and Law and Order*, 2nd ed. Houndmills, Basingstoke: Palgrave Macmillan.

Marx, K. 1852/1968. *The Eighteenth Brumaire of Louis Bonaparte*. In Marx and Engels (1968: 94–179).

Marx, K., and F. Engels. 1968. *Selected Works in One Volume*. London: Lawrence and Wishart.

Sartre, J.-P. 1960/1976. *Critique of Dialectical Reason I: Theory of Practical Ensembles*, trans. A. Sheridan-Smith, ed. J. Ree. London: New Left Books.

Sartre, J.-P. 1963. *The Problem of Method*, trans. and intro. H.E. Barnes. London: Methuen.

3

Conjunctural Analysis Part Two: The Case of *Policing the Crisis*

Although *Policing the Crisis (PTC)* was being researched and written at the same time as *Resistance through Rituals (RTR)*, by many of the same personnel, it was a significantly different project in several ways. It is these differences, I believe, that has made it so widely recognised as a major contribution to both cultural studies and criminology. In the first place, it was the result of a sustained piece of empirical research, not a provisional 'work-in-progress'. Secondly, it started out, *not* as an attempt to analyse a conjuncture, but as an attempt to understand the particularly savage sentences meted out on three juveniles. Thirdly, it turned out to be remarkably prescient, thus making its analysis broadly true. What follows will attempt to demonstrate each of these points by showing, step by step, what we did; and, in doing so, how we, inadvertently and without conscious intent, produced what has become the paradigm example of a contemporary conjunctural analysis.

A Short Detour via Marx

PTC starts with two events. The first was the robbery that took place in November 1972, in Handsworth, Birmingham, which we first became aware of in March 1973 when the three boy 'muggers', as they were labelled, were severely sentenced, the oldest (at 16 years old) to 20 years. It was the reporting of this that horrified us sufficiently to get involved, determined to do something. This was partly because it involved local boys and partly because our special interest, and to some extent expertise, was 'youth'.[1] The second was the reporting of the stabbing to death of an 'elderly widower' in London—labelled 'a mugging gone wrong' by a police officer. This was the first time the term mugging had been used in the UK to refer to a specific crime. The book starts with this press report. Why is this important? Answering this requires a short detour via Marx.

In the same year, 1973, that we started the research for *PTC*, Marx's *Grundrisse*—the rough drafted notebooks written during 1857–1858 that he intended as an outline of his entire project—appeared in English translation. Later that same year, Hall produced a 'reading' of the Introduction to the text which became the very first Centre for Contemporary Cultural Studies (CCCS) *Stencilled Paper* (Hall 1973/2007). Marx's text is not an easy read: condensed, provisional and one Marx himself later partly redrafted. But it was one of his 'most pivotal' (ibid.: 83); crucially, for present purposes, it was Marx's 'fullest methodological…summary-text' (ibid.: 84). Whatever changes Hall's relationship to Marxist concepts underwent in subsequent years, he remained true to Marx's method. It was, and remains, foundational to the notion of conjunctural analysis.

What Marx had to say about the appropriate starting point for 'the method of political economy' (Marx 1857–1858/1973: 100) was one of those issues that caused him most trouble, and about which he was to change his mind. Broadly speaking, Marx ended up arguing against starting with an abstract whole, like 'population', because it is already

---

[1]The local dimension was enhanced by the community activist work in Handsworth of one member of the *PTC* team. This led to the establishment of a support Committee for the accused boys, which produced a pamphlet called *20 Years* (Paul and Mustafa Support Committee 1973).

a composite of many elements. Rather, he suggested a simpler starting point, 'such as labour, division of labour, need, exchange value' (ibid.: 100–101) from which to trace the determinations to a new, concrete, not abstract, 'whole'. This Marx then concluded was 'obviously the scientifically correct method. The concrete is concrete because it is the concentration of many determinations' (ibid.: 101). In a later reworking of these ideas, Marx simplified matters even further: '"the reader who wishes to follow me at all must resolve to climb from the particular up to the general"' (Marx in *Marx-Engels Werke* XIII, p. 7, quoted in Nicolaus 1973: 38).

Marx (1857–1858/1973: 102) also wondered about the role of history in all this: if his 'simpler categories' did not 'also have an independent historical or natural existence predating the more concrete ones?'. This led to lengthy ruminations on where, historically, one should start thinking about these simpler relations: from the beginning of history or…? Marx concluded that the proper starting point is how these relations appear in the present: in his case 'their relation to one another in modern bourgeois society' (ibid.: 107). This radical historicity is the other methodological protocol underpinning conjunctural analyses and their attempts to be histories of the present.

PTC Part I: From Particular 'Mugging' Trials to the Determinations of an Over-Reaction

Returning to *PTC*, our historically located, 'particular' starting point, the reports of two trials, established the empirical co-ordinates of what we needed to address: the media, since they reported the cases, the 'mugging' label, since apparently novel, the police, since they 'produced' the cases at court, and the courts, since they sentenced the 'muggers'. But, first, we needed to establish what was wrong with the existing explanation for tough sentencing, why what we called 'the "rising crime rate" equation' was inadequate (rising violent crime plus courts being 'too soft' meant a new 'toughness' was needed). When we concluded that, whichever way we looked at it, the conventional theoretical common sense did not stack up and that we were witnessing an 'over-reaction', then we needed a new theoretical model that could accommodate this idea. Enter the notion 'moral panic', recently introduced to the sociological community by Stan Cohen (1972). The over-reaction to 'mugging' seemed to have all the hallmarks of a moral panic.

Having reconceptualised our object of enquiry, we returned to the origins of the label and what was happening in the police, courts and media to produce this particular moral panic. In other words, we moved from the phenomenology of the panic to the 'mediations' (in Sartre's terminology), or 'determinations' (in Marx's terminology), producing it. Exploring the immediate histories of each of these began to provide new determinations: for example, the courts had been getting 'tougher' for some time; the police in London had set up 'anti-mugging' squads; the 'mugging' label had acquired a host of negative connotations before it was used to label particular crimes.

Take the 'mugging' label. Being able to establish, empirically, that it made an appearance in the British press with all its scary American-derived connotations of 'race, crime, riot and lawlessness' and the associated '"law and order" backlash' (Hall et al. 2013: 31), began to make sense of the 'over-reaction', helped us understand better a part of its determining complex. Or take the apparent unanimity with which the police, courts and media seemed to speak on the topic. Here, our empirical examination, a painstaking dissection of how mugging was reported, commented upon, editorialised and so on, was able to reveal precisely how three apparently independent agencies—the police, the judiciary and the media—effectively combined together to produce '*an effective ideological and control closure*' (ibid.: 80) around mugging. Though some will not be surprised by this, given the simplistic, reductive uptake of the Marxist generalisation about the age's ruling ideas being those of the ruling class, what this close examination revealed, and which could not have been found without such an examination, was that this outcome was determined partly by the professional ideologies of news journalists, with their sense of themselves as independent, non-partisan arbiters charged with calling the state to account. Methodologically, then, the important point is that it was only by staying close to the data that new determinations were found. More generally, one could say, remain empirically driven as long as possible: do not go reaching for a theoretical (hence, inevitably, reductive) explanation too soon. So long as the 'facts' on the ground, the empirical data, are revealing their determinations, remain theoretically parsimonious. It is only when no new determinations have been revealed and existing explanations remain inadequate as responses to the data that they will need to be critiqued and replaced with a better theoretical offering.

Part II: From the Reception of Media Messages to the Determinations of Ideologies of Crime and Punishment

Part II is a less discussed part of the book. It was, on the one hand, a detailed further look at the press coverage of the Handsworth case, in this case the local press. On the other hand, it began to examine the reception of this media coverage: how was the 'effective ideological…closure' going down with the public? To get at this, we examined letters to the editor in both the national and the local press, and the abusive letters, sent privately, to the mother of the oldest of the convicted boys. Part II concluded with a chapter attempting to make sense of these manifold offerings, all of which, directly or indirectly, in their various different formats, constituted data about 'explanations and ideologies of crime' (ibid.: 138), the title of Chapter 6. This look at public opinion about crime attempted to show the dominance of the traditionalist view of crime, its roots in common sense, and to explain its relationship to the 'social anxiety' that underpinned the moment of the 1960s and 1970s. This explanation began to call on the work of Gramsci (1971), since such moments coincide with a sense of lost authority. Thus was introduced the quote from Gramsci that delivers that for which perhaps the book is best known: 'A "crisis of authority" is spoken of: this is precisely the crisis of hegemony, or general crisis of the state' (ibid.: 175). Methodologically this chapter started with empirical data and attempted to make sense of it with theory. In this it was probably theoretically top heavy, more speculative about the determinations than would be ideal; a conclusion it readily acknowledged. However, the available empirical data were limited. The analysis did not shy away from the need to understand how audiences responded to media images and messages; to ideologies of crime and punishment. In a historical moment of global populism, this continues to be an important issue.

Part III: From Moral Panics to the Determinations of a Crisis of Hegemony

Chapter 7, which commenced Part III, set out the theoretical tools needed to understand the 'moment' of mugging that the Handsworth case crystallised. In so doing, it appears to reverse the previous methodological strategy of starting with empirical material: Marx's historical particulars. However, that is only partly true. What Chapter 7 does is reprise the empirical contours of the argument about the reaction to mugging being an example of a moral panic before announcing its new theoretical move: beyond the transactionalism of moral panic theory to 'a more historical and structural view' (ibid.: 183). The chapter's endpoint stated that the following two chapters would provide the empirical basis to justify this theoretical move. Ultimately, a reversal such as this, presenting the theoretical justification in advance of the research-based, empirical evidence upon which it was built, is a rhetorical choice: What works best to make the argument accessible to the readership? And readers, ultimately, decide that. However, before embarking on the theoretical justification, there was an attempt to make clear that this move to the historical and structural level was not at the expense of empirical specificity, even though readers would have to be patient for such a reveal.

A further point about the ordering of material relates to Sartre's notion of the progressive-regressive method, the idea that there is a constant movement between the moments as one re-theorises (regressive moment) en route to the ultimate goal of a new 'concrete' whole. We have seen this already in the shift from conventional common sense on mugging to moral panic theory and beyond. The inadequacy of common sense 'theorising' was first demonstrated by a critical look at relevant empirical data (regressive moment 1) before being replaced by more adequate theorising (attentive to the empirical data), namely, moral panic theory (progressive moment 1). But, the inadequacies of moral panic theory conceptualised within a transactional rather than a historical and structural framework, meant it failed to answer the question, 'why then'? Addressing this question involved revealing new determinations, which in turn required yet another return to empirical data: further historical/empirical research on moral panics and the media (regressive moment 2). This provided (in Chapters 8 and 9) the empirical support, and new determinations, that justified the theoretical conclusion already delivered in Chapter 7 (the reaction to mugging as a manifestation of the 'crisis of hegemony' in the British state): progressive moment 2, our new 'concrete' whole and ultimate goal.

The newly uncovered determinations resulted from the finding that moral panics changed shape somewhat from the early 1960s (the time of the mods' and rockers' seaside clashes that provided the empirical basis of Stan Cohen's classic study) to the early 1970s. The 'discrete' panics of the 1960s began to be mapped together in a 'speeded up sequence' during the later 1960s and, by the early 1970s, began to exhibit what we construed as an 'altered' sequence, one in which the initiating 'dramatic event' of Cohen's classic moral panic—that which was thought to precipitate the over-reaction—was no longer necessary before the 'control culture' made its presence felt. In 'anticipating' the dramatic event, as it were, the 'control culture' became, in effect, the initiator of the subsequent panic. Trying to make sense of what we were finding entailed the production of new mediating concepts, namely, 'signification spirals' (based on the recently developed 'new deviancy' notion of 'deviancy amplification spirals'), 'thresholds', and 'convergence'. Once again, we were attempting to remain empirically driven, to be theoretically parsimonious, developing only those concepts that we felt necessary to organise and comprehend an enormous amount of data. These concepts were attempting to illuminate the way the threat potential of particular events was amplified through the way it was being signified ('signification spiral'). The amplification was achieved by linking one apparent threat with another, like student protest with violence ('convergence'). If the linked threat was worse, as is the case with protest and violence, we talked of a 'threshold' having been crossed, with the 'threshold' of 'extreme violence' being the ultimate one. These new types of 'anticipatory' panic combined with this changed pattern of signification whereby the threats to the social order were continually being amplified had begun to repose the question of how to understand moral panics at the level of the social formation as a whole:

> To put it crudely, the 'moral panic' appears to us to be one of the principal forms of ideological consciousness by means of which a 'silent majority' is won over to the support of increasingly coercive measures on the part of the state, and lends its legitimacy to a 'more than usual' exercise of control. (ibid.: 218)

Demonstrating the 'more than usual exercise of control' that characterised 'the *moment of mugging*' (ibid.: 317) is the empirical subject matter of Chapter 9. It was also evidence of the coercive tilt that signified the crisis of hegemony and the movement 'Towards the "Exceptional State"' (the chapter's title and theoretical endpoint). This was the form the 'crisis of hegemony' took and thus the other element of our new 'concrete' whole. However, this new 'progressive moment' which ended the chapter did not end the book, although many appear to think so, based on how the book is usually discussed. In fact, there is a whole new Part (IV) to follow, which consists of one long chapter, 10, on 'The Politics of "Mugging"'.

Part IV: From the Lives of Black Youths to the Determinations of the Politics of Mugging

Although the reporting of two 'mugging' trials was the book's starting point, there would have been nothing to report without the crimes that led to the trials. And, although we chose to start with the former because the harshness of the sentences in the Handsworth case provoked us politically and puzzled us intellectually, and went on to devote the lion's share of research attention to the issue of the social reaction to 'muggings', we were well aware that similar detailed attention needed to be paid to the act of mugging. This then became the subject matter of the final chapter, albeit a more tentative offering than the earlier chapters. Its inclusion made the book, inadvertently, an empirical test case of 'a fully social theory of deviance' recently called for by Taylor et al. (1973: 269), in their influential book *The New Criminology* (*TNC*). The fact that, even today, it remains the only such attempt merely reinforces this book's central argument, namely, the failure by criminologists to take up the conjunctural message from *PTC*.

Although many may find the chapter theoretically top-heavy, methodologically it proceeds in identical fashion to the rest of the book. It starts with two empirical observations that were derived from the media reportage that provided so much of the book's data. The first was that, although the mugging label arrived 'connotatively rich in its racial reference' (Hall et al. 2013: 322) in the early 1971–1972 period, it was not unambiguously seen as a black crime. By the mid-1970s, this had changed: 'mugging' had become overwhelmingly associated with black youth and the multiply deprived areas they came from. And although the statistics remained as fraught as ever, some black youths in some areas were 'involved in petty crime, including those which are labelled "mugging"' (ibid.). These empirical starting points provided the question about the meaning of mugging that needed to be addressed: what was it about black youth and their conditions of existence in that historical moment that made 'mugging', for some, a potential 'option'. Or, expressed in the terms I have been using throughout, what determinations/mediations lay hidden within the crime of 'mugging'? What needed to be addressed in ascending from the apparently concrete phenomenon of a particular crime to a new, concrete, 'general' whole? As with the work on *RTR*, essentially this entailed trying to identify black youth's 'class problematic': in their case, attending to what we might call their 'raced', class problematic.

This meant interrogating the key structures impacting the lives of black youth, namely, school, the labour market and the housing market.

In each case we noted that these were 'structures of "secondariness"' (ibid.: 333), i.e. they placed black youth, systematically, not incidentally, in a 'secondary' position in relation to their similarly working-class white counterparts. In schools, this racially specific disadvantage entailed devaluation of their cultural capital, including their language (with patois seen as sub-standard English), and the labelling of disproportionate numbers as educationally 'sub-normal'. In terms of the labour market, the position of black immigrant labour—'sucked in and expelled in direct relation to the swings and dips of capital accumulation' (ibid.: 336)—meant the recession and unemployment that characterised the 1970s hit black labour first and hardest and their 'miseducated' children even harder: by the mid-1970s, the black unemployment rate was approximately twice the national average (which was around 5%) and black school leavers four times that. As for the housing market structure, this worked to concentrate the black immigrant communities in multiply-deprived, inner-city areas, the only places where they could afford to rent the relatively cheap, multi-occupancy housing available. As the mid-1970s housing market conditions led to a decline in this kind of property, making the finding of accommodation harder for black families, the prospects for young black men and women seeking to find accommodation on their own became even bleaker. The result: a growth in 'drifting', sleeping rough, squatting and homelessness among young blacks.

The argument here was both empirical and theoretical. Methodologically, in terms I have been using throughout, there is a constant oscillation between the descriptive moment (what was happening to black youth empirically: culture and language devalued in schools, high unemployment, etc.) and Sartre's 'regressive' moment: 'In each of the structural areas dealt with so far, we can see that the general way in which class position and the division of labour is reproduced for the working class as a whole assumes a specific and differentiated form in relation to the stratum of black labour…Not only are these mechanisms race-specific; they have a differentiated impact on the different sexes and generations *within* the black labour force' (ibid.: 338). However, other mediations remained to be uncovered because race was not only the medium through which the class position of black youth was structured: 'it is also the principal modality in which black members of that class "live", experience, make sense of and thus *come to a consciousness* of their structured subordination...Race is not only an element of the "structures"; it is a key element in the class struggle - and thus in the *cultures* - of black labour' (ibid.: 340).

What followed, in the section 'Culture, Consciousness and Resistance' (ibid.: 341) was a potted history of the responses of the black, West Indian community to life in England (black youth 'muggers' at this time meant Afro-Caribbean)—from attempted assimilation or accepting one's subordinate lot to building a life of one's own, separate from the host community. The latter entailed constructing relatively self-sustaining communities—ghetto 'colonies'—which, in turn, provided the basis for new colony-generated identities and survival strategies to emerge. Of these, 'that range of informal dealing, semi-legal practices, rackets and small-time crime classically known in all ghetto life as *hustling*' (ibid.: 345), was perhaps the most relevant mediation for second-generation black youth born into the colony. With no other 'home' to relate to, miseducated and with few prospects other than 'shit-work' or the dole queue, constantly subjected to street racism and police harassment, too angry and disaffected to live peacefully at home and too poor to move out, except onto the streets, hustling as a survival strategy had a definite appeal. Not only was the hustling image 'cool', for when the going was good these were men with a certain style, but the politicisation of the American ghettos during this period, which had been undertaken by ex-hustlers like Malcolm X and members of the Black Panther Party, also made hustling signify a form of resistance to 'the man'. Closer to home, British ghettos were also producing their own resistant forms of street life with 'reggae, rastas and rudies'. All this marked the generational divide: 'The commitment of first-generation migrants to steady if unrewarding labour, and of the second generation to the life of the street and hustling rather than labouring, are the *principal* forms in which the "generation gap" is articulated in the black community' (ibid.: 346). Again, the oscillation between description and analysis continued. Much of the description derived from the many, detailed, interview-based accounts, of the lives of black youth, emerging during this period; what I earlier called, secondary ethnography.

The section ended with a composite biography of a 'mugger' (p. 354). It was a short, summarising attempt to imagine how a black youth coming to consciousness in that historical moment, inhabiting those particular structures of secondariness, might have lived them such that 'mugging' became a potentiality. Though not based on direct ethnography, by carefully tracing the particularity of the structural and cultural mediations of black youth at that historical moment, we managed to produce an account which captured much of the secondary ethnographies that we consulted.

Some would have stopped there. We had produced an account addressing the structures underpinning the situation of black youth, some of their relevant cultural responses, and attempted an imaginative reconstruction of their collective, 'lived' experience. However, while our journey from the act of 'mugging' to its biographical, cultural and structural mediations was in line with a conjunctural analysis, such an approach demands more. Remember that the ultimate point of such work is political, not merely academic: it is to reveal 'the exact balance of forces…to which political tactics must be applied'. So, we needed to answer a further question, namely, what could 'mugging' in the 1970s, a particular crime in a particular historical moment, tell us about the then current political balance of forces? What was its relation to political struggle in the conjuncture of the 1970s?

Having already offered an account of how the social reaction to 'mugging' was symptomatic of a crisis of hegemony partly manifested by 'exceptional' state measures, we needed to offer a similar account from the other side: what could the act of 'mugging' tell us about resistance to such measures. Before doing so, it is worth remembering that such a move was in line with Hall's earlier work on the hippies, where his ultimate interest lay in the same question: what could their social deviance reveal about their viability as a political project? It was also in line with another early paper of his, written at much the same time as *PTC* but based on empirical work he was undertaking with the CCCS media group, where the topic was the relations among 'deviance, politics, and the media', the paper's title (Hall 1974). It was a typically wide-ranging paper embracing symbolic interactionism, media sociology, French structuralism, semiology, Marx, Althusser and Lefebvre. But Gramsci and conjunctural analysis were in command, as this justification for a long theoretical detour made clear:

> [Processes of signification] can only be clarified by the study of a specific conjuncture between the different levels of practice and institution in a historical moment…but the route by which such insight is gained into the specificity of ideological discourse cannot be the final resting place of theory. Phenomenology teaches us to attend…to the level of *meaning*: symbolic interactionism presses on us the decisive level of 'definitions of the situation' as critical intervening variables: ethnomethodology refers us to the interactive work by which normative features of interpreted social situations are sustained, and the indexable character of expressions. Yet, in the end, these different aspects of the process by which abnormal political events are signified must be returned to the level of the social formation, via the critical concepts of power, ideology, and conflict'. (Hall 1974: 298)

Getting to the level of the social formation that included the activity of 'mugging' in the 1970s also required a theoretical detour, a regressive moment, to establish the historical relationships that have obtained between crime and politics. This entailed a consideration of the historical role of riots, mobs, rural unrest, social bandits, the 'dangerous classes' and the *lumpenproletariat*, an engagement with Marx on the *lumpenproletariat* and productive and unproductive labour, and with differing theoretical takes on the meaning of black wagelessness in the 1970s. This is not the place to reprise these arguments. What is important is that, rendering arguments about the *lumpenproletariat* historically and geographically specific revealed important differences between Marx's classical *lumpen*—'the criminal detritus of *all* classes' (Hall et al. 2013: 358)—and its subsequent appearances. Mao was happy to recruit criminal elements into his Red Army, for example, and the dispossessed 'underclass' of the third world were a key component of Fanon's 'spontaneously' radical 'wretched of the earth'. The Black Panther Party actively sought out *lumpen* ghetto hustlers; in the context of the UK in the 1970s, these would have been included in the wageless refusers of 'shit-work'.[2] Some of these black youth resorted to 'mugging'. In the case of these youths, it was their link not only with their metropolitan history but also with their colonial history, and thus its connection with the third world dispossessed, that provided a key to why they could not simply be regarded as contemporary members of a 'reserve army of labour' or *lumpenproletariat*, as perhaps their white counterparts might have been.

Ultimately, we were not able to resolve the questions about the politics of mugging that this historical/geographical journey threw up, although we hoped to have offered 'the component elements of an explanation, and thus the basis of a political judgement' (ibid.: 381). The indecisive nature of our answer echoed that of 'reality', since the successful revolutions in the third world, in which the new *lumpen* played a significant (though not uncontested) part, had not been repeated in 'the metropolitan heartland of capitalism' (ibid.: 385). However, in establishing that 'race is intrinsic to the manner in which the black labouring classes are *complexly constituted* at each of …[the] levels [economic, political and ideological]' of the social formation, we were able to conclude that 'race is the modality in which class is lived' (ibid.: 386). Insofar as this applied to the white working class too—'capital reproduces the class as a whole, structured by race' (ibid.: 387)—the state of race relations becomes indicative of the balance of class forces. A racially divided class is a politically divided class, and 'black crime functions as one of the vehicles of this division. It provides the separation of the class…with a material base [as]…one part of the class materially "rips off" another. It provides this separation with its ideological figure, for it transforms the deprivation of the class, out of which crime arises, into the all too intelligible syntax of race, and fixes a false enemy: the black mugger' (ibid.: 388). We are now back where we started, but now read from the subordinate side:

> The fact is that there is, as yet, no active politics, no form of organised struggle, and no strategy which is able adequately and decisively to

---

[2] For different takes on the meaning of black youth wagelessness at that time, see copies of *Race Today* and *The Black Liberator*.

intervene in the quasi-rebellion of the black wageless such as would be capable of bringing about that *break* in the current false appropriations of oppression through crime - that critical transformation of the criminalised consciousness into something more sustained and thorough-going in a political sense. (ibid.: 389)

In other words, the same balance of class forces—including the significant role played by racism—that produced the ideological and political offensive symptomatic of the crisis of hegemony characterising 1970s Britain, was also responsible for the above bleak conclusion.

Conclusion

A conjunctural analysis such as this, can only be judged, ultimately, by its ability to illuminate the historical moment it covered, which is why the book is remembered more for its analysis of the social reaction to mugging than for this final part on the act of mugging. While the latter analysis, reflecting reality, could only end indecisively, the former, in tracing the drift into the 'Law-and-Order Society' with its increasing authoritarianism, offered an early, prescient glimpse into 'Thatcherism', the term Hall (1979/2017) minted in his era-defining *Marxism Today* essay 'The great moving right show'. The notion of 'Thatcherism' as a momentous, global shift in capitalist social relations inaugurating neoliberalism is now a widely accepted understanding of the contemporary world.[3] Perhaps more than anything else, it is this, the ability to shed a little light on some aspect of contemporary reality, that accounts for the text's canonical status. What I hope to have achieved in this chapter is to show how the production of this 'truth' was made possible only via the methodology of conjunctural analysis.

---

[3] At the time, the meaning of Thatcherism, especially its novelty, was contested by many on the Left. See especially the exchanges between Jessop et al. (1984, 1985) and Hall (1985).

References

Cohen, S. 1972. *Folk Devils and Moral Panics*. London: MacGibbon & Kee.
Gray, A., J. Campbell, M. Erickson, S. Hanson, and H. Wood (eds.). 2007. *CCCS Selected Papers*, vol. 1. London: Routledge.
Gramsci, A. 1971. *Selections from the Prison Notebooks*, ed. and trans. Q. Hoare and G.N. Smith. London: Lawrence & Wishart.
Hall, S. 1974. Deviance, politics, and the media. In McIntosh and Rock, eds. (1974: 261–305).
Hall, S. 1985. Authoritarian populism: A reply to Jessop et al. *New Left Review* 1 (151).
Hall, S. 1973/2007. A "reading" of Marx's 1857 introduction to the *Grundrisse*. In Gray et al., eds. (2007: 83–111).
Hall, S. 1979/2017. The great moving right show. In Hall (2017: 172–186).
Hall, S. 2017. *Selected Political Writings: The Great Moving Right Show and Other Essays*, ed. S. Davison, D. Featherstone, M. Rustin, and B. Schwarz. London: Lawrence and Wishart.
Hall, S., and T. Jefferson (eds.). 2006. *Resistance Through Rituals: Youth Subcultures in Post-war Britain*, 2nd ed. London: Routledge.
Hall, S., C. Critcher, T. Jefferson, J. Clarke, and B. Roberts. 2013. *Policing the Crisis: Mugging, the State and Law and Order*, 2nd ed. Houndmills, Basingstoke: Palgrave Macmillan.
Jessop, B., K. Bonnett, S. Bromley, and T. Ling. 1984. Authoritarian populism, two nations and Thatcherism. *New Left Review* 1 (147).
Jessop, B., K. Bonnett, S. Bromley, and T. Ling. 1985. Thatcherism and the politics of hegemony: A reply to Stuart Hall. *New Left Review* 1 (153).
Marx, K. 1857–1858/1973. *Grundrisse: Foundations of the Critique of Political Economy (Rough Draft)*, trans. with a Foreword by Martin Nicolaus Harmondsworth: Penguin.
McIntosh, M., and P. Rock (eds.). 1974. *Deviance and Social Control*. London: Tavistock.
Nicolaus, M. 1973. Foreword. In Marx (1973: 7–63).
Paul, Jimmy, and Mustafa Support Committee. 1973. *20 Years*. Handsworth, Birmingham: The Action Centre, Handsworth.
Taylor, I., P. Walton, and J. Young. 1973. *The New Criminology: For a Social Theory of Deviance*. London: Routledge & Kegan Paul.

Part II

Cultural Criminology, Theorising and Stuart Hall

4

Cultural Criminology Part One: The Problems with a Theory-Driven Methodology

In Chapter 1, I showed briefly how cultural criminology and cultural studies came to have less in common intellectually than might be expected. There I noted that cultural criminology's failure to think conjuncturally lies at the heart of this difference. My aim in this and the next chapter is to show, using selected examples from cultural criminology, what this failure means in practice and what difference it makes. Since cultural criminology covers a wide variety of topics and approaches, to make this task manageable I will confine myself to some of its foundational, introductory texts and to four other texts, one from each of the key authors of those introductory texts. Between them these cover the broad orienting vision, theoretical ambition and methodological scope of cultural criminology, as well as some specific examples of the approach. I start out in this chapter with a critical overview of the introductory texts—*Cultural Criminology* (Ferrell and Sanders eds. 1995), *Cultural Criminology Unleashed* (Ferrell et al., eds. 2004), *Cultural Criminology: An Invitation* (Ferrell et al. 2008)—before focusing on two others, *City Limits: Crime, Consumer Culture and the Urban Experience* by Keith Hayward (2004) and Jock Young's (2003) article, 'Merton with energy:

© The Author(s), under exclusive license to Springer Nature Switzerland AG 2021
T. Jefferson, *Stuart Hall, Conjunctural Analysis and Cultural Criminology*, Palgrave Pioneers in Criminology, https://doi.org/10.1007/978-3-030-74731-2_4

Katz with structure: the sociology of vindictiveness and the criminology of transgression'. Both of these latter examples show that the strengths of cultural criminology's approach—its ambition, imaginative sweep and wide-ranging attempt to synthesise a variety of authors and theoretical positions—are also the source of its weaknesses. Not being anchored by the historical specificity of a particular moment, both authors became seduced, albeit unintentionally, by the holy grail of a general theory of crime. In short, they demonstrated the problems that arise from a theory-driven as opposed to a conjunctural methodology.

By way of reminder, a conjunctural methodology is a historically located attempt to make sense of a particular event or series of events, both in terms of what is apparently happening and in terms of what these events reveal about the underlying social relations. Stemming from a commitment to research as a form of political intervention, its ultimate objective is an understanding of just how the power relations in play produce, in all its complex specificity, the particularity of the event in question. Easy to say; anything but easy to achieve, as we saw in the last chapter with the example of *Policing the Crisis (PTC)* and its lengthy attempt to trace the connections between the response to a series of 'muggings' and the underlying shift in the nature of state power that it signified. In short, such a methodology is driven by historical particularities (the unusually harsh response to 'muggings' in the 1970s), and theory gets used to assist an understanding of their connection to underlying power relations (the 'crisis of hegemony' of the state).

An Overview of the Cultural Criminology Project

The cultural criminology project emerged tentatively in the 1990s and gradually developed from 'Fragments of a manifesto' into a full-blown manifesto (Ferrell and Sanders 1995a, b; Ferrell et al. 2004, 2008). It was an eclectic response to the 'new times' of Thatcherism and beyond, partly reflecting the diversity of the intellectual formations of its founding authors: critical criminology, left realism, postmodernism and ethnography. Unfortunately for the project's coherence, how all these strands were meant to hang together was never addressed in a principled fashion. Rather, there was a persistent tendency to produce formulations that either failed to recognise unresolved problems or claimed that these had already been resolved within cultural criminology.

In broad terms, the project originally aspired to integrate the study of crime, criminalisation and culture, both in terms of everyday dynamics and underlying structures: legal, political and symbolic (broadly, the mass media). This was reminiscent of a cultural version of *The New Criminology*'s (*TNC*) call for a 'fully social theory of deviance' (Taylor et al. 1973: Chap. 9), one attentive to the social dynamics, the social psychology and the political economy of both the criminal act and the reaction to it. However, as *TNC*'s authors themselves admitted, these were only the 'formal requirements' of a fully social theory (which was where they ended the book, and with it the idea of a fully social theory, to which, unfortunately, they never returned). What was needed, they insisted, 'is that these formal requirements must all appear in the theory, as they do in the real world, in a complex, dialectical relationship to one another' (ibid.: 277). One reading of *PTC* is that it was an attempt to do just that: to show how these 'formal requirements' appeared in a 'real world' example. My MA thesis (Jefferson 1974), based on our mugging materials, explicitly used their terminology, both in the title ('For a Social Theory of Deviance: The Case of Mugging, 1972-3') and in structuring the argument. But, the cultural criminology project quickly retreated from even these 'formal requirements'. Given the array of theories that they wished to include under the cultural criminology umbrella—interactionist, subcultural, constructionist, critical, anarchist, neo-marxist, feminist, cultural studies and postmodernist—they felt obliged to adopt a pluralistic approach (Ferrell and Sanders 1995b: 297).

In addition, the call for pluralism was accompanied by claims that the formal requirements had already produced substantive results; apparently so successfully that a core problematic of the social sciences—the relation between agency and structure, self and society—had been resolved: these were no longer separate spheres but 'exist…as social strands so tightly interwoven in the construction of crime and control as to be indistinguishable one from the other' (ibid.: 304). Or, talking specifically about media studies, 'the most viable model is one in which media presentations, real-life events, personal perceptions, public policies, and individual actions spiral about each other in a complex, mutually affecting and ever-changing structure of inter-relationships' (ibid.: 308). Such a chaotic model provided no clue as to how it might be analysed; nor could it, since, like all pluralistic approaches, it evaded the crucial issue of determinacy, without which it is impossible to trace back, through an event's many determinations, to the operation of power in any given situation (thus making conjunctural analysis impossible too).

As for methods, the anything goes anarchistic approach of Paul Feyerabend (1978), which echoed their theoretical pluralism, was combined with advocacy for the 'attentiveness' of 'the ethnographic case study' (Ferrell and Sanders 1995b: 306). However, there was no attempt to move beyond the perennial problem of the ethnographic case study and discuss how to theorise the relation between the ethnographic moment and underlying structures. Rather, the expanded discussion of methods in *Cultural Criminology* (Ferrell et al. 2008) introduced several new notions—'instant ethnography', 'liquid ethnography', 'visual criminology' and 'ethnographic content analysis' (ibid.: 179–91). Basically, the notions of 'instant' and 'liquid' ethnography suggested that the speed, chaos, confusion, unpredictability, transitoriness, etc. of contemporary life required an ethnography that somehow echoed these features. For example, because 'crime can occur in an instant', it was suggested that ethnography could also be done instantly, thus undercutting a fundamental tenet of ethnography that considerable fieldwork time is necessary to get to understand a culture. None of the examples that were proffered to demonstrate this postmodern ethnography undercut this fundamental tenet: the unpredictable can only be known as such if you have been around long enough to differentiate it from the predictable. The analogy with a butterfly house seems appropriate here: the faster the butterflies flutter about, the more you see, not by moving around with them, but by simply standing still, the longer the better. 'Visual criminology' seemed to be a plea to take the visual seriously, to use the visual to bear witness politically, rather than a novel method. As for 'ethnographic content analysis', the description of what this entailed—close reading of texts, sensitivity to nuance, capability of making connections beyond the text—was not new but had a long-standing history in media analysis. The media analysis in *PTC* came to mind when reading this; more generally, the close reading of texts had been a core method of cultural studies since its origins in literature and Leavisite literary criticism.

This failure to mention, much less build upon, this long-standing, more sophisticated history of media analysis was all the more odd since it had a big presence in criminology, especially through the volume, *The Manufacture of News: Deviance, Social Problems & the Mass Media*, edited by two National Deviancy Conference (NDC) stalwarts, Stan Cohen and Jock Young (1973)—the latter, of course, one of the authors of the volume being discussed here. It included two articles by Stuart Hall, one an analysis of news photographs (Hall 1973), which was an early example of visual criminology. The second, revised and expanded edition published in 1981 had grown to 30 articles, many of them now much-cited classics of the genre. Using the argument that others have already summarised and critiqued work in this area, Ferrell and colleagues settled for brief reductive summaries of relevant research. Ignoring previous contributions is not the way to build a more adequate model, which can only happen by first critiquing existing contributions and transforming them in some way as a result.

Despite the advocacy of pluralism and ethnography, the project is committed to a politically engaged criminology. For example, there is a wish to understand the contemporary crime moment in its particularity (Ferrell et al. 2008: 63); which looked like a plea for conjunctural analysis. However, this wish turned out to be a concern to understand crime/criminalisation in late modernity, a period roughly co-terminus with the dominance of neoliberalism. As we shall see later in the chosen examples of their empirically-based work, this largely involved making some general connections between the characteristics of a period and the crime/criminalisation it produced. Moreover, the discussions about the relationships among capitalist and other structural inequalities and crime begged a series of questions that remained unanswered.

A radical, political engagement requires that the question of the state be addressed. And, there was such an attempt (ibid.: 75–79). Although only a tentative offering, it was, nevertheless, unsatisfactory in many ways. For a start, existing attempts within criminology to address the issue were ignored. Like that of *PTC*, where the introduction of the notion of the state was a significant part of what was innovative about that work[1]: how it was a development of moral panic theory, not simply another example of it.[2] Rather, Guy Debord and situationism were cited—whose work was not specifically about the state—but not the later theories of Althusser, Gramsci and Poulantzas informing *PTC*, which did advance Marxist theorising of the state. So, rather than offer some thoughts about how to understand state power, Ferrell and colleagues suggested a series of empirical areas to be covered. The one time they did raise a theoretical issue, about the 'paradox' of nation states 'becoming more rigid and aggressive in...maintaining sovereignty' in a world of global capitalism 'increasingly characterised by the erosion of...borders' (Ferrell et al. 2008: 76), they again missed an obvious connection with *PTC*: the idea of the crisis of hegemony producing more authoritarian state responses (massively in evidence on a global scale today). Instead, they offered a simple, general redescription of the paradox as a contradiction between the economic demands of contemporary capitalism and the new security demands of the post-9/11 war on terror without any attempt to explain the contradiction. This was another example of failing to think conjuncturally. The call to 'research and expose the full collateral damage of mass incarceration' (ibid.: 78) felt particularly poignant in the absence of mentioning 'authoritarian populism', the concept Hall (1988) made central to understanding Thatcherism: exposing the damage of mass incarceration made the general, transhistorical point that if only

---

[1] A year after *Cultural Criminology* was published, an edited text appeared called *State, Power, Crime* (Coleman et al., eds. 2009), that specifically made the notion of state power underpinning the analysis of mugging in *PTC* its starting point and the focus of their contributors' attempts to reconsider the contemporary relevance of the notion within particular areas of criminological interest. Stuart Hall contributed the Preface.

[2] Which was, unfortunately, exactly how the authors did see it. Listed along with Cohen's 'study of mods and rockers' (Cohen 1972) and 'Young's study of cannabis and hippies in *The Drugtakers* (1971)' as one of 'the three original studies of moral panics' (Ferrell et al. 2008: 50), the originality of *PTC*'s notion of the state was reduced to a shared revelation of 'major structural and cultural changes in advanced industrial societies, as refracted through the prism of youth' (ibid.). While this may have been true of the studies of Cohen and of Young, it seriously misrepresented what *PTC* was attempting. Interestingly, a few years prior to this, Jock Young (1998: 28) had been much more willing to recognise the full Marxist scope of *PTC*. Calling it the 'apotheosis of radical criminology', he regarded it then as 'by far the most complete expression' of *The New Criminology*'s call for a fully social theory of deviance.

we knew the scale of the problem we would do something to change it; the historically specific notion of authoritarian populism problematised that assumption since mass incarceration may be a populist vote winner. Rendering an idea historically contingent is to think about it conjuncturally.

If the engagement with Marxism was marked by an avoidance of all the issues that needed to be addressed, the engagement with postmodern theory was largely unclear. Take, for example, the issue of the speed of today's culture, for which Paul Virilio was a key influence. Was this a difference that made a difference: were the faster 'spirals' of late modernity qualitatively different from earlier spirals (such as the 'deviancy amplification spirals' of radical criminology in the 1970s) simply because they were, we were told, speeded up? Was meaning recoverable when the linear sequencing of modernity gave way to late modern 'loops'? The use of gangsta rap to think more about loops and spirals did not clarify matters. The examples used to discuss the commodification and commercialisation of violence and transgression seemed merely to update empirically rather than transcend theoretically the already known about the relationship between fictional and real violence. But, after all this novel looping and spiralling, we were told that the job of cultural criminologists was rather similar to the traditional one of critical criminologists, namely, 'to find the political and economic contradictions unfolding amidst the loops and spirals of contemporary culture' (Ferrell et al. 2008: 150). Rather than say more about what this entailed in the new historical moment, we were presented with another example of looping and spiralling, the case of graffiti. It was as if whenever a theoretical issue was raised, a new empirical example was needed to deflect attention from the fact that they were attempting the impossible: to be both pluralistic postmodernists and Marxists at the same time. The suggested resistance to all this drew on a similarly eclectic mixture of ideas and theorists, which had become, by this point in the book, a familiar, if not very enlightening, trope.

One reason why so much that should have been presented at length in Ferrell et al. (2008) was dealt with summarily (and hence unsatisfactorily) was because so much space was given over to what could and should have been lesser concerns: the list-like additive approach to exemplification that I have already alluded to; and the disproportionate space—a dozen pages—given over simply to rubbish survey-based, quantitative research of mainstream criminology. Conducted in a dismissive rather than a dialogic fashion, it felt pointless: a bit like Jeremy Corbyn trying to convince Boris Johnson of the need to convert to socialism. The issue of space may or may not have been the reason for one peculiar but fateful omission: the decade of the eighties. Having dealt with the theoretical origins of the project up until the 1970s moment of the NDC and the early years of the Centre for Contemporary Cultural Studies (CCCS), the following chapter leapt straight into 'the world of late modernity' (ibid.: 56). This not only neatly bypassed the knotty theoretical problems thrown up by 'new times' and marxism's encounter with postmodernism,[3] but it removed completely the many struggles—political, economic, ideological—of that period induced by Thatcher's ruthless enforcing of her 'strong state/free market' neoliberal project. Imagining new trajectories may well have been necessary, but what will always be crucial for any project with radical, political objectives, is how everyday particularities are connected to social forces of one kind or another. Caught between an unexamined Marxism and a pluralistic postmodernism, this issue was either dealt with reductively or not at all.

In moving on to selected examples of the more focused, research-based work of these cultural criminology pioneers, we will encounter a range of topics but similar problems. In the first two examples that I introduce below, it is the role of theory in their accounts that is the principal source of the problem. To demonstrate this, I start with Keith Hayward's ambitious *City Limits*, followed by Jock Young's equally ambitious attempt to combine Merton's structural account of crime with Katz's phenomenological one. As I hope to show, this theoretical ambitiousness is a large part of the problem.

---

[3]The 1980s was also the decade of the atomisation of the NDC project and the development of 'left realism', an attempt by Jock Young and others to 'take crime seriously' (Lea and Young 1984). At that point in time, because of its primary focus on the over-reaction to crime, *PTC* was regarded by such 'realists' as an example of 'left idealism'. Perhaps this was another reason for bypassing the decade.

City Limits and the Limitations of Theory

Keith Hayward's *City Limits* (2004) was an argument about how what he called 'late modern consumer culture' was producing profound changes in the city's physical or spatial environment and, concomitantly, in our subjective experience of urban life—all of which was contributing to the commission of certain kinds of crime. Although he asserted that his was not an attempt to produce a general theory of crime, his ambition to connect, albeit tentatively, social (structural, situational, environmental) and individual theories of crime, suggested otherwise. For the sake of brevity, I will overlook the early chapters on the city and urban life since the mid-nineteenth century, and move straight to his new conceptual framework. Ultimately, despite the theoretical sophistication constantly on display, the framework failed to convince; not just because it was over-ambitious, but because its method was theory-driven. All three of Hayward's starting concepts—the city, consumer culture and crime—are general abstractions, like Marx's 'population'. As we saw in Chapter 3, Marx abandoned this apparently concrete but actually abstract starting point, since it was already comprised of many elements, in favour of a method that started with the particular and worked up to the general, as the correct route to uncovering the many determinations in play. Starting abstractly also transgressed a key methodological protocol of conjunctural analysis. Consequently, Hayward's resulting framework could only end up being, in Marx's dismissive words, 'merely speculative, merely theoretical' (Marx 1857–1858/1973: 102).

Although the book started with the city, the attempted theoretical framework started with the act of crime; more specifically with Jack Katz's influential *Seductions of Crime* (1988). But whereas Katz attempted to show what was involved in the actual commission of various different crimes, from murder and gang violence to robbery and shoplifting, Hayward started with the general ideas that these explorations gave rise to: crime as emotionally driven, pleasurable, exciting, a means of transcending the self, escaping the mundane routines of everyday life. Moreover, Hayward wished to add to Katz's list other crimes—'vandalism, theft and destruction of cars, fire-starting, mugging, hoax emergency service call-outs, car "cruising", peer group violence and other forms of street delinquency' as well as 'drug use' and 'football hooliganism' (Hayward 2004: 149–150)—which he believed to be similarly motivated because they appeared to have similarly expressive, rather than rational, dimensions. Leaving aside Katz's different phenomenologies for different types of crime, and the conventional viewpoint that many of these crimes would seem to involve different motivations (or, express different emotions), the starting point had shifted from particular crimes to the general, abstract idea of the 'thrill of transgression' (ibid.: 149).

Part of Hayward's attempt to link individual behaviour and structural conditions involved addressing the historical issue of why the thrill of transgression seemed to be more in evidence at the time of writing (although this had not been shown to be the case). Hayward suggested this was because it also 'offers a way of seizing control of one's destiny' in late modern societies characterised by 'a pervasive sense of insecurity and disembeddedness' (ibid.: 152), which he thought was best captured by Jock Young's (1999) notion of 'ontological insecurity'. What began as an attempt by R. D. Laing (1959) to differentiate the ontologically secure from the ontologically insecure had become, apparently, a general condition, common to all, which begged many questions. Perhaps such insecurity, he suggested, was a result of each of us trying to 'reconcile our (still partly modern) selves, to the fundamental changes' of postmodernism: 'might the common feelings of ontological insecurity…be best understood as a congress of feelings that together can be described as the *dilemmas of transition*'…? (Hayward 2004: 153).

Exerting a sense of control was also about creating an 'authentic' sense of self in uncertain, inauthentic times, which was where 'edgework' entered the argument. Edgework is a term originally embracing activities that have a metaphorical 'edge' to them, such as risky sports, like skydiving, and supposedly dangerous occupations like firefighting and police work[4] (see Lyng 1990). The appeal of edgework was heightened by the paradox that late modern insecurity was accompanied by the feeling of being 'over-controlled'. Translating edgework to contemporary youth culture and run down, deprived neighbourhoods, Hayward

---

[4] Although common sense regards police work as dangerous, this is not borne out statistically. It is much less dangerous than many other occupations.

suggested that these offered many opportunities for risk-taking, illegal and otherwise, and cited the growing pervasiveness of risky behaviours like using drugs and binge drinking as evidence.

Showing how consumer culture played into this notion of postmodern subjectivity and certain criminal transgressions required another theoretical detour, namely, a renewed look at both Merton's 'strain' theory (the notion that when opportunities to achieve society's goals are blocked, the resulting strain on individuals eventuate in the exploration of alternative, including criminal, routes to society's goals) and the idea of relative deprivation. This detour produced a revised, less instrumental, more expressive notion of need: '*what people are now feeling deprived of is no longer simply the material product itself, but, rather, the sense of identity that products have come to bestow on the individual*' (ibid.: 161). Moreover, needs had, apparently, become rights—most of us in Britain, we were told, now regarded a foreign holiday as such a right—and desires had become needs. This produced unprecedented strain: '*the essence of a consumer society*' was '*a constant sense of unfulfillment*' (ibid.: 161). And this was 'a recipe for criminality' (ibid.: 162). An interim summary followed:

> Drawing this together, we thus go beyond Katz's simple model of escape from/transcendence of the routine to present, instead, a 'control-excitement' - model (understood via risk, hedonism, expressivity and the concept of edgework). Put simply, many forms of crime frequently perpetrated within urban areas should be seen for exactly what they are: attempts to achieve a semblance of control within ontologically insecure social worlds (ibid.: 165).

An argument about the market's contribution to promoting transgression followed, with a series of examples—from advertising, film, video games, television, board games—of how important were images of crime to contemporary capitalism's youth market. (Unfortunately, there was nothing to show how these images were 'read' by today's youths.) What the state sought to control, the market celebrated and commodified. Bauman and others were used to expand on the idea of the insatiability of contemporary desire. Late modern subjects endlessly chasing the new had been called '"neophiliacs" or lovers of novelty' by Campbell (1989) and 'sensation-gatherers' by Bauman (1997: 146), the latter characterised by 'impulsivity, dissatisfaction, narcissism and spontaneity' (Hayward 2004: 174). Since they were the objects of aggressive lifestyle advertising and responsible for most crimes, it was apparently unsurprising that young men were attracted to 'novel, unconventional and illegal forms of excitement' (ibid.: 175). This may be true, although it is questionable how novel were some of the crimes listed to illustrate the point, namely, 'joyriding, football hooliganism, drug-use, mugging and gang membership' (ibid.).

Desires needed to be satisfied immediately in the continuous present of late modern, consumer culture, apparently. The emphasis on novelty and the now encouraged a reckless disregard for consequences in young people impulsively chasing excitement, something conventional 'right realist' criminologists erroneously critiqued in moral terms, thus failing to see the 'obvious' connection with consumer capitalism. By contrast, economic psychology and consumer research had noticed the contemporary, consumer-related importance of emotional factors and thus had eventually moved beyond the rational actor presumption of conventional consumer research. Perhaps, Hayward concluded, there was hope in all this for 'criminology to reconcile many of its polarised theoretical positions?' (ibid.: 179). This was the hope that was the book's constant shadow: for a general theory of crime.

The final section attempting to put all these ideas to work in establishing his new framework repeated much of what had already been established. The addition of a spatial or areal approach to the contemporary city did not advance matters substantially. The discussion of 'spaces of deprivation' essentially suggested his arguments had even greater weight in such spaces since the excluded and frustrated poor, denied conventional avenues to do so, used consumer goods to achieve status, identity and a sense of control. Carl Nightingale's (1993) ethnography of a poor, black neighbourhood in Philadelphia, which as we shall see figured prominently in Jock Young's argument too, was the warrant for this notion of 'over-identification' with consumer goods. Lyng's notion of risk-taking being a way of regaining control was also particularly pertinent in such spaces where, we had already been told, plenty of opportunities for illegal edgework existed. The consideration of 'centripetal spaces' was both a brief overview of the situational crime prevention literature and an argument about how it could be counterproductive with edgework crimes, since preventative measures could contribute to the transgressive 'thrill'. 'Spaces of consumption and pleasure' was about the death of the shopping mall, both as a postmodern pleasure dome and as a site for youthful transgressors. The obsession with security and surveillance had ruined their appeal to illicit thrill-seekers. Finding new exciting, transgressive spaces proved elusive, but a range of cities across the globe were cited as offering new, hedonistic offerings. However, the examples given of such novel attractions—'lap-dancing and strip bars…Internet-advertised brothels, rave venues…bars catering for niche market sexual fantasies' (ibid.: 192)—seemed remarkably old school and gendered (and hardly accessible to the average kid from a run-down neighbourhood).

In sum, a journey that had taken us from the emergence of the modern city to contemporary spaces in its late modern version, had offered up a thesis suggesting that the present, late modern epoch, defined primarily by a pressure to consume, produced insatiable desires and massive insecurity. Together with the over-control that was also a late modern feature, these omnipresent characteristics of contemporary life produced subjects that felt powerless and out of control. This was particularly the case among youthful inhabitants of run-down, deprived urban spaces. The delinquency of such a group was thus an emotionally-driven attempt to regain a sense of control and engineer excitement through dicing with danger and pursuing the thrill of transgression. Such an endpoint felt like meagre reward for so much theoretical effort. More importantly, at many points it didn't persuade. The characterisation of late or postmodernism in terms of consumption and control may have some empirical warrant but these remain theoretical abstractions without further analysis. Simply overviewing similar claims of theorists, which was largely the path taken by Hayward, cannot substitute for critical analysis—what works and what doesn't in a particular line of theorising—and a grounding in a set of social relations. This abstract starting point became compounded with the discussion of subjectivity. The idea that cultural characteristics are simply reproduced at the level of identity is both reductive theoretically and wrong empirically. The most sustained attempt yet to link a social order and individual personality, Adorno et al.'s (1950) *The Authoritarian Personality*, also found a 'conventional' personality type as well as the authoritarian personality of the study's title. Individuals are never simple imprints of the cultural order. The 'type' that Hayward offered may be a logical deduction from his notion of consumer culture, but it does not exhaust all empirically possible responses.

Finally, crime(s). The powerless, over-controlled, ontologically insecure postmodern subject resorted to crime for its transgressive excitement and to regain a sense of control. The theoretical warrant for this was largely Katz. Here, too, there was a reductive thrust that resulted in characterisations of crime that are non-Katzian and unrecognisable. Katz's project was to try to capture the 'lived experience of criminality' (Katz 1988: 3), to portray what actually occurred in the process of committing particular crimes together with the accompanying interpretations and emotions. For each crime considered, the results of this process differed. However, for Katz, 'central to all these experiences is a member of the family of moral emotions: humiliation, righteousness, arrogance, ridicule, cynicism, defilement, and vengeance. In each, the attraction that proves most fundamentally compelling is that of overcoming a personal challenge to moral - not to material - existence' (ibid.: 9). For each crime considered, then, a different 'member' of this 'family of moral emotions' was implicated: what was general to them all was 'overcoming a personal [moral] challenge'. Hayward's reading of this was to bypass the process altogether, reduce the emotional element simply to 'excitement' and the immediacy of the personal moral challenge involved (the foreground) to the desire to regain a general sense of control (a background factor). Moreover, the crimes Katz considered embraced a range of difficult, negative emotions. Ironically, the largely positive emotion of 'excitement' was not one of them. To reduce Katz to the thrill of transgression and 'explain' him in terms of regaining control—the 'excitement-control' model—did him a double disservice: more importantly, it seemed to have lost touch with the reality of the crimes considered. This was theory reflecting upon theory, and not always critically. A less ambitious project, one that started with a particular problem, perhaps something thrown up by Katz's work, for example, might have managed to work back to the general 'whole' in a way that, identifying new determinations, transformed our theoretical understanding of late modern consumer culture in some way rather than simply finding correspondences between postmodern theory and crime. The politics of such a position could only be gestural: voicing resistance to 'an all-consuming consumer society' (Hayward 2004: 198). Young's use of Katz, as we shall see in the next section, is similarly reductive.

'Merton with Energy, Katz with Structure': An Imaginary Synthesis

Jock Young's 2003 article, 'Merton with energy, Katz with structure', was attempting to produce an explanation of crime and punishment that combined a Mertonian structural approach with a Katzian phenomenological one, hence the title. The argument, broadly speaking, went something like this. The 'late modern' world, a period which for him dated from the 1970s onwards, was characterised by 'economic and ontological insecurity…and an exclusionary tendency towards the deviant' (ibid.: 390)—in contrast to the preceding, less divided and more secure post-war years. However, this exclusionary tendency was complicated by another characteristic of late modernity, what Young called the 'crossing and blurring of boundaries' (ibid.: 389). It was this that provided the key to understanding 'the changing characteristics of crime and punishment today'. This was ambitious stuff: to explain both changes in crime and in punishment, hence the paper's subtitle: 'the sociology of vindictiveness and the criminology of transgression'. Such ambitiousness inevitably entailed reductionism: 'blurring the boundaries' as '*the* key' to explaining, not 'some' or 'a', but '*the* changing characteristics' of both 'crime and punishment' (ibid.: 390; emphases added). This ambitiousness, and related reductiveness, did not stop there, however; for, as well as the 'strong parallels between the dynamics of crime and the desire to punish', Young also intended to argue 'that there are close similarities between violence associated with "common" criminality and the violence of war and terrorism' (ibid.). Finally, notice that we had not, at that point, encountered anything particular to be explained, only general, abstract ideas ('crime and punishment today'): as was the case with Hayward, this was a theory-driven methodology.

What immediately followed part reprised and part anticipated the argument. In the interests of brevity, I intend to move directly to the argument itself. It is significant that the only actual crimes mentioned had been a list—'joyriding…murder…telephone kiosk vandalism…rape'—that purported to show that 'an awful lot of crime…involves much more than an instrumental motivation' (ibid.: 391). These were part of 'the wide swathe of [expressive] crime' that had been cultural criminology's subject matter. This raises the point about whether all the crimes mentioned (never mind the 'awful lot' that weren't) can conceivably be reduced to a single entity—expressive crime—requiring a single explanation. Remember, this was an identical theoretical move to that made by Hayward, as we saw earlier, with the same problem: again, you don't have to be a criminologist to be puzzled by the alleged similarities between crimes as diverse as vandalism and rape or joyriding and murder.[5]

The argument about the 'blurring of boundaries', conceptualised as 'spatial, social and moral', being the key to understanding crime and punishment in the world of the early 2000s rested on the idea that this blurring produced mutual antagonisms: 'of the poor towards the well off and of the better off to those below them' (ibid.: 392). The warrant for the idea that the excluded underclass and the included mainstream shared the same morality was based on Young's reading of 'Carl Nightingale's (1993) brilliant ethnography of the black ghetto of Philadelphia, *On the Edge*'. There, Nightingale found, in Young's (2003: 394) words, 'the apotheosis of the USA…full immersion in the American dream: a culture hooked on Gucci, BMW, Nike, watching television 11 hours per day, sharing the mainstream culture's obsession with violence…worshipping success, money, wealth and status'. The ghetto's problem was thus 'not exclusion but inclusion/exclusion' (cultural inclusion/structural exclusion), a process Young likened metaphorically, somewhat ill-advisedly, to 'bulimia of the social system' (ibid.), i.e. a system

---

[5] Although, if you are a criminologist, especially if also a feminist, you might wonder at the absence of any reference to gender in relation to the particular crimes cited.

that simultaneously included (like the bulimic taking in food) and also excluded (like the bulimic vomiting up the same food). This was then oddly glossed as 'a society that choruses the liberal mantra of liberty, equality and fraternity yet systematically…practises exclusion' (ibid.).[6] At this point, the argument introduced Merton and strain theory: 'All of this is reminiscent of Merton' but amplified because 'the implosion of the wider culture on the local is dramatically increased', thus increasing the strain for those lacking the means to achieve success in the wider culture (ibid.).

The idea of a spatially shared city was apparently supported empirically by studies in Glasgow and Milwaukee where the working class and the 'underclass' poor existed next door to each other, not on segregated estates. The idea of blurred boundaries between social groups was argued on the basis of regular border crossings for work: 'maids, nurses, clerical staff move across into work every day [as do]…bellhops, taxi drivers, doormen [and] maintenance men' (ibid.: 396). This, and a shared language—'the language spoken on each side [of the border] is remarkably similar' (ibid.)—together with a 'daily ration' of media messages extolling 'the virtues of work and the stable nuclear family', meant that the poor had 'direct and often intimate knowledge of the lives of the affluent' and thus a heightened 'sense of relative deprivation' (ibid.). Reading this reminded me of 'upstairs/downstairs', of a time when domestic service was a major form of employment and of the inevitable sharing of social space involved, and thus did not feel particularly new.

These blurred boundaries, collectively, underpinned the idea that modern societies were bulimic, and this was what 'helps to explain the nature and tenor of the discontent at the bottom of the social structure. It is rooted *quite simply* in the contradiction between ideas that legitimate the system and the reality of the structure that constitutes it' (ibid.: 398: my emphases). The simplifying thrust of that 'quite simply'

---

[6]Earlier, cultural inclusion for ghetto residents meant their embrace of conspicuous consumption, violence, and the idea of success. Their relationship to the 'liberal mantra of liberty, equality and fraternity', given their structural exclusion, was less clear. Was this a recurrent 'chorus' to their lives or was it just an abstract, largely meaningless notion without any concrete relevance?

(a phrase that occurs also in Hayward's *City Limits*) was echoed in the simple Mertonian contradiction to which it referred. Everyday evidence suggests that the contradiction between an ideology of equality and a reality of economic inequality can be variously lived out.

Crucial to the argument of blurred boundaries was the idea that problems did not stop at imagined borders. Both the excluded and the included had problems of economic precarity and domestic uncertainties. Spelling out 'the precariousness of inclusion' involved a reminder that late modernity had undermined two principles of justice that underpinned 'advanced industrial societies' (ibid.: 399): that rewards are distributed on the basis of merit; that all are equally respected as individuals. Both principles had become 'chaotic' as rewards had become divorced from merit and 'discontinuities of personal biography' had unravelled people's sense of self worth and produced 'an ontological insecurity - an identity crisis' (ibid.: 400).[7] We were then told that 'the most ready response to this' was 'the evocation of an essentialism that asserts the core unchanging nature of oneself and others' (ibid.). This amounted to an assertion of the cultural or biological superiority of those who possessed the valued 'core' qualities and the denigration of those who didn't; in short, racism, classism, sexism and the like. In turn, this produced a similar hardening of those who had been othered, 'in order to combat their humiliation and exclusion from society'. Violence by both sides, those doing the othering and those being othered, was the result. My problem with this is not with the notion of essentialised identities producing racist and sexist violence, something the hate crime statistics readily endorse, but with the argument that this somehow stemmed from the notion of blurred boundaries and the late modern undermining of the 'two principles of justice' of 'advanced industrial societies'.

What mobilised the aggression that produced violence was 'a feeling of economic injustice (relative deprivation of some sort) and feelings of ontological insecurity'. These feelings helped produce 'enemies' who were 'the cause of…our problems' and who were 'intrinsically different from us…evil…wicked, etc' (ibid.). Conceptualising enemies in this way

---

[7]These are not interchangeable terms, if the Laingian origins of 'ontological security' are to be respected.

was a 'technique of neutralization [that] permits the transgression of our general prohibition against violence' (ibid.). As an account of violence it was both reductive and purely theoretical, not based on any empirical examples. 'Our general prohibition against violence' universalised the culturally specific. Contemporary macho working-class cultures, then and now, have no such prohibition; indeed, there is a prohibition on refusing to respond violently to a violent challenge as many a working-class male kid, threatened with a beating for not fighting back when picked on in school, knows to his painful cost (there were concrete examples of this, ironically, in Nightingale's, *On the Edge*, the book that Young generally found so inspirational). Similarly, the idea that 'relative deprivation especially when coupled with misrecognition and disparagement can readily lead to crime' (ibid.) prompts the response, or to religion, the madhouse or a life of quiet desperation.

Young's section on '*Globalization and the generation of domestic and global discontent*' was about the parallels between the generation of discontent globally and on the domestic front. 'For brevity's sake' the process was outlined 'schematically' (ibid.: 402). Since no new arguments were introduced, as the 'parallels' were so 'compelling', for brevity's sake I will not repeat them here but move on to the next section, 'Towards a sociology of vindictiveness' (ibid.: 403), which was Young's attempt to explain the angry vindictiveness of the 'included'. This started with the notion that 'relative deprivation downwards, a feeling that those who work little or not at all are getting an easy ride on your back and your taxes, is a widespread sentiment' (ibid.). Characterised by 'disproportionality, scapegoating and stereotyping', or the production of 'late modern folk devils' (ibid.: 404), such resentment disguised envy. Operating, as they did, in the late modern conditions of 'restraint and sacrifice' was what 'turns simple displeasure (a sense of unfairness) into vindictiveness' (ibid.: 405).

A similar dynamic underpinned 'the feelings of exclusion' of those at the bottom. This served to introduce the next section 'Towards a criminology of transgression' (ibid.). But, in the case of those at the bottom, it was compounded by the disrespect and humiliation encountered daily, partly from the disrespect heaped on them by the discontented included as we have just seen, but also in their encounters with the police. As was argued earlier, the resulting 'crisis of identity'—more severe among the excluded than among the precariously included because 'poverty among abundance [is] the most humiliating stigma of all' (ibid.: 406)—could result in essentialising or hardening certain values. This produced, among young ghetto males, a hypermasculinity accompanied by an othering of a range of groups: 'not the rich and the celebrated' (ibid.: 406) outside the ghetto, but 'others' within the ghetto, or in similar circumstances beyond its confines, like women, other ethnic groups, other gangs, etc.[8] Vindictiveness, as with the discontented included, was similarly motivating the excluded, which was why the 'criminality of the underclass is not simply a utilitarian affair…but…has a transgressive edge' (ibid.: 408).[9] This transgressive edge was fuelled 'by the energies of humiliation' which can produce 'a delight in excess, a glee in breaking the rules, a reassertion of dignity and identity' (ibid.). This was best captured by Katz's phenomenology of the foreground of crime. But, in Katz's rejection of the structural background (including Merton), Young suggested Katz 'throws the baby out with the bathwater…Our job is to emphasise both structure and agency and trace how each constitutes the other' (ibid.). The quote that ends this section summarised these ideas:

> the structural predicament of the ghetto poor is not simply a deficit of goods - as Merton would have it - it is a state of humiliation. And crime, because it is driven by humiliation not by some simple desire to redistribute property, is transgressive. The theory of bulimia which I have proposed involves incorporation and rejection, cultural inclusion and structural exclusion, as with Merton, but it goes further than this, emphasizing that this combination of the acceptance followed by rejection generates a dynamic of resentment of great intensity. *It is Merton with energy, it is Katz with structure.* (ibid.)

---

[8] Here, gender was introduced into the analysis, in the form of 'young ghetto males', 'hypermasculinity', and the sexist othering of women, as well as racism, in the form of ethnic othering; but neither term was interrogated. Consequently, the relationship of gender or race to the master concept, transgression, was left hanging in the air.

[9] The difference between utilitarian and transgressive criminality was never defined, despite the fact that the *Shorter Oxford English Dictionary* effectively makes crime and transgression all but synonymous—'passing beyond the bounds of legality or right'. Jenks' short text, *Transgression* (2003), published in the same year as Young's article, did make the effort to distinguish between transgressive and non-transgressive crime, albeit not entirely convincingly.

One of the problems about Young's use of Katz, which echoed Hayward's earlier use of him, was turning Katz's phenomenological use of the term 'humiliation', which Katz saw as a contingent state precipitating the commission of certain crimes, into a structural feature of late modern exclusion: deprivation and disrespect produced (permanently) humiliated subjects.[10] Without at this point evaluating these different usages, it is important to note that they were different and lead to different, and not necessarily compatible, theories of crime: the structural background of Katz's criminal subjects could be various since humiliation was but a temporary state producing the crime. They need not have been feeling a Mertonian strain. Consequently, Young's endpoint was a rhetorical flourish, not a serious attempt to 'trace how each [agency/structure] constitutes the other'.

Summary and Conclusion

As stated at the beginning of this chapter, cultural criminology's ambitiousness was the source of both its strengths and its weaknesses. For example, wanting to connect crime and society is fine as an ambition. But that means taking a particular crime seriously and interrogating it for what it can reveal about its social conditions: its many determinations. Take rape, for example. There is a large body of feminist literature that has looked at crimes of rape and revealed much, especially about the workings of patriarchal social relations in particular societies at particular moments. But, bundling rape together with a host of apparently dissimilar crimes and labelling them all as in some way 'expressive' of the humiliation of the excluded in late modern times was both insensitive and reductive.[11] Its reductionism was a consequence of attempting too much—explaining a host of crimes—too quickly: moving from late

---

[10]Although Young talked of 'the ghetto poor', it was clear from his earlier discussion that he meant 'a state of humiliation' that affected young males. Women's humiliation, which is often experienced in the home at the hands of controlling males, is not simply a feature of late modern times but has a much longer history.
[11]And somewhat surprising since Young, in his 'left realist' phase, certainly took the crime of rape seriously in its own right.

modern society to its imagined effect on the presumptive criminal perpetrators. This was also the wrong way to proceed, but at this level of generality—both of society and crime(s)—it hardly mattered. It hardly mattered because the strength of the article's 'imaginative sweep' also produced largely imaginary results. While it is likely that some of Young's discontented included and humiliated excluded conformed broadly to the picture he painted, many would not. In order to advance thinking here, one would need more detailed work on responses to economic insecurity and identity crises. For a start, they are not inevitably conjoined, as they seemed to be here. One can exist without the other, even in our late modern world, even in the ghetto. Properly pursued empirically, rather than using empirical examples to illustrate an already made argument, such an analysis would reveal more determinations than Young uncovered. Ironically, as we shall see in the next chapter, Nightingale's much lauded ethnography, for example, revealed some of these, such as parenting styles or the extent of trauma. More generally, there is a literature on resilience factors that mediate the impact of economic deprivation. As for the synthesising ambition, it needed to be done with more care than was exhibited here.

These criticisms echo those I levelled at Hayward's *City Limits*. By not following the conjunctural injunction to start with an historically specific event/crime but with a theoretical depiction of our late modern times, both writers were only able to offer 'merely speculative' findings. What happened in both instances was that the characteristics attributed to the system—disembeddedness, rampant consumerism, economic insecurity, biographical dislocations—were transcribed to the level of the subject without any serious attention to mediations (other than the mass media) and with minimal empirical support. Any non-supportive data that might have contradicted the theorising was ignored. These, largely theoretical, subjects were then held responsible for a host of crimes which were said to be expressive of their alienation. It was all too simple because largely theoretical, unconstrained by empirical data. As much of it could be contradicted by a few readily accessible examples, it was partly wrong. Despite their many criticisms of mainstream criminology's attempts to produce a general theory of crime, cultural criminology, as evidenced in this chapter, was in danger of falling into the same trap. Not a universal, transhistorical notion of crime since it was crime in late modernity that was at issue; but in wanting to reconceptualise what was previously thought of as utilitarian crime as expressive crime, it was a general theory of crime *in late modernity* that was the implicit goal. And not, as must be the case with conjunctural analysis, using crime as a route to understanding the power relations that underpin both the act of crime and the responses to it.

References

Adorno, T., E. Frenkel-Brunswick, D. Levinson, and R.N. Sanford. 1950. *The Authoritarian Personality*. New York: Harper and Row.

Bauman, Z. 1997. *Postmodernity and Its Discontents*. Cambridge: Polity.

Campbell, C. 1989. *The Romantic Ethic and the Spirit of Modern Consumerism*. London: Blackwell.

Cohen, S. 1972. *Folk Devils and Moral Panics*. London: McGibbon & Kee.

Cohen, S., and J. Young (eds.). 1973. *The Manufacture of News: Deviance, Social Problems and the Mass Media*, 2nd rev. ed., 1981. London: Constable.

Coleman, R., J. Sim, S. Tombs, and D. Whyte (eds.). 2009. *State, Power, Crime*. London: Sage.

Ferrell, J., and C.R. Sanders. 1995a. Culture, crime and criminology. In Ferrell and Sanders, eds. (1995: 3–21).

Ferrell, J., and C.R. Sanders. 1995b. Toward a cultural criminology. In Ferrell and Sanders, eds. (1995: 297–326).

Ferrell, J., and C.R. Sanders (eds.). 1995. *Cultural Criminology*. Boston: Northeastern University Press.

Ferrell, J., K. Hayward, W. Morrison, and M. Presdee. 2004. Fragments of a manifesto: Introducing *Cultural Criminology Unleashed*. In Ferrell et al., eds. (2004: 1–9).

Ferrell, J., K. Hayward, W. Morrison, and M. Presdee (eds.). 2004. *Cultural Criminology Unleashed*. London: Glasshouse Press.

Ferrell, J., K. Hayward, and J. Young. 2008. *Cultural Criminology: An Invitation*. London: Sage.

Feyerabend, P. 1978. *Against Method*. London: Verso.

Hall, S. 1973. The determinations of news photographs. In Cohen and Young, eds. (1973: 176–90).
Hall, S. 1988. Popular-democratic vs authoritarian populism: Two ways of "taking democracy seriously". In *The Hard Road to Renewal: Thatcherism and the Crisis of the Left*, S. Hall, pp. 123–49. London: Verso.
Hayward, K. 2004. *City Limits: Crime, Consumer Culture and the Urban Experience*. London: Glasshouse.
Jefferson, T. 1974. For a Social Theory of Deviance: The Case of Mugging, 1972–3. MA Thesis, University of Birmingham.
Jenks, C. 2003. *Transgression*. London: Routledge.
Katz, J. 1988. *Seductions of Crime: Moral and Sensual Attractions in Doing Evil*. New York: Basic Books.
Laing, R.D. 1959. *The Divided Self: An Existential Study in Sanity and Madness*. London: Tavistock.
Lea, J., and J. Young. 1984. *What Is to Be Done About Law and Order? Crisis in the Eighties*. Harmondsworth: Penguin.
Lyng, S. 1990. Edgework. *American Journal of Sociology* 95 (4): 851–86.
Marx, K. 1857–1858/1973. *Grundrisse: Foundations of the Critique of Political Economy (Rough Draft).*, trans. with a Foreword by Martin Nicolaus. Harmondsworth: Penguin.
Nightingale, C.H. 1993. *On the Edge: A History of Poor Black Children and Their American Dreams*. New York: Basic Books.
Taylor, I., P. Walton, and J. Young. 1973. *The New Criminology: For a Social Theory of Deviance*. London: Routledge & Kegan Paul.
Walton, P., and J. Young (eds.). 1998. *The New Criminology Revisited*. Basingstoke: Macmillan.
Young, J. 1971. *The Drugtakers: The Social Meaning of Drug Use*. London: Paladin.
Young, J. 1998. Breaking windows: Situating the new criminology. In Walton and Young, eds. (1998: 14–46).
Young, J. 1999. *The Exclusive Society*. London: Sage.
Young, J. 2003. Merton with energy, Katz with structure: The sociology of vindictiveness and the criminology of transgression. *Theoretical Criminology* 7 (3): 389–414.

5

Cultural Criminology Part Two: Ethnography, Carnival and the Need for Critique

In this chapter, which is a continuation of my exploration of key texts in cultural criminology, I intend to compare and contrast two pairs of texts: a pair of ethnographies, since ethnography is a key methodology of cultural criminology; followed by a pair exploring the notion of carnival, since this had become a key concept within cultural criminology: the expressive crimes of cultural criminology were said to be, like carnival, transgressive and, hence, carnivalesque. In each pair, the first chosen example predates the example from one of the pioneering figures from cultural criminology that follows. The point of the comparisons, generally, is to explore whether each of the cultural criminology studies constituted a significant development of the older, pre-existing studies and how their relationship to conjunctural analysis affected matters in this regard. Unfortunately, as I shall demonstrate, the cultural criminology texts did not advance understanding in their chosen areas: partly because, as we saw was the case with our exemplary texts in the last chapter, of the over-reliance on theory and a failure to be disciplined by the specificity of the particular (even in the case of our example of ethnography); and partly because of an apparent unwillingness to start with a critique of existing approaches in order to transform them into better, more revealing, explanations. One might call this a failure to be disciplined by the specificity of the existing knowledge field.

The first of the ethnographic pair to be examined is Nightingale's *On the Edge* (1993), chosen because, as we saw in the last chapter, it was an oft-cited and much-admired text within cultural criminology. This is a traditional ethnography; that is, one based on long hours of fieldwork over many years with, in this case, a small group of poor black children and their extended families in inner city Philadelphia. It has an historical dimension achieved by poring over the welfare case records of an earlier generation of similarly poor kids from the same area. The comparator cultural criminology ethnography is Jeff Ferrell's *Tearing Down the Streets* (2001), chosen because, of all the pioneer figures, Ferrell is the committed ethnographer. Ferrell calls it an 'existential ethnography - that is direct, ongoing, open-ended immersion in the disorderly moments and diverse communities of everyday life' (2001: 33), specifically, the graffiti writers, street musicians, cycling activists, microradio operators, hobos, BASE jumpers, gutter punks and skate punks that Ferrell variously hung out with and participated alongside over long periods of time.

Both of our next pair of texts, *The Politics and Poetics of Transgression by* Stallybrass and White (1986) and *Cultural Criminology and the Carnival of Crime by* Presdee (2000), used Bakhtin's notion of carnival to think through their respective theses. Fortuitously, then, we are presented with the possibility of a direct comparison between two different approaches to the same topic: Stallybrass and White's informed by conjunctural thinking and Presdee's informed by the theory and methods of cultural criminology. In addition, my choice of them was determined by the fact that each has a significant place in their respective fields: Stuart Hall (1996: 289) regarded *The Politics and Poetics of Transgression* as a '"landmark text"…in cultural studies'; *Cultural Criminology and the Carnival of Crime* is widely regarded as a foundational text for cultural criminology.

A Tale of Two Ethnographies

A Traditional Ethnography: Carl Nightingale's *On the Edge*

Nightingale started with commonly used descriptions of his kids ('ghetto kids', 'alienated youth', the 'underclass', etc.), contrasted these with the kids own preferred terms ('hustlers', 'b-boys', 'baaad niggers', etc.) and both with the absent term—'American'—which, given their love of all things American, from television and Coca-Cola to fancy cars and the military, might have seemed the obvious choice. However, American was not the term used because, being poor, on welfare and dark-skinned, his kids had been alienated from mainstream America and segregated by area and schooling. In addition, the growing tendency to live in single-parent households and the growing numbers of black-on-black homicides had exacerbated their differences from the mainstream. The violence of the inner city riots accentuated the process and marked black youth out as looters, criminals, 'muggers'. As such, they became the source of a widespread fear of crime and a revival of racist stereotypes. These were used by authorities to justify 'get tough' policies which led to the mass incarceration of black youth, including several of the kids Nightingale was involved with. As Nightingale (1993: 5) summed it up:

> Poor, on welfare, left behind by emigrating employers and community leaders, racially excluded, feared and despised by many Americans, then thrown into prisons: how could the children in this book be more alienated from the American mainstream than that?

Yet they enthusiastically embraced American consumer culture and a host of American values. Explaining this apparent conundrum, between their alienation and their embrace of Americanness, lay at the heart of the study. Empirically, the research covered two-time periods: the late 1950s and early 1960s when the kids Nightingale encountered through welfare records were coming of age (what I call the secondary ethnography) and 1987–1992, the period of the direct ethnography which began with an accidental encounter with some of the kids who lived near Nightingale (they offered to mow his lawn and he became a regular customer). Getting close to the youngsters' leader, a boy Nightingale named as Chauntey Patterson, led to the establishment of a voluntary organisation (called the 'kids' club' in the book). This was originally suggested by Chauntey and was designed to counter the violence and drug dealing of the streets by variously helping kids with alternatives: schoolwork, play and job-seeking. By this point, Nightingale had his sample, a sponsor, Chauntey, and a participatory role, albeit one as a surrogate parent or teacher rather than a peer-based one.

The first chapter of the book was devoted to establishing, statistically, the nature of the 'historical tragedy' that had afflicted 'poor urban black American communities' from 'about 1960' (ibid.: 16): the family stresses—between men and women, fathers and children—consequent upon 'the virtual disappearance of marriage as an institution among poor black people'; and the 'extraordinary surge in levels of fatal violence' which 'has threatened to overwhelm' all the informal and formal neighbourhood institutions of social control (ibid.). These changes were shown to be 'both historically unprecedented and exceptional' (ibid.), i.e. not shared with other groups of the urban poor. Subsequently, the chapter detailed the accompanying street code 'espousing manipulative and aggressive behavior' that contradicted the more traditional code of neighbourly cooperation and mutuality. However, relationships to the code varied: whether or not particular kids 'act out in ways that threaten community life' depended 'greatly on [their] personal subconscious struggles…with often-overwhelming memories of painful emotional experiences' (ibid.: 8). Finally, the chapter suggested that understanding these changes and the accompanying 'drastic erosion of community life in late-twentieth-century American inner cities' would entail attending to 'the sources of aggressive values and the reasons for increasingly widespread memories of pain in the upbringing of young poor Americans' (ibid.).

Chapter 2 critiques existing attempts to explain the tragedy which, variously, centred on the notion of alienation: economic, social or cultural. While he agreed with significant elements of arguments stressing economic alienation—how the deindustrialisation of American cities, leading to job losses and poverty, resulted in the 'deeply painful feelings of frustration, disappointment, humiliation, and shame' (ibid.) that underpinned aggressive and manipulative behaviour—these failed to explain why the black experience had been so much worse than that of other poor urban groups. To give but one example of why 'joblessness remains a necessary part…but…does not suffice as a complete explanation', Nightingale offered up some statistics: 'Measures of unemployment and joblessness, like those of poverty, have correlated only moderately with high rates of homicide' (ibid.: 62). Similar problems arose with the other forms of alienation. The 'social isolation' thesis underpinning the notion of social alienation, the idea that poor blacks were increasingly living in isolated pockets of concentrated poverty, was also less than complete since also undermined by murder statistics. For example, Washington DC and Los Angeles, which had notoriously high murder rates in the 1980s 'were among that half of American metropolitan areas that saw a decline in the percentage of poor blacks living in high poverty neighbourhoods during the 1970s' (ibid.: 66). More importantly, none of the alienation theories, social, economic or cultural, could account for that which could only have been revealed by doing ethnographic work, namely, 'the precise historical heritage of values of manipulation and aggression at the heart of community-threatening behavior or inner-city kids' ways of compensating for painful feelings' (ibid.: 67).

Having demonstrated 'the limits of alienation' as an explanation of the historical tragedy of poor, black, urban America, Part II set out to supply the missing elements of a fuller explanation. This entailed attending to 'the ways that inner-city kids have actually become more American, not less, during the late twentieth century' (ibid.: 9). Nightingale identified four such ways: the violent nature of social control, by both parents and the criminal justice system, to which the kids were subjected (which both undermined traditional notions of cooperative values and disabled any emotional awareness of their hurt-filled aggression); their compensatory embrace of racist stereotypes of the violent 'baaad nigger' to combat hateful, racist exclusions; their 'desire for compensatory status' (ibid.: 10) via conspicuous consumption; their enthusiasm for mass-mediated images of 'newly glorified versions of the age-old values of American violence…America's violent television shows...blockbuster action-adventure and horror film images' (ibid.: 11). In short:

> although economic exclusion from job markets and social exclusion need to take a central place in our explanations for changes in poor urban communities, the twentieth-century history of black inner-city culture has not been, overall, one of increasing isolation, but one that has proceeded from relative isolation to greater participation in the larger American culture. But in their embrace of the values associated with American law and order, racial caricatures, abundance, and violence, black inner-city children have also increasingly lost contact with more autonomous African-American traditions such as expressive religion or the rituals of 'toasting' and 'playing the dozens' that may have actually been more successful in curbing violent expressions of pain. (ibid.: 11–12)

As with all good ethnographies, these conclusions were arrived at by closely observing and listening to the kids themselves. Nightingale's hope was that their 'words...stories and lessons...will help - if just a little - to give more Americans new kinds of voices in their conversations about and with the American people they have most often and most viciously ignored and despised' (ibid.: 12). Practically, such new kinds of voices would need to be guided by 'two inter-related goals: the creation of employment for poor African-American city-dwellers, and the creation of a national culture of commitment and community that is emotionally expressive, ethnically diverse, and compelling to children and young people' (ibid.: 191). Not easy to achieve, of course, but a vision nonetheless; and one that stemmed organically from the research. Our next ethnography reads very differently.

A Cultural Criminology Ethnography: Jeff Ferrell's *Tearing Down the Streets*

Ferrell (2001: 1) started with a dramatic statement, one that implicitly raised questions: 'Something's gone wrong. Something has shifted away, away from...a sense of the city as an open, inclusive community'.

What followed were brief intimations of the shifting away from inclusivity, delivered, as would be the case throughout the book, through Ferrell's autobiographical involvement in the miscellaneous outsider street subcultures that were the book's subject matter. He first noticed the change in the 1990s with the media hysteria about graffiti writing and its tougher policing (which led to the author's conviction for destroying private property). Some years later, it was the city-issued permits that his 'busking' friend possessed that signalled the shift, and, then, being 'busted' with radical cycling friends for collectively 'impeding traffic' on their bikes. As we shall see in the chapters that followed, he continued, 'young gutter punks and old hobos, skaters and skate punks, bicyclists, daredevil BASE jumpers, microradio operators - all sense the shift, feel the changing rhythm, understand the ways in which their lives are more and more regulated, their activities outlawed, their living spaces closed down' (ibid.: 3). While, at this stage, Ferrell said it 'may not be exactly clear' what was 'happening here in the streets of America and beyond', what 'is clear [is] that it involves contested practices of public life and urban community' (ibid.). Thus he introduced the book's other key theme: resistance to what had 'gone wrong'.

At this point, a litany of examples was introduced, purportedly of similar developments of greater control of public space, each apparently demonstrating the new 'exclusionary model of public life' (ibid.: 5): a military veteran prevented by his housing association from flying a US flag; civil injunctions against the 'loitering' of suspected gang members; seminars on 'Crime Prevention through Environmental Design'; urban gentrification; and the Disneyfication of New York's Times Square. Adapting Marx's (1852/1968: 96) oft-quoted remark from *The Eighteenth Brumaire*, about history occurring 'twice…the first time as tragedy, the second as farce', Ferrell suggested that what we were then witnessing was a shift from cities being 'forged…out of industry, commerce and labour' [history as tragedy] to them being the product of 'the careful marketing of consumption, symbol, and amusement' and thus becoming 'corporate theme parks, selling idealised images of themselves and cartoonish echoes of their former identities' [history as farce] (Ferrell 2001: 9). Although these transformations were presented as necessary for economic salvation, they were also seen as necessary for social and cultural reasons too: to restore/impose a version of the 'good life'. Such a version did not include Ferrell's subjects and friends: the 'misfit' outsiders. If successful, these transformed urban spaces 'will 'attract growing numbers of middle-class consumers - consumers eager to embrace the sanitised hyperconsumption of revitalised downtown shopping districts as a glossy doppelganger for their own little lives' (ibid.: 10).

Regarding this re-segregating and sanitising of city spaces as perhaps signalling the end of American claims to be a melting pot, Ferrell asked, rhetorically, what might be the point of all this, beyond creating a cleaner, safer environment for the middle classes. Ferrell's answer—'perhaps the point would be a police state' (ibid.: 13)—upped the stakes considerably. Of course, 'In a putatively democratic society', these new forms of controlling the 'undesirables' had to be sold as something else: restoring 'community' or protecting the 'common good' (ibid.). In other words, control was as much about ideology, controlling the meaning of outsider groups and the spaces they inhabited, as it was about regulating their existence. The chapters to follow promised to offer both sides of this perceptual struggle, partly through the words of the participants.

Then followed a run-through of historical parallels to the present attempt to control public spaces, both in the USA and beyond—a slightly odd mixture including twentieth-century urban ethnographic research as well as work on the English vagrancy laws and their importation into the USA—before Ferrell offered 'a second parallel history…of *resistance* to emerging spatial controls…This history, this jagged line, is the history of anarchism' (ibid.: 19–20). A brief look at this history, we were told, 'can provide not only a bit of perspective on contemporary conflicts…[but] a sort of guidebook to the anarchist actions and orientations that will surface repeatedly in the following chapters' (ibid.: 20). This started with the Paris Commune of 1871, which was seen as a revolt 'as much against spatial authority as political authority' (ibid.: 21), 'a carnival of insurrectionary pleasure' (ibid.: 22), that remained inspirational to 'contemporary battles to revitalize public spaces and restore communities rendered sterile by those who control them' (ibid.: 23). Emma Goldman had a similar anarchistic sensibility, as did the Wobblies, the 'defiantly anarchistic union' (ibid.: 23) operating in the early twentieth century. Though defeated politically, their inspiration and tactics lived on, among contemporary street anarchists, as did the underlying strategy of direct action. Ultimately, the struggle was one over what constituted community: the sanitised, 'manufactured security and preplanned pleasure' (ibid.: 31) of the developers, politicians and the police, or the 'do-it-yourself uncertainty' and 'goofy federation of difference and disorder' (ibid.: 32) favoured by anarchists. The opening chapter ended reminding us of Ferrell's lifelong commitment to anarchism, of his long-time, active involvement in the various outsider communities that would be the subject matter of the chapters to come.

Comparing the Ethnographies in Their Own Terms

Two very different ethnographies: one explored the lives of poor black kids in Philadelphia in two historical periods, the late 1950s/early 1960s and the late 1980s/early 1990s; the second the lives of various outsider groups from all over the USA, and beyond, during the 1990s. Addressing the broad issue of whether the later, cultural criminology ethnography constituted an improvement on the traditional approach requires that we ask, first, how well they work as ethnographies in their own terms. Part of the answer to this involves a consideration of their 'attentiveness': How well has each attended to their subject matter? It is ethnography's defining methodological principle, as Ferrell has himself acknowledged (Ferrell and Sanders 1995: xvii). A second part of the answer entails examining how well they answered the questions, explicit and implicit, that oriented their respective studies. This requires an examination of the relationship between data and theory to see whether the answers proposed have been demonstrated rather than simply asserted and whether the research produced something new, something hitherto unknown that was only revealed as a result of the research.

The Question of Attentiveness

One of the obvious advantages of spending a long time with a small group is that you can get to know them very well: their life stories; their behaviour in a variety of social settings; their changes over time; their relationship to a variety of authority figures including parents, teachers and criminal justice professionals; their reputations; their strengths and vulnerabilities; and so on. Nightingale's six years with his kids, as trusted, adult friend and neighbour, enabled him to get to know his kids very well indeed. Unsurprisingly, the most memorable was his key sponsor and 'teacher', Chauntey. Like Phillipe Bourgois' (1995) key informants, Primo, Caesar and Candy, in his ethnographic study of Puerto Rican crack-dealers in New York's Spanish Harlem—still, for me, the gold standard for ethnographic work—Chauntey remains a vividly etched and complicated character, constantly torn between the macho world of the streets and a desire to move on. When Nightingale first met him, Chauntey is the neighbourhood bully; but setting up the kid's club was his idea. He led two burglaries of Nightingale's house, became a drug dealer, and ended up in and out of custody; but also sprayed the neighbourhood with 'C.A.D', which, in one of their 'more trusting and close moments' (Nightingale 1993: 38) he told Nightingale, 'stood for "Chauntey against Drugs"' (ibid.: 39), which he later 'changed to "Chauntey and Drugs", encircled with a heart' (ibid.). The explanation for his changeable behaviour, which I have no time to rehearse here in detail, lay partly in the realm of the social (all the kids were caught between two moral codes, the collaborative cooperation of the neighbourhood and the manipulative aggression of the streets) and partly in his personal biography, namely, 'the overwhelming emotional crisis he endured...[in the] summer of 1988, when he was on the eve of his twelfth birthday' (ibid.). This level of detail is simply inaccessible to those who have not been inside a community for an extensive period of time, with an open mind and a non-judgemental, respectful attitude.

Ferrell's very different strategy, on the move between outsider groups and geographical locales, made achieving Nightingale's level of detail impossible. However, there were several other, related problems. One was the object of study. The presumption seemed to be that all the groups studied were similar enough to be part of a single ethnography. But were they? Were homeless hobos—most of whom would not have been on the streets through choice—similar to graffiti writers who clearly did choose to be doing what they were doing? Were buskers and graffiti writers—whose activities are in some ways connected to an art form—and BASE jumpers similarly motivated, for example? Were the cycling outsiders who were attempting to challenge the precedence given to cars on city roads similar to skaters? Both groups are in some way connected to a sport or physical activity, but beyond that would seem to have little in common. Part of being attentive is to *show* us, the inattentive reader, what it is that these apparently disparate groups and activities have in common. But that didn't happen, although we were constantly *told* they are all part of the resistance to contemporary gentrification/Disneyfication/regulation of public spaces: latter day descendants of the Parisian communards and the American Wobblies.

The same problem emerged within any one of these 'subcultures'. Take graffiti-writers. Were they all similarly motivated? Greg Snyder's (2009: 9) conclusion, after a ten-year ethnographic study of the New York graffiti scene, that the activity 'meant different things to each writer' seems far more likely: 'For some it was strictly art, for others a vandalistic thrill, for others a means to communicate one's worth. For some it was an addiction, a medium that produced endorphins, but ultimately proved to be self-destructive'. As for busking, my own personal experience of a Grandmother who busked for money to help feed her nine children and to save towards her first house, tells me that the motivations for busking are various: she was not an anarchistic 'resister'. The only thing she was resisting was poverty and, unlike those of Ferrell's respondents who actively chose the streets over working in clubs or a recording studio, she would have happily swapped the streets for a recording studio, had she been offered the chance.

The flip side of this is the presumption that all the things that Ferrell talked about as part of what's 'gone wrong'—greater control, regulation and policing, gentrification, Disneyfication and so on—were all but synonymous, part of a single phenomenon. While I can agree that they are all in some way related to attempts by cities to remake themselves as post-industrial urban centres, there are many conflicting things going on here. Take gentrification and Disneyfication. They are not necessarily the same thing although they may overlap in any particular development project. One pattern of gentrification starts with artists. Always seeking lower rent studios, they enter an area in decline with comparatively low rents. These also attract independent businesses. Thus starts an area's uplift. The middle-class people who follow tend to be attracted by somewhat lower rents, but also the emergent vibe, which, emanating from a mixture of artists, independents and the remaining locals, will not entirely have lost its 'edge'. When the corporations and developers arrive, whether they accommodate to the vibe or transform it will depend, ultimately, on the local community struggles that underpin all such changes.

Disneyfication suggests a particular commercial, entertainment-based ethos underpinning development projects: escapist, fun-filled, child-friendly and, in a quintessentially American way, optimistic. Not my scene; but to describe it as bland and dystopian does a condescending disservice to the millions of visitors to the Disneylands around the world. More importantly for present purposes, the term is inadequate to characterise the transformations of Times Square. To describe the old 42nd Street 'peep shows and gay movie houses…[as] places of vibrant marginality' and the new as defined by 'tourist shops and corporate theme cafes…overrun by homogenised safety and middle class consumerism' idealised the past's vaguely threatening seediness and overplayed its difference from the new look square (of the 1990s, given when Ferrell was writing). Given its central location at the heart of the theatre district, tourists, commerce and consumption have long been the Square's lifeblood.

However, the Square has since gone through further revamps, which leave me wondering quite what Ferrell would make of them. Talking of the post-2017 present, there is still plenty of tourists, commerce and consumption, but also a different, more communal, kind of vibrancy. Any time of the day or night it is a brightly lit sea of people, tourists and locals from all classes, moving through or sitting on the newly installed steps and benches, chatting, smiling, laughing, taking pictures, often consuming little more than the communal atmosphere and friendly vibe. Should they be visiting during a summer afternoon, they could well stumble across live street music: jazz, folk, pop or whatever, part of the city's programme of free concerts that takes place in all the parks and many of the squares throughout each summer (busking with a permit, perhaps, but invariably quality offerings). Is the Square's partial pedestrianisation, which is spreading throughout the city, part of Disneyfication—or a small victory for the New York equivalent of Ferrell's radical cycling, anti-automobile friends, 'Critical Mass'? Or, where does yoga in the square fit in? And is the transformation of the Square fundamentally different (and if so, in what ways) from the construction of the hugely popular High Line, an old elevated railway line that has been converted into an urban park running above the city Streets on Manhattan's West Side? I would find Disneyfication off-putting: but I regularly enjoy the vistas, public art and free music of the High Line.

A second problem is Ferrell's omnipresence: we learn far more about Ferrell's 'adventures in urban anarchy' than we do of anyone else. Take 'Barry', his temporary busking friend, who figured throughout the dozen or so pages devoted to 'sidewalk music' or busking (Ferrell 2001: 55–69) and was probably the informant given the most space in the entire book. We were presented with a history of Ferrell's busking 'career' around the globe, but learned nothing of Barry's life story. We were also presented with a sort of diary of their occasional night-time 'gigs' over an eight-month period. Once again, Ferrell's voice dominated with an occasional quote from Barry as support. Piecing together these supportive quotes, we learned that Barry enjoyed playing on the streets for the interest, because you never knew who you might meet or what might happen, for the feeling of solidarity with other buskers, for the energy, for the freedom to come and go as he pleased, and to be able to offer an alternative to an advertising driven media culture. Whether these added up to anarchist resistance he never said since it was Ferrell's words again and not Barry's that constructed their larger meaning:

> BMXers and hoedown dancers, homeless folks and club drunks, locals and tourists - all flow in and out of the little sonic space that Barry and I construct each night, finding there a conversation, a dance, a moment of pleasure. In turn, Barry and I jump genres, play requests, invent new songs, rolling with the ever-changing rhythms of the street as much as orchestrating them. In this way, we and other street performers put into

practice the anarchist ideal of fluid, give-and-take negotiation as a human alternative to the rigidity of rules and preplanning. (ibid.: 67)

A third problem was the anarchistic anything goes approach to method. Take triangulation, a key element of ethnographic method, used when, for example, somebody says something which is contradicted by someone else. The ethnographic participant observer attempts to resolve such contradictions by virtue of his or her own observations and participation in the culture: by becoming, effectively, the third side of a triangle. In one of Ferrell's conversations with a homeless man attempting to hitch hike to the local bus station, he was told by the man that you needed a ticket to be allowed to wait in the bus station. So, Ferrell drove him to the bus station, bought him a ticket and waited for the Phoenix bus with him. When, months later, Ferrell was back in the same bus station, he decided to ask about the policy of tickets and waiting in the station. An employee assured him a ticket was not needed to wait in the bus station: 'As long as they're not causing trouble'. Against a background of a boy playing a violent, noisy video game, Ferrell wondered what might constitute trouble and for whom: 'Does he [the boy] have a ticket? And who's causing trouble' (ibid.: 41). And that is where it was left. We had the homeless man's experience contradicted by a statement of official bus policy, but no resolution: just an idle rumination about trouble. In the context of an argument about greater control and regulation, resolving such an issue matters.

Data and Theory

The second double-headed question concerning how well the ethnographies work in their own terms concerns the relationship between the data and theory: How well has the data demonstrated, rather than asserted, the answer provided to the underlying research question; and is the resulting understanding saying something new? What Nightingale was proposing was that his long period inside his poor, black community could not be understood simply in terms of alienation, though his kids were certainly alienated. This was because he noticed at least two things that seemed unaccounted for in alienation theorising: the extent of his kids Americanness, both in relation to consumption patterns and in relation to many mainstream American values. Violence was one such value, which was implicated in his noticing something else hitherto overlooked, namely, the extent of the punitive violence to which his kids were subjected by parents. The question of violence and parents got him looking at the statistics about changing family patterns and the rise in black-on-black violence. Thinking about how all this hung together—the growth of the one-parent household, rising homicide stats, forceful parenting, the kids' commitment to mainstream consumption and violence, their economic alienation and subjection to all kinds of racism—was resolved, ultimately, by noticing, beneath the hurts, frustrations, disappointments and anger of alienated children, the underlying pain of their lives as abused children. This pain was then linked to their aggressive street performances and eager consumption via the notion of compensation. Violent street performances and purchasing branded sneakers were the unconscious paybacks, to themselves, for past pains: the more painful the past, the more important was the compensatory activity likely to be.

It is here, I believe, where Nightingale's real theoretical novelty lies. In noticing the different levels of commitment to consumption and violence, and how some were relatively inoculated from their appeal, while the pain of others, like Chauntey, was such that they could not resist the compensatory seductions of the drug dealer's lifestyle, he was able to demonstrate the biographically unique dimension of involvement in crime/violence. That pain emanated originally from inside the family, which could only have been noticed through a long-term commitment to ethnographic study. It is not that others, like Young (1999) who referred to the book often, had not seen the importance of pain in the kids' lives. But because the book's novelty was understood in terms of the paradox of social and economic exclusion and cultural inclusion (which was key to Young's understanding of much contemporary crime, as we saw in the last chapter), the source of the kids' pain was effectively reduced to their experiences of alienation. Noticing and then theoretically incorporating a biographical dimension is still largely too difficult a theoretical task for an overly social sociology and an overly cultural criminology (or cultural studies, for that matter). So, Nightingale was saying something new, theoretically, even if it was not what some of his most enthusiastic supporters think it was.

The problems with Ferrell's *Tearing Down the Streets* when it comes to the relation between data and theory all stemmed from the same source: the diversity of the data—from homeless hobos to daredevil BASE jumpers and more—and the singularity of the explanatory theory: anarchistic resistance. This was also true of the control side: diverse processes like gentrification, Disneyfication, greater regulation and tougher law enforcement were all regarded as part of the same anti-anarchist quest for a particular, sanitised version of civic order. In short, it suffers all the problems of reductionism. Whereas Nightingale's deep immersion enabled him to see something others hadn't and thus was able to offer a subtly different and new theoretical understanding of what he was witnessing, Ferrell's encounters seemed comparatively shallow and inattentive to the particularities of what he was witnessing. One reason for that was the apparent failure to render his observations and conversations 'anthropologically strange': to approach his subjects without preconception, as if visiting a strange 'tribe', a key methodological protocol of traditional ethnography. Rather, entering as an anarchist member of the various 'tribes' he covered, or sponsored by known anarchist members, he appeared to already know what he was witnessing. Nothing, it seemed, was observed that contradicted his theoretical predilection. This was theory chasing confirmatory data, not data-led ethnography challenging existing theoretical accounts, forcing some novel rewriting of theory, as we saw with Nightingale.

Comparing Ethnographies in Terms of their Relationship to Conjunctural Analysis

Conjunctural analysis involves, essentially, unpacking the many determinations or mediations that, operating together, produce the precise balance of forces in a given, historical moment. How might Nightingale's ethnography fit with such an approach? Fortuitously, his historical moment, which started in the 1960s with his 'secondary' ethnography, overlapped that of *Policing the Crisis (PTC)* with its notion of a crisis of hegemony originating in the mid-1960s. His framing of the 'historical tragedy' that afflicted his alienated youngsters was provided by two sets of statistics: those demonstrating the virtual disappearance of marriage in black communities and those showing a rise in fatal violence, both of which he dated to around 1960. In other words, while *PTC*'s historical frame was pitched at the level of the social formation as a whole, Nightingale's ethnography alerted him to the importance of familial relations and hence to systemic changes in that particular area. Expressed in terms of determinations or mediations, Nightingale's work pointed to the importance of the new familial relations and particularly the 'forceful' parenting that accompanied this change. This was a new mediation. Linking all this to *PTC*, what we would appear to be witnessing in the case of Nightingale's alienated, hurt, frustrated, angry 'coming of age' children, some of whom progressed to criminal lives, was something similar to what the *PTC* team were witnessing, albeit only via secondary ethnography and hence only via a composite biography, in the case of their hypothetical 'young mugger' (Hall et al. 2013: 354).

Although the geographical location was different, we know that both countries, the USA and the UK, albeit each in their own particular way, were experiencing a crisis of hegemony and a consequent 'law and order' response. How Nightingale's ethnography potentially complemented *PTC*'s conjunctural analysis was its identification of another level of determination, that of family violence, to the making of a mugger. How *PTC*'s conjunctural approach potentially complemented Nightingale's ethnography was its ability to track the determinations of his historical tragedy, manifested in the (unproblematised) statistics that framed his study, back to the underlying, crisis-laden social relations. An historically located ethnography like Nightingale's can provide the detailed phenomenology that a complete conjunctural analysis requires; conjunctural analysis should be able to situate such an ethnography within the operative balance of forces in a given conjuncture. We need both.

Ferrell's reductionism disabled it from being able to offer what is ethnography's specific strength, the ability to discover new determinations. As we saw, Ferrell's confirmatory approach precluded new discoveries. The further problem was the lack of historical specificity. Although Ferrell's work largely took place in the 1990s, the issue of timing (sometimes his work seemed to be based on short periods of immersion, at other times on decades-long, even life-long, commitments), as with location, was not spelled out or given any prominence. This atemporal approach also affected his use of history. We were not given, as we might have expected, histories of the diverse activities he covered but rather a history of what they all represented, namely, anarchism. But, this was not a history of the shifting balance of forces that we would expect from a conjunctural analysis: how the balance of forces that underpinned the Paris commune, or the 'moment' of the Wobblies, or 1968—three of Ferrell's constant reference points—led to their respective defeats; but a history of how, despite their defeats, the spirit of anarchistic resistance lived on (among hobos, punk skateboarders, etc.). I have said enough already about how this latter point was not convincingly demonstrated. However, it was odd that the question of the succession of defeats was not addressed. How else can we learn the lessons of the past? It is the defining political point of conjunctural analysis. Symptomatic of the distance between Ferrell's approach and conjunctural analysis was his summary dismissal of 'hegemony': 'a word not much used anymore, and with good reason, since it was generally associated with an exaggerated analysis of political and ideological domination' (ibid.: 99). Ironically, this dismissed term, which remains an indispensable term for conjunctural analysis today, as I shall demonstrate in the chapters on Brexit, would have helped him understand better the forces in play in controlling public spaces than the rather loose idea of a police state.

The next section takes a similar comparative approach to two different texts on the relationship between carnival and transgression, one from outside cultural criminology and one from within.

Comparing a Conjunctural and a Cultural Criminological Approach to Carnival

A Conjunctural Approach to Carnival: Stallybrass and White's *The Politics and Poetics of Transgression*

The Stallybrass and White (1986: 16) text, which was not a criminology text, started with the idea of 'carnivals, fairs, popular games and festivals' being sites of struggle between the labouring poor and the authorities from the eighteenth century onwards. However, these struggles could best be understood in their historical specificity: 'the politics of carnival cannot be resolved outside a close historical examination of particular conjunctures: there is no a priori revolutionary vector to carnival and transgression' (ibid.). Moreover, unless Bakhtin's celebratory notion of carnival—the hierarchical order upturned, the popular temporarily in command—was transcended, 'none of the problems...concerning the politics of carnival: its nostalgia; its uncritical populism (carnival often violently abuses and demonizes *weaker*, not stronger social groups...); its failure to do away with the official dominant culture; its licensed complicity' (ibid.: 18) could be resolved. Thus, the authors began with a critique of Bakhtin since 'only by shifting the grounds of the debate, by transforming the "problematic" of carnival' can 'these issues...be solved' (ibid.). With this transformation in place, the authors went on 'to consider carnival as one instance of a generalized economy of transgression and of the recoding of high/low relations across the whole social structure...the body, the household, the city, the nation-state - indeed a vast range of interconnected domains' (ibid.: 18–19).

The critique of Bakhtin involved first noting that he sometimes adopted a binary model (where 'the grotesque [or low] is simply the opposite of the classical [or high]', ibid.: 44) and at other times a hybrid one, where 'the grotesque is formed through a process of hybridisation or infixing of binary opposites, particularly of high and low' (ibid.). With this hybrid model in place, they argued that they were able to accommodate the 'symbolic processes at work' in 'any specific historical location' of carnival (ibid.: 56).

Since 'the division of the society into high and low, the polite and the vulgar…the civilised and the grotesque body' also 'cut across the social formation' as a whole, 'subject identity cannot be considered independently of these domains' (ibid.: 191). In other words, 'the bourgeois subject continuously defined and redefined itself through the exclusion of what is marked out as "low" - as dirty, repulsive, noisy, contaminating'. But the excluded remained 'constitutive of…identity': it was still 'internalized [but] under the sign of negation and disgust'. And, as we know, 'disgust always bears the imprint of desire. These low domains, apparently expelled as "other", return as the object of nostalgia, longing and fascination' (ibid.). Once again, the complexity of this process could only properly be grasped by conceptualising two different forms of grotesque, the binary and the hybrid, since 'the *exclusion* necessary to the formation of social identity [binary model]…is simultaneously a *production* at the level of the imaginary…of a complex hybrid fantasy emerging out of the very attempt to demarcate boundaries, to unite and purify the social collectivity' (ibid.: 193).

Although this truncated summary does scant justice to a detailed and closely argued text, I hope it demonstrates the importance of four 'Cs': critique, conjuncture, complexity and contradiction. Using Bakhtin's notion of carnival as a jumping off point, the celebratory (or simple binary) way this was conventionally understood had first to be *critiqued* (which revealed two distinct, but often conflated, models of the grotesque) in order to make sense of the different symbolic processes variously at work in differing historical *conjunctures*. This more *complex* understanding enabled an argument to be made, not just about carnival, but about the symbolic classifications 'high' and 'low' more generally and how these contrary classifications necessarily produced *contradictory* bourgeois subjects. As Hall said in his glowing review of the book, it was a classic example of 'how to "think" in a non-reductionist way, the relations between "the social" and "the symbolic"…[which is] the paradigm question in cultural theory' (Hall 1996: 287). As we saw earlier, this was broadly the paradigm question for cultural criminology too; but the phrase, 'in a non-reductionist way' tended to be forgotten, as we shall see with the work of Presdee.

A Cultural Criminological Approach to Carnival: Mike Presdee's *Cultural Criminology and the Carnival of Crime*

Although published fourteen years after the Stallybrass and White text, and evidently aware of it since it was referenced, there was no evidence of Presdee attempting to build on it. Although he acknowledged the argument of Stallybrass and White when he wrote of 'a number of critics [who] have found a wide variety of instances where elements of carnival [i.e. high/low] have emerged in other contemporary forms of social and symbolic activity ['across the whole social structure']', he attempted to subsume it within his argument: 'It is as if, through the dual processes of scientific rationality and containment, carnival has shattered and its fragments and debris are now to be found in a wide variety of contemporary forms'. This was not at all what Stallybrass and White were saying.

Bakhtin's binary, celebratory model of carnival (the social order temporarily turned upside down) was reinstated *tout court* and utilised as a universal, ahistorical, not as a conjunctural, category. Presdee did point out that carnival's 'transgressive excitements...are not assumed to be all positive...In the ecstatic, marginal, chaotic acts of carnival, damage is done, people are hurt' (Presdee 2000: 32). Moreover, he also appeared at one point to complexify the binary model: 'On a simple level carnival may be seen as a time when low becomes high and vice versa, but more deeply carnival throws into question certain fixed notions of high and low' (ibid.: 41). However, these qualifications were never followed up nor were their implications explored. Thus, he effectively reduced carnival to a binary model with his notion that 'the performance of excitement and transgression' was the frame 'most appropriate' to the book's concerns. It's as if, having acknowledged that the picture is complex, not simple, he could then proceed reductively with a clear conscience. Complexity was thus replaced by reductionism and the only contradictions were those that appear inadvertently in the argument and were, in consequence, unaddressed. In place of Stallybrass and White's four 'Cs', Presdee explored the relations among another four 'Cs', namely, crime, criminalisation, consumption and culture. In terms of broad questions, these became: Why were horrendous/'meaningless' crimes endemic? Why did the media treat these as entertainment? Why were we fascinated/excited by such 'events'? Why were the young routinely blamed for much of this?

In attempting to answer these big, general questions without narrowing them down to questions about specific crimes at specific historical moments, the answers could only ever be equally general, i.e. theoretical, speculative. The attempted answer was twofold, with the second part somewhat in contradiction with the first, which I'll call the 'crime is fun' thesis. In an era of postmodernism, authority, truth and order were under challenge while consumerism and the commodification of everyday life were the order of today's capitalism. These cultural trends had served to collapse the distinction between carnival—periods of licensed misrule, excess, disrespect—and non-carnival and had led to the commodification of violence and crime. The result was that the transgressive excitements and pleasures formerly regulated by carnival had spread into everyday life, including in criminal acts, aided and abetted by the media packaging all this as commodities for consumption by a public desperate to escape the demands of rationality. As Presdee summarised the process, 'it is no longer enough to "do" carnival once, twice or three times a year. Under the "unbearable" rationality of modern life, acts of carnival become a daily need for social survival' (ibid.: 33). And, 'the more cultural aspects of …postmodernism have provided the context for a hugely complex fragmentation and reworking of carnival where the debris of carnival litters everyday life…not only does contemporary mass culture make free use of the idea of carnival in the service of the promotion of excitements, but its very nature is carnivalesque' (ibid.: 43–44). Within this context, 'the acts of body modification, S & M, raving, recreational drug-taking, hotting and rodeo, gang rituals, the Internet, festivals and extreme sports', all contain 'the marginal performance of carnival fragments in the late twentieth century' (ibid.: 47). The authorities attempt to criminalise much of this, as always, in the name of order and reason.

Shadowing the crime is fun thesis is a second thesis, which I summarise as 'crime as resentment of the dispossessed'. This felt more traditional, familiar, modern. Those left behind in this brave new world of transgressive excitements—leisure, pleasure and endless consumption—were left with the negative emotions of anger, rage, and hatred with which to express their injuries, hurts and sense of injustice. The punctuation of the text with Presdee's autobiographical experiences, *The Muck of Ages*, appeared to illustrate this second thesis rather than the first. Whether a crime could be, simultaneously, both pleasurably transgressive and hatefully kicking against the pricks was unclear, and Presdee did not enlighten on this point. Perhaps the two notions were meant to be resolved in the idea that everyday life under postmodernism was, it was claimed, so boring that transgressive excitements were necessary outlets: 'as everyday life becomes less and less interesting, so it also becomes less and less bearable and there is felt a general desire for daily excitement that becomes an essential ingredient in a consumer commodity culture' (ibid.: 62). This did not clarify matters. For whom was life becoming 'less and less interesting'? All of us or only the dispossessed? And why was life losing its interest, given the apparent spread of transgressive excitements?

One concrete example Presdee used to explore his idea of the continuation of the carnivalesque in the everyday world of late modernity was the 1987 trial and convictions of a group of gay men for engaging, consensually, in sadomasochistic sex: the notorious 'Operation Spanner' trial. Here was a particular, historically situated event of the kind that appeared to invite a conjunctural analysis, not least because it took place against a backdrop of the growing popularity and acceptability of S & M. In this context, the trial was an unusual event. (The waters were muddied by Presdee's assertion that consensual, sadomasochistic sex between adults had been successfully criminalised in the recent past, thus demonstrating that S & M sex was effectively still illegal. Be that as it may, his explanation of this disjunction between popular acceptance and continued criminalisation is what is at stake here.)

Having detailed the many ways that S & M activities had become popular, a part of everyday life, in films, literature, magazines, advertising, promotions, clubs, piercings and bodily alterations, he asked how such a popular activity could be criminalised and demonised. But, rather than go back to the trial directly, and thus be anchored by its conjunctural specifics, he rephrased the question in the most general terms: 'how is it that the popular becomes criminal' (ibid.: 98). Freed from the discipline of a concrete case, he reminded us that S & M was still regarded as a mental disorder by the World Health Organization, that attempts to explain such practices had not helped much, that the relation of sexuality to confession had linked it to 'wrong-doing' and thus to 'punishment and pain' and that 'confessing our transgressions has become a great entertainment/play commodity as punishment was so often in the past' (ibid.: 99). Having segued into the world of commodities, he was able to make his argument about why S & M was currently popular:

> So it is not remarkable that the world of S & M and other extreme pleasures is often the world of confession, punishment and pleasure woven together to become the commodification of confession and the consumption of pain. (ibid.)

So, why criminalisation? Here, Foucault and the importance of power relationships was invoked since 'playing with power' was 'an essential ingredient of S & M consensual play' (ibid.: 100). This was not just patriarchal power since women play all kinds of roles in S & M. Demonstrating this with a couple of long quotes, Presdee concluded that

> what is apparent and visible is the extent of the carnivalesque pleasures enjoyed by many women and men which are profoundly different in style to those of the past. Carnival has "come out" and in so doing will come into conflict with the aspirations and fantasies of the State. That is political conflict. (ibid.: 101)

And the State, it appeared, remains wedded to seeing it all through a traditional discourse of deviance and sickness, not sexuality, in which ideas of mutuality and consent have no part, only those of 'coercion, victims, violence and evil' (ibid.: 102).

Having made the case, in general, for how the popular became criminal—not very convincingly—the trial was returned to by way of endorsing this conclusion:

> As Lord Templeman stated in his Spanner Appeal ruling in the House of Lords, 'Society is entitled and bound to protect itself against a cult of violence. Pleasure derived from the infliction of pain is an evil thing. Cruelty is uncivilised'. (ibid.)

I remain as confused by the trial's verdict (upheld by the Appeal court, the House of Lords, and The European Court of Justice, apparently) as I was before reading Presdee's account and convinced that had the trial been used as the route to its 'many determinations', and not a general thesis about carnival, a more enlightening explanation of this odd prosecution would have resulted. As even a cursory examination of the case, which took place in 1987 in Thatcher's Britain, reveals, there were a whole host of relevant issues swirling around the case, issues to do with piercing and body modification, video 'nasties', the role of the Obscene Publications Squad, HIV Aids and homophobia, that a conjunctural analysis would have explored and that surely would have helped explain this particular verdict at this particular moment; but these were not mentioned in Presdee's account. I write this weeks after seeing a terrestrial television programme on dominatrixes and their consensual male, temporary 'slaves'. Among many 'cruel' practices, nailing clients' genitals to boards was similar to the practices that led to the assault charges in the Operation Spanner trial. But in this case, there were no subsequent prosecutions, so far as I know, and the perpetrators talked, undisguised, to camera. Clearly something is different from 1987 that Presdee's general notion of the state versus the carnivalesque was not equipped to explain.

Summarising the Differences Between the Two Approaches

The key difference between the two approaches to methodology lay in their relationship to historical specificity and, hence, to critique. As Stallybrass and White showed, Bakhtin's celebratory notion of carnival simply could not explain the historically variable politics of carnival, at some moments revolutionary, at others complicit with the authorities, for example. To understand such variation required a critique of Bakhtin's notion in order to produce a more serviceable, transformed, 'hybrid' notion of carnival with which they could begin to make sense of the politics of carnival in any given historical moment. This transformed concept also enabled the authors to make sense of transgression, now symbolically recoded as high/low, more generally. In other words, a conjunctural approach requires the discipline of historical particularity and, relatedly, the discipline of a critical approach to existing theorising, something to be transformed via critique rather than as something simply to be, eclectically, adopted. Lacking neither discipline, as was the case with Presdee's cultural criminology approach, enabled him to treat a particular historical event, the 'Operation Spanner' trial, as a general example of the state versus the carnivalesque utilising a notion of the latter based on an untransformed, 'celebratory' Bakhtinian notion of carnival. Leaving aside the many unanswered questions such an analysis provoked, it is hard to see more generally how Presdee's claims for carnival could be disproved. If fragments of carnival were to be found everywhere in everyday life, and the state, in the interests of reason and order, was generally opposed to the carnivalesque, it is hard to see what areas of crime and criminalisation would escape such an explanation. In explaining too much, a theory inevitably loses its usefulness.

Cultural Criminology and Conjunctural Analysis: A Summary Conclusion

I have now looked at a range of work, including introductory overviews and focused research, from some of cultural criminology's pioneer figures. I have presented these in some detail, quoting extensively, in order for their arguments to be, so far as is compatible with concise presentations, effectively in their own words. The object of such diligence has been, broadly, twofold: to see how well they succeeded in their own terms; and to see how compatible they were with the axiomatic methodology of cultural studies, namely, conjunctural analysis. On both counts, I found them consistently wanting: they failed to persuade with their own arguments, and they proved to be incompatible with conjunctural analysis. At first sight this might seem surprising since, in terms of broad aims, cultural criminologists and conjunctural analysts share a desire to relate the symbolic and the social. However, the discipline of historical specificity in conjunctural analysis compels the work away from reductionism and towards complexity. Herein lies the first difference between the two approaches: the constant reductionism evidenced in the cultural criminological work under review.

The source of this reductive thinking provides a second major difference: the role of theory in both cases. What for conjunctural analysis is a necessary moment in the analysis, because, as Hall (1997/2019: 250) put it, 'appearances are…largely wrong', became all pervasive in the work of cultural criminology's pioneers. As we have seen throughout, their work started and ended with theory: 'expressive' crimes, 'ontologically insecure' subjects, 'late modern' times; shuffle these terms any way you want but you will never escape the fact that these reference theoretical ideas about society, individuals and crime, not particular events involving particular people at particular historical moments. Or, the particular was used to try to demonstrate the correctness of the theory: the Operation Spanner trial exemplifying the idea of the 'carnival of crime'; or Ferrell's subordination of his 'misfit' street people to the idea of a struggle between gentrification and latter-day anarchist resistors. Unanchored by the discipline of understanding something specific in the real world, putting theory in command inevitably reduces the messy disorderliness of reality to a more manageable set of ideas.

Cultural criminology's preference for the theoretical over the conjunctural stemmed, knowingly or otherwise, from a desire to contribute to general theory, whether that be Hayward's wish to bridge the divide between social and individual theories of crime, Young's desire to produce both 'the sociology of vindictiveness' and 'the criminology of transgression', Presdee's attempt to link carnival and crime, or Ferrell's efforts to subsume his subjects within a theory of anarchism. Conjunctural analysis, on the other hand, uses the act of theorising to illuminate the realities of specific historical moments: it thus starts with the particular and is disciplined by it, not by theory. As we saw with the Marx quote in Chapter 3, 'the reader who wishes to follow me at all must resolve to climb from the particular up to the general'. Such a climb will, with the help of theory, progressively uncover the many determinations hidden in the appearance of the empirical particular, en route to a new understanding of the 'general'. Why all this matters is because the truth of this new synthesis can never be established merely theoretically. As Stuart Hall put it (in the second part of his quote above about the necessity of theory): 'What theory will never do is tell you either what you ought to have done or act as a guarantee that the choices that you've made are right'. Only actuality or practice can determine that: the always historically contingent truth of a theory or rightness of an action. Reality disciplines truth, not theory.

References

Bourgois, P. 1995. *In Search of Respect: Selling Crack in El Barrio*. Cambridge: Cambridge University Press.
Ferrell, J. 2001. *Tearing Down the Streets: Adventures in Urban Anarchy*. New York: Palgrave.
Ferrell, J., and C.R. Sanders. 1995. Preface. In Ferrell and Sanders, eds. (1995).
Ferrell, J., and C.R. Sanders (eds.). 1995. *Cultural Criminology*. Boston: North Eastern University Press.
Hall, S. 1996. For Allon White: Metaphors of transformation. In Morley and Chen, eds. (1996: 287–305).
Hall, S. 1997/2019. Politics, contingency, strategy: An interview with David Scott. In Morley, ed. (2019: 235–62).
Hall, S., C. Critcher, T. Jefferson, J. Clarke, and B. Roberts. 2013. *Policing the Crisis: Mugging, the State and Law and Order*, 2nd ed. Houndmills, Basingstoke: Palgrave Macmillan.
Marx, K. 1852/1968. *The Eighteenth Brumaire of Louis Bonaparte*. In Marx and Engels (1968: 94–179).
Marx, K., and F. Engels. 1968. *Selected Works: In One Volume*. London: Lawrence and Wishart.
Morley, D. (ed.). 2019. *Stuart Hall Essential Essays Vol. 2: Identity and Diaspora*. Durham and London: Duke University Press.
Morley, D., and K.-H. Chen (eds.). 1996. *Stuart Hall: Critical Dialogues in Cultural Studies*. London: Routledge.
Nightingale, C.H. 1993. *On the Edge: A History of Poor Black Children and Their American Dreams*. New York: Basic Books.
Presdee, M. 2000. *Cultural Criminology and the Carnival of Crime*. London: Routledge.

Snyder, G.J. 2009. *Graffiti Lives: Beyond the Tag in New York's Urban Underground*. New York: New York University Press.
Stallybrass, P., and A. White. 1986. *The Politics and Poetics of Transgression*. London: Methuen.
Young, J. 1999. *The Exclusive Society: Social Exclusion, Crime and Difference in Late Modernity*. Sage.

6

Hall's Theorising: The Importance of a Principled Eclecticism

This chapter is an attempt to contrast the principled eclecticism evident in Hall's use of theory to that of the pluralistic eclecticism, the fairly arbitrary selection of theory that was evident in cultural criminology's use of theory that we saw in Chapters 4 and 5. I use the term 'principled eclecticism' because Hall was called many things in his lifetime, from Marxist and post-Marxist to postmodernist and post-structuralist, and found theoretical sustenance from diverse sources. However, his use of theoretical ideas was always principled, not random. Central to these principles, which will be fully explained below, were a historically materialist and not idealist starting point (material reproduction of social life precedes ideas about it), a dialogic rather than a dismissive approach to critique (broadly, an attempt not to throw the baby out with the bathwater) and a recognition of the diverse forms of power underpinning social relations and thus a commitment to a complex and not a reductive understanding of social forces. These principles will provide the thread linking this selective, broad-brush look at Hall's theorising.

Up until now my focus has been on conjunctures and conjunctural analysis: particular historical moments and how to understand them. As

© The Author(s), under exclusive license to Springer Nature
Switzerland AG 2021
T. Jefferson, *Stuart Hall, Conjunctural Analysis and Cultural Criminology*,
Palgrave Pioneers in Criminology,
https://doi.org/10.1007/978-3-030-74731-2_6

I have been arguing throughout, Hall's genius lay in such an approach, which is why earlier I called him Gramsci's natural heir. To understand a particular moment in all its complex specificity demands theoretical tools that are sufficiently sophisticated to grasp that complexity. It was, for example, the conjuncture of 1848 in Europe, the moment of continent-wide insurrections that were everywhere defeated, which sent Marx back to the library to fashion new theoretical tools (which would produce the ideas that became *Capital*) with which to understand these defeats. Such tools, as with all theory, are designed to have a more general explanatory power, beyond the conjuncture that might have precipitated their re-fashioning. The theory of surplus value that Marx's labours eventually produced, and the contradiction between capital and labour that this is necessarily built upon, provide a core element in understanding capital's growth. In other words, wherever the capitalist mode of production operates, the theory of surplus value remains true.

The conjunctural moment that was to produce new political defeats for the working class in Europe, and thus the need for re-theorising Marx's ideas, was the revolutionary period during and after the First World War which produced victories for fascism in Italy and Germany, dictatorships in Portugal and Spain, and the first successful communist revolution in Russia, which was to morph into Stalinism. These seismic events eventually served the theoretical, although not the political, death knell for what came to be called 'economistic' marxism. (This is the idea that everything, ultimately, was determined by, or could be reduced to, capitalist relations of production.) A raft of revisions to marxist theorising followed, all attempting, ultimately, to make sense of these new situations. Gramsci's theoretical revisions (written inside a fascist prison cell) were occasioned by the success of Italian fascism and Althusser's by Stalinism (as well as the problematic responses to it). Jointly these provided two of the key sets of revisions that influenced Hall in his attempts to find new tools with which to understand various conjunctures. Thus, in addition to the conjunctural work of *Resistance through Rituals (RTR)* and *Policing the Crisis (PTC)* that we have looked at in some detail, Hall produced a range of theoretical writings that, among other things, provided the conceptual frameworks that guided his conjunctural work.

As with anyone whose intellectual output spans many decades, especially decades marked by massive political changes and huge intellectual shifts, the problem of periodisation arises in Hall's writings. Much has been made of the differences between Marx's early, middle and late work, for example. Hall thought Althusser's later theorising tended to become over-structuralist when compared with his earlier work. More generally, he often remarked that he preferred 'people's middle period…where they have gotten over their adolescent idealism but their thought has not yet hardened into a system', a reference on this occasion to the work of Marx, Althusser and Laclau (Hall 1986/2019: 240). Although Hall's work never hardened into a system, he constantly rethought his ideas as the political and theoretical conjuncture altered. This issue of changes of theoretical approach over an intellectual lifetime is compounded in Hall's case by the oddities of publication. For example, the lectures he gave in America in 1983 and which led to the massive expansion of cultural studies in the USA remained unpublished until 2016 (Hall 2016), and his Du Bois lectures of 1994, given at Harvard University, were not published until 2017 (Hall 2017). However, my concern is not with the details of his re-theorising efforts but with the principles informing these changes. Put another way, I am concerned with what does not change in Hall's theorising: how he decided, when approaching the novelty of postmodern theorising, for example, what was important enough to shift his thinking and what was not. It is this focus on Hall's core theoretical principles that enables me to move freely between early, middle and late Hall in exemplifying my argument.

Principle 1: A Historically Materialist Starting Point and Problematic

> Men…reproduce themselves as 'social individuals' through the social forms which their material production assumes. No matter how infinitely complex and extended are the social forms which men then successively develop, the relations surrounding the material reproduction of their existence forms the determining instance of all these other structures…This

is the basis for a *materialist* understanding of social development and human history; it must also be the basis of any materialist or non-idealist definition of culture…Marx's 'materialism' adds …that the relationship must be thought within determinate historical conditions. It must be made *historically specific*. (Marx quoted in Hall 1977a/2019: 298–99)

This is Hall interpreting the Marx of *The German Ideology* to begin his explanation of culture's 'roots' in material production in his influential essay 'Culture, the media and the "ideological effect"'. Whatever his other differences with Marx, and especially with various forms of Marxism, this remained Hall's starting point for understanding the cultural. Quite how to understand the relationship between this 'determining instance' and 'all these other structures', a relationship 'normally referred to, within Marxist analyses, by way of the metaphor of "base" and "the superstructures"' was, he thought, 'perhaps the most difficult aspect of a materialist theory' (ibid.: 299). It was to preoccupy Hall throughout his life and went through many rethinks as old models failed to match the complexity of a constantly changing historical present. However, the attempt to hang on to an historically materialist grounding was never abandoned. What he said of Marx could equally be applied to himself: 'If Marx's thought on the subject subsequently developed, what changed is how he came to understand determinacy by a mode of production, not whether it determined or not. When we leave the terrain of "determinations", we desert, not just this or that stage in Marx's thought, but his whole problematic' (Hall 1977b/2019: 151–52). Years later, when talking about his relationship to discourse theory and how 'the discursive position' can lose touch with materialism, he restated his commitment to the principle: 'Material conditions are the necessary but not sufficient condition of all historical practice', adding, in case that be read reductively, 'Of course, we need to think material conditions in their determinate discursive form, not as a fixed absolute' (Hall 1986/2019: 241–42). Hanging on to the necessity of material conditions to historical practice in a non-reductive way involved continuing to engage or dialogue with theoretical ideas, like Marxist ones, which others had begun to dismiss because some of its elements were flawed, inadequate or no longer fit for purpose, which brings me to Hall's second principle in considering theory: dialogue with existing approaches, even when you disagree with them in some way, in order to see what continues to remain serviceable. Avoid simply dismissing them.

Principle 2: A Dialogic Approach to Critique

Hall's 'Rethinking the "base" and "superstructure"' metaphor' (1977b/2019) was an early attempt to grapple with the issue of a historically materialist understanding of 'the determining instance'. In mapping the field, thematically rather than purely chronologically, from the early Marx of *Economic and Philosophical Manuscripts* and *The German Ideology*, through the "1859 Preface" to *The Critique of Political Economy*, *The Eighteenth Brumaire*, *Capital*, 'Engels's Letters on historical materialism', Gramsci and Althusser, Hall is engaged in a critical dialogue with the texts and authors: demonstrating when and how the relationship was, or needed to be, rethought. The broad thrust of the critique is away from the reductive historicist assumption in some of Marx's writings, that the base ultimately determines what happens in the superstructures. This is the essentialist or economistic reading of the relationship with the social formation seen as an expressive totality: the superstructures being a simple expression of the base.

This move away from economism was inspired by Althusser's reformulation of the superstructures in terms of relatively autonomous practices or levels (economic, political, ideological and, briefly but soon abandoned, the theoretical), with their own specificities and effectivities. Together these practices constituted 'an ever pre-given structured complex whole' which required, in turn, a new conception of determinacy, 'not as the simple determination of one level (e.g., the economic) over all the others, but as the structured sum of the different determinations, the structure of their overall effects' (Hall 1977a/2019: 312). Althusser called his new conception of determinacy 'overdetermination', a concept he borrowed from Freud (for whom it meant that the genesis of neuroses was usually the result of the convergence of several factors, hence overdetermined[1]). This attempted resolution to the base/superstructure problem bequeathed by Marx, of how to reconcile the *'relative autonomy of the superstructures'* with *'determination in the last instance by the (economic) mode of production'* (Althusser 1969: 111), did not satisfy everyone. Some thought Althusser was attempting to reconcile the irreconcilable and effectively abandoned Marxism as a viable intellectual project. Hall's dialogic approach enabled him, guided as always by his theoretical principles, to recognise the important achievements of Althusser while disagreeing with other parts of his theorising: 'despite my disagreements, Althusser's break with classical Marxism opened up a new perspective on the question of ideology and thus made it possible for me to rethink it as well' (Hall 2016: 127). I shall return to the nature of this new perspective when I consider Hall's third guiding principle.

One reason why Hall does not abandon Marx's problematic but continues his critical dialogue with him is the discovery, in his close reading of Marx's writings, of ways in which Marx himself was aware of the problems of his early formulations and attempted to clarify them, albeit that these attempts remained incomplete and untheorised. For example, his historical writings, paradigmatically *The Eighteenth Brumaire* (Marx 1852/1968), clearly demonstrate Marx's practical awareness of the complexity of the relationship between everyday politics and the economic level: of how changes in the political superstructure were not simple expressions of the economic base (a point that was central to Sartre's Marxism, too, as we saw in Chapter 2). Or the distinction Marx makes, in *Capital*, between 'phenomenal forms' and 'real relations': how appearances under capitalism fail to tell the whole story; how apparently equal exchange relations hide the extraction of surplus value from labour, capitalism's 'real' exploitative and unequal social relations. Moreover, Marx goes on to argue that our ideas of freedom and equality stem from this sphere of exchange. Hall would regularly use the apparent freedom and equality of the wage relation—'a fair day's work for a fair day's pay', freely entered into—in contrast to the hidden inequality of the extraction of surplus value to illustrate the point. He thought this an

---

[1] See Freud's 'The psychotherapy of hysteria' (1893/1974: 346).

'essential starting point…to found a theory of the superstructures' (Hall 1977b/2019: 163).

This critical dialogue was not just with Marx, however. Although Marx's historical materialism offered an essential and never-to-be-abandoned starting point and guiding principle, the fact that Marx's own theoretical writings were undeveloped beyond the economic level made it necessary to seek out other areas of knowledge that did have something to say about these other levels. Like the concept of culture, for instance. Disciplines like literature, with its notion of 'high' and 'low' culture (Shakespeare and comic books), and anthropology, with its notion of culture as a whole way of life, had developed notions of the meaning of culture. Cultural studies' first critical dialogue, consonant with its origins in the study of literature, was with the literary critic F. R. Leavis, not with Marx. Leavis's close reading of texts was adopted but put to work sociologically on understanding the lived meanings of working-class culture, for example in Hoggart's foundational text, *The Uses of Literacy* (1957). Consequently, in the early days the Centre for Contemporary Cultural Studies (CCCS) had two 'working groups': one doing close readings of literary texts; the other reading widely in other disciplines (Hall 2007/2019: 40).

Unsurprisingly, given this early interest in understanding working-class culture, critically dialoguing with sociology became a central and enduring feature of cultural studies. However, this dialogue, as with all Hall's many dialogues, was guided by a Marxist problematic. Hence, an important early attempt by Hall at mapping the sociological field centred on 'ideology and the sociology of knowledge', to quote from the subtitle of his 1977 article (Hall 1977c/2019). If Marx's phenomenal forms/real relations distinction constituted an essential starting point for thinking further about the superstructures, it was specifically pivotal for Hall in theorising ideology (Hall 1977a/2019: 308). And so Hall (1977c/2019) conducted his critical dialogue with an entire catalogue of major thinkers on the topic: the ideologues of the French revolution, then Kant, Hegel, Dilthey, Lukacs, Weber, Nietzsche, Schutz, Durkheim, Mauss, Levi-Strauss, Althusser, Barthes and Bourdieu (to name only those credited with initiating an important 'break' in the debate). As with his

'Rethinking the "base" and "superstructure"' metaphor' article, it historically situates contributions, critically evaluates them and traces 'lines of descent'. Hall often jokingly said that 'we made up cultural studies as we went along', implying we read randomly; this article belies that claim; for here was Hall working his way systematically through a body of literature with a firm sense of direction supplied by his guiding principles.

Threading its way through this mapping exercise are two metaproblems: ideology (as a set of ideas) versus 'truth'; and the issue of the historical locatedness of ideas which underpins the materialist (ideas as a product of their historical moment) versus idealist (ideas as the motor of history) understandings of the notion. This latter issue was at the heart of the first principle, about the importance of a materialist starting point, as we saw earlier. The problem for those opposing a materialist notion of ideology was what they saw as the reductionism of a Marxist theory of ideology. Max Weber was one such, who saw his own work, correctly according to Hall, as explicitly anti-Marxist (Hall 1977c/2019: 119–20). Nevertheless, Hall was a great admirer of Weber's *The Protestant Ethic and the Spirit of Capitalism* (1930), calling it 'by any reckoning an intellectual *tour de force*' (1977c/2019: 121) and thought that it was possible to read it through a Marxist lens. The book is 'Weber's best-known contribution to the substantive analysis of an ideology' (ibid.: 119). It uses his methodological ideas about the study of Culture needing to be understood both objectively, at the level of historical causality, and subjectively, at the level of meaning, and his compromise solution: the ideal type (a simplified attempt to approximate reality in order to make it thinkable). Thus, Protestantism and Capitalism are conceived as ideal type constructions. The core argument is that there was an 'elective affinity' between the structure of ideas animating Puritanism and those underpinning capitalism (the importance of planning, regulation, routinisation, the idea of work as a vocation, for example), and this produced a particular 'character structure'. This affinity was secured through what Hall calls the 'startling...paradox that the most secular, materialist of economic systems - capitalism - emerged at the level of ideology, paradoxically, *not* through the gradual erosion and secularization of Catholicism but through the intensified *spiritualization* of Puritanism' (ibid.: 122). In other words, the alignment of the economic and the ideological is 'articulated through the *differences*, rather than through the correspondences, in their respective logics' (ibid.). This is compatible with a non-reductionist Marxist reading: 'a theory of the "relative autonomy" of ideology *could*, therefore, be rescued from Weber's work without doing violence to his argument' (ibid.).

This is an example, one of many in the article and grossly simplified, of Hall's critical dialoguing with those with whom he was ultimately intellectually at odds but from whom, nevertheless, he felt we could learn something. There is nothing dismissive in the approach, despite Hall's disagreements over Weber's enduring methodological individualism and neo-Kantianism. Rather, in line with his dialogic approach in which critique is used as a basis for rethinking and not simply to criticise, there is a generous acknowledgement of the achievements of the approach:

> It is worth noting that the move from content to 'homologies of structures' [both references to Weber's approach to ideas] is the key theoretical advance represented in Goldmann's *Hidden God*: and that the attention to 'character structure' is an aspect to which both the 'Frankfurt School' and Wilhelm Reich were, later, to pay considerable attention. (ibid.: 121)

Here, Hall is attentive to the relationship among intellectuals, how those coming after borrow from and develop ideas: how intellectual work is an ongoing and ever-changing dialogue. This dialogic approach to critique presumes an openness to complexity, which constitutes Hall's third guiding principle and to which I now turn.

Principle 3: A Complex Understanding of Social Relations

For ease of presentation, I am going to discuss Hall's changing understanding of power and social relations in terms of three key moments. In reality, of course, these moments were not sharply demarcated but part of a gradual evolution of his thinking: his constant 'wrestling with the angels', as he described his theorising and re-theorising. Moreover, the headings used to encapsulate each moment are also, inevitably, simplifications. In a section designed to demonstrate the complexity of Hall's thinking this is especially ironic. Nevertheless, the three moments are: (1) Relative autonomy and the effectivity of the superstructures; (2) The role of language and the discursive turn; and (3) Identity and articulation.

Relative Autonomy and the Effectivity of the Superstructures

I opened the last section by noting that the broad thrust of Hall's critique of the base/superstructure model was away from a reductionist or expressive understanding of the relationship towards Althusser's notion of the relative autonomy of the practices or levels of the superstructures possessing their own specificities and effectivities. In classic Marxist theory, the key site of political power is the State, conceptualised (in a theoretically undeveloped fashion) purely as a repressive instrument for securing the domination of the ruling classes and thus, in capitalist social formations, enabling capitalist exploitation to continue. Althusser's rethinking of the superstructures included a seminal essay retheorising the nature of the capitalist state: 'Ideology and ideological state apparatuses' or, as it became known, the ISAs essay (Althusser 1971/1977). Although Althusser regarded it as a series of preliminary thoughts (hence his bracketed subtitle: 'Notes Towards an Investigation'), it provided a crucial stimulus to Marxist thinking on the issue of class power. In suggesting that, as Hall (1977b/2019: 169) put it, 'the specific "effectivity" of the superstructures is to be understood in terms of their role in *the reproduction of the social relations of production*', it offered innovative theorising about the state's ideological role. Moreover, this new focus on the state's role in social reproduction enabled much new Marxist theorising on the family, education, communications, and so on, all of which were now, in Althusser's terms, ISAs.

As it happens, Hall's relationship to the essay was mixed: he welcomed 'the attempt to reconceptualize the base/superstructure problem in terms of "social reproduction"' for being 'in much closer conceptual touch with the starting point of Marx's mature work (production, reproduction)' (Hall 1977b/2019: 170). However, he regarded the idea that the ISAs' 'function' is to reproduce capitalist relations of production as reductively functionalist. He had other misgivings about the essay and, in line with his preference for middle periods, preferred the less developed formulations, on ideology as well as determinacy, in the earlier essay 'Contradiction and overdetermination':

> 'Contradiction and overdetermination' in *For Marx* contains a richer notion of determination than *Reading Capital*, though not so rigorously theorised. *For Marx* has a fuller notion of ideology than does "Ideological State Apparatuses", although it is not as comprehensive. Again, I prefer the early Althusser to the late Althusser. (Hall 2016: 142)

This is where, for Hall, Gramsci enters the picture. Both Gramsci's *Prison Notebooks* and Althusser's ISAs essay were first published in English in the same year: 1971. Althusser fulsomely acknowledges his debt to Gramsci, a sentiment that Hall powerfully endorsed: 'Both [Althusser and Poulantzas] are *massively* indebted to Gramsci, in seminal not just in marginal or incidental ways' (Hall 1977b/2019: 166–67):

> The concept of 'Ideological State Apparatus'…is a direct reworking of a few seminal passages on apparatuses of consent and Gramsci's 'State and Civil Society' essay (*Prison Notebooks*), though, of course, translated - with effect - into a more structuralist Marxist language.

The 'with effect' is a recognition of the theoretical gains a more structuralist Marxism could achieve (something he could recognise despite his reservations). Hall's theoretical achievement was to get the best of both worlds: by reading Althusser through his indebtedness to Gramsci, he could counter the functionalism of Althusser's structuralism ('overstructuralism' as he sometimes referred to it); by reading Gramsci somewhat systematised by an Althusserian structuralism, he could counter the incipient expressive relativism of Gramsci's historicism (the idea that theories and ideologies are simple expressions of their historical conditions of existence).[2]

What Gramsci added, in broad terms, was an enlarged role for the superstructures, and specifically the state and civil society, in conforming all areas of social life to the needs of capital—the state as educator with a key role in the production of consent to class rule—along with a swathe of new, if undeveloped, concepts with which to think about all this. Hegemony was one of these, which, as we have seen, became one of Hall's core concepts for thinking conjuncturally:

> In Gramsci's concept of hegemony…we discover the beginnings of a way of conceptualizing how classes, constituted at the fundamental level of production relations, come to provide the basis of the social authority, the political sway and cultural domination of a 'class alliance on behalf of capital', without reducing the idea to what Marx once called the 'dirty-Jewish' question of class interest, narrowly conceived. (Hall 1977b/2019: 165)

'Common sense' was another of Gramsci's core concepts that he used to think about ideology at the level of everyday talk. This was also influential for Hall as we saw in the analysis of popular sentiments of crime and punishment in *PTC*. Its relevance in today's conjuncture for thinking about authoritarian populism should not be under-estimated and I shall return to it in the chapters on Brexit.

One of the reasons that, in the end, Hall was more Gramscian than Althusserian can be summed up in the different ways they conceptualised civil society. For Althusser, all the essentially private institutions of civil society (family, schools, trade unions, etc.) are absorbed within his new notion of ISAs: the family ISA, the educational ISA, etc. His justification for this was that the public/private distinction was a purely legal one with no impact on how ISAs function. Somewhat confusingly, Althusser's warrant for this abolition of the private/public distinction is Gramsci, who is also credited with the 'remarkable' idea that the State

---

[2]For a detailed examination of the complexity of Hall's reading of the relationship between the two authors, see Hall et al. (1977/2007).

could include institutions from civil society (Althusser 1971/1977: 136–67). The pages from Gramsci's *Prison Notebooks* that Althusser cites (12, 259, 260–63) in footnote 7 (ibid.: 136) do indeed tend to elide the State and civil society at many points. However, I am inclined to read these passages and other similar examples from the quoted pages as saying that the necessary hegemonic functions of the State, as opposed to its coercive functions, are undertaken by the private institutions of civil society and that consequently these institutions perform State functions while remaining private institutions of civil society. Hall certainly read him in this way. He thought that Althusser's rethinking of all the diverse institutions of civil society as State apparatuses with an ideological function was a reductive move since it undercut their specificity.

On the other hand, maintaining the civil society/State distinction as in his view Gramsci succeeded in doing was a distinction that mattered: the way institutions are articulated with the State, among other things, 'have *pertinent effects*':

> For example, in the British case, the functions of the press (privately owned) and of television (indirectly coordinated with the state) are different because of their different modes of insertion; and these differences have *pertinent effects*. (Hall et al. 1977/2007: 294)

In the light of the upcoming struggle over the fate of the BBC and public broadcasting generally, and the prospect of entirely privatised television networks, this is an apt reminder of just why this distinction matters. More generally, Hall's own work on the media over many years is a testimony to the complexity of the relationships among ownership, professional and organisational practices and the social reproduction of dominant ideologies. Ultimately, Hall was more Gramscian than Althusserian because Gramsci's attempts to rethink the base/superstructure relation, 'the proper posing' of which he thought 'was the seminal issue in a Marxist theory of politics' (Hall 1977b/2019: 164), were both more complex and more productive. Althusser's more systematic ideas about social reproduction tended to produce rather functionalist Marxist readings of the family, education, etc. Gramsci's less developed notions, such as common sense and hegemony continue to provide indispensable tools for thinking the specific effectivity of Althusser's relatively autonomous instances. Althusser himself (1969: 114 n29) considered hegemony to be 'a remarkable example of a theoretical solution outline to the problems of the interpenetration of the economic and the political'. However, none of this should undermine how seminal a contribution the ISAs essay was when it first entered Centre discourse; ultimately it was the dialogue between Althusser and Gramsci that enabled Hall to make his own seminal contributions; he needed both of them. The importance of the idea of hegemony and the production of consent necessarily implicates language and discourse. Hall's relationship to these topics constitutes the second key moment in Hall's theorising.

The Role of Language and the Discursive Turn

In discussing the importance of Richard Hoggart's *The Uses Of Literacy* to the formation of cultural studies, Hall used the term 'cultural turn' to describe the growing significance of all things cultural 'across Western societies', especially 'after the Second World War' (Hall 2007/2019: 35–36). Hoggart's work was seminal in expanding the use of the term culture to include class and its whole way of life. Hall continued to expand this exploration of culture with his early theoretical journeyings within Marxism and elsewhere to try to understand how the cultural level could be thought about systematically in relation to the social totality. This was Marxism's base/superstructure problematic. Central to understanding culture within the Marxist tradition has been the issue of ideology, one of Hall's key examples in his attempts at re-theorising the base/superstructure relationship. It is the realm of experience that is specific to the ideological level—'the level of …*ideology proper*' as Hall (1977a/2019: 306) once put it, in order to distinguish it from culture as 'lived'. By 'experience' he meant how people become conscious of, think about, make sense of, represent to themselves, and generally give meaning to their experience of their lives and their place in the world. Central to thoughts, ideas, representations and meanings is language, the pre-eminent medium for providing meanings.

The notion of language is not problematised in Marx. Problematising the form in which ideas are formulated and made meaningful, entailed, for Hall among others, a theoretical detour beyond Marxism; to the revolutionary ideas about language associated with Saussure and the emergence of modern linguistics. In cultural studies, this was sometimes called the 'linguistic turn'. Saussure's revolutionary break was with reflective and intentional views of how language gives meaning to reality—language imitates or reflects nature; language expresses an individual speaker's intended meanings. Instead, Saussure inaugurated a constructionist view of language: things have no meaning in themselves but are made meaningful only through the system of signs and concepts that has been socially constructed. Saussure argued that 'signs' produce meaning by uniting an essentially arbitrary form, the four letters, t-r-e-e, comprising the word tree, with a corresponding concept (in this case, the concept 'tree'). The former he called the signifier, the latter the signified. As Hall (1997: 31) put it in his discussion of Saussure's legacy, 'both are required to produce meaning but it is the relation between them, fixed by our linguistic and cultural codes, which sustains representation'. This relationship between signifiers and signifieds, the sign system that collectively constitutes a culture's meaning system at any given time, is thus subject to the operative linguistic and cultural codes. These are not fixed for all time but are subject to the play of history: thus new meanings to old signs constantly make an appearance. One of the consequences of this constant slippage of meaning is to open up the potentiality for a gap between what Hall (1973/2019) called encoding—the sign as produced—and decoding—the sign as consumed, or read, by an audience, a potentiality heightened when the issue of power is introduced (although this was not something that Saussure addressed).

Saussure also introduced the idea that many things in a culture, not just language, can operate as signs, the general study of which he called semiology. However, it was left to others to carry forward this aspect of the work, most famously by Barthes with his semiotic readings of everyday objects (like 'Steak and Chips') and events (like 'Striptease') in *Mythologies* (1972). Take clothes. Semiotically speaking, these are a sign system in which a particular arrangement of material is the signifier (like the word 't-r-e-e' in the earlier linguistic example) and our concept of it as, say, 'shirt' or 'dress' is the signified (like the concept 'tree' in the earlier linguistic example). What Barthes added was another level of signification that enabled the sign system to be connected to the world of culture and ideology. The descriptive, widely shared meaning of signs like 'clothes', Barthes called the level of denotation. The second, broader level of meaning he called the level of connotation. For example, when we decide what to wear each day, deeming this combination too casual for a job interview, that too formal for attending a music festival or that too bohemian for the office, we are basing our decision on this second level of meaning: what our choice of clothes connotes in the wider culture. Clothes are something the fashion industry exploits endlessly for commercial reasons by reworking their connotations. Think of the history of jeans and trainers, for example, and the conversion of their connotations of workwear and sportswear into the new, highly lucrative, connotations of casual fashionableness, wearable by everyone and anyone, anywhere at anytime.

Approaching culture semiologically, inspired particularly by Barthes' distinction between denotation and connotation, was a key methodological aspect of *RTR* as we attempted to read youth subcultural styles like a language; to decode them as meaning systems and connect these to broader changes in class cultures. What is important here, in the present context, is to emphasise that 'this "world of signs"…has its own internal rules, codes, and conventions, its own modes and mechanisms' (Hall 1977a/2019: 313). This is a different question about ideology to the notions of its relation to 'truth' or to history, the questions that dominated Hall's mammoth survey of 'ideology and the sociology of knowledge' as we saw earlier. Here it is about what mediates ideology, principally language but also, as we have just seen, other sign systems. As a mediation with its own specificities and effectivities, it needed to be understood in its full complexity before being reinserted into the social formation and thought about in relation to history and power. Hall undertook that necessary theoretical detour, most comprehensively perhaps in the Open University teaching text *Representation: Cultural Representations and Signifying Practices* (1997) which he edited as well as writing the Introduction and two long chapters.

The next major contributor to the debate on representation, for Hall, was Foucault. Less concerned with language and meaning than with knowledge and power, his approach to the question of representation restated the centrality of history while abandoning the concept of ideology in favour of the notion of discourse.[3] He was someone from whom Hall learned much, even as he disagreed with him about core elements, namely Foucault's abandonment of two key concepts of Marxism: ideology and the state. Discourse, for Foucault, was a broader concept than language. As Hall understood it, 'a discourse is a group of statements which provide a language for talking about - i.e. a way of representing - a particular kind of knowledge about a topic'. Discourses are historically specific 'groups of statements', but they also implicate practice: 'Discourse is about the production of knowledge through language. But it is itself produced by a practice: "discursive practice" - the practice of producing meaning. Since all social practices entail *meaning*, all practices have a discursive aspect' (Hall 1992: 291). It was this aspect above all, and the potential it provided for slippage between discourse and practice such that discourse effectively swallowed up practice and everything became discursive, that was to become the crucible of all the other differences Hall had with Foucault.

Although discourse and ideology are both knowledge-producing groups of statements, Foucault rejected the latter term because it relied on a distinction between the 'truth' of science and the falsity of ideology: false because, within Marxism, it represented class-based ideas ('the ruling ideas of any age are the ideas of the ruling class'). This idea Foucault found reductive. Nevertheless, Foucault understood the 'truth' of a discourse as a product of power relations, not a product of scientific reasoning:

> Truth isn't outside power…Each society has its regime of truth, its 'general politics' of truth: that is the types of discourse which it accepts and makes function as true; the mechanisms and instances which enable one to distinguish 'true' and 'false' statements; the means by which each is sanctioned; and the techniques and procedures accorded value in the

---

[3]Within criminology, Foucault's historical work on the changing nature of punishment in *Discipline and Punish* (1977) was more influential than his work on discourse.

acquisition of truth; the status of those who are charged with saying what counts as true. (Foucault 1980: 131)

This is not very different from Hall's understanding of ideology, as he himself recognised (Hall 1986/2019: 227). It was both the similarity to and difference from the Marxist problematic that led to much discussion of the compatibility or otherwise of Foucault with Marxism, and to Hall's continuous engagement with him.

Importantly for Hall, Foucault greatly expanded our conception of power, from a top-down model—oppressor/oppressed; dominant class/subordinate class, etc.—emanating from a single source to one where power is everywhere, in every nook and cranny of social life. Moreover, this power was not merely repressive but also productive, as in the way that the power to punish produces, among other things, the whole industry that is criminology. As Hall (1997: 50) put it: 'without denying that the state, the law, the sovereign or the dominant class may have positions of dominance, Foucault shifts our attention away from the grand, overall strategies of power, towards the many, localized circuits, tactics, mechanisms and effects through which power circulates'. However, in so doing, he neglected to theorise the state. Overall, Hall welcomed and admired the historicising thrust of his work. He welcomed the detailed attention to the micro-physics of power and the gains to specificity that this enabled. However, to the extent that Foucault abandoned some of the core principles underpinning Hall's approach to theorising, Hall parted company with him. In response to an interview question about postmodern theorists abandoning, among other things, the issue of ideology, Hall had this to say about Foucault:

> while I have learned a great deal from Foucault... about the relation between knowledge and power, I don't see how you can retain the notion of 'resistance', as he does, without facing questions about the constitution of dominance in ideology. Foucault's evasion of the question...[ensures that] Nobody knows where it comes from. Fortunately, it goes on being there, always guaranteed: in so far as there is power, there is resistance. (Hall 1986/2019: 227–28)

Here the issue is Foucault's abstract conception of resistance, in stark contrast to his empirically-based and historically located discussions of power. The consequence, Hall goes on to argue, is that Foucault cannot address the actual relations between power and resistance at any given time:

> But at any one moment, when you want to know how strong the power is, and how strong the resistance is, and what is the changing balance of forces, it's impossible to assess because such a field of force is not conceptualizable in this model. Why? Because there is no way of conceptualizing the balance of power between different regimes of truth without society conceptualized, not as a unity, but as a 'formation'. (ibid.: 228)

In other words, once you introduce a historical dimension, conceptualising the changing balance of forces requires a differentiated not unified concept of society. Once you do that, a concept of ideology, whatever you want to call it, is unavoidable:

> as soon as you begin to look at a discursive formation, not just a single discipline but as a *formation*, you have to talk about the relations of power which structure the inter-discursivity, or the intertextuality, of the field of knowledge. I don't much care what you call it: ideology or not. What matters is not the terminology but the conceptualization. The question of the relative power distribution of different regimes of truth and social formation at any one time - which have certain effects for the maintenance of power in the social order - that is what I call 'the ideological effect'. (ibid.)

This is a classic Hall argument. Start with a generous acknowledgement of what he has learned from the theorist in question, followed by a detailed, reasoned critique of what is problematic in its own terms. In Foucault's case, this amounts to him not recognising the need for a broadly Marxist notion of ideology if his claim that 'where there is power there is resistance' is to make historical as opposed to merely formal sense.

One of the things Foucault's work did, because it was largely read through a postmodern rather than Marxist lens, was to legitimate a host of studies of discourse without any attempt to relate them to the existing balance of forces. The problem was partly the undeveloped notion of resistance as we have just seen, but perhaps a bigger issue was the notion of discursive practice and the elision of discourse as system of knowledge with the practice of its production. Earlier I called it the crucible of all the differences that Hall had with Foucault. Let me elaborate, since it leads into the work of another theorist, Ernesto Laclau, to whose work, generally, Hall was much indebted. However, Laclau was another theorist whose middle period work (Laclau 1977) Hall preferred because it remained within a Marxist tradition, unlike his later work (like Laclau and Mouffe 1985) which had become purely discursive.

The relation between discourse and meaning is at stake here, as Hall explains:

> The idea that 'discourse produces the objects of knowledge' and that nothing which is meaningful exists *outside discourse*, is at first sight a disconcerting proposition...Is Foucault saying - as some of his critics have charged - *that nothing exists outside of discourse*? In fact, Foucault does not deny that things can have a real, meaningful existence in the world. What he does argue is that '*nothing has any meaning outside of discourse*'. (Foucault 1972, cited in Hall 1997: 44–45)

Here, Hall absolves Foucault of the charge of reducing everything to discourse while acknowledging that some have read him that way. It is a charge he was to make against Laclau and Mouffe (1985): 'the...-book thinks that the world, social practice, is language, whereas I want to say that the social operates *like* a language' (Hall 1986/2019: 240). However, we need to start with the issue of 'articulation', since this is the concept that both Laclau and Hall used to rethink Marxist theorising of ideology in a non-reductive way. And since Laclau uses the Althusserian term 'interpellation' in his definition, we also need a brief return to Althusser's ISAs essay.

Identity and Articulation

I said earlier when we looked at the ISAs essay in relation to relative autonomy that Hall welcomed its attempt to think its way out of the base/superstructure problem by its focus on social reproduction but had misgivings about its latent functionalism. In the second part of the essay, Althusser (1971/1977: 160) addresses the question of the ideological subject, how individuals come to inhabit ideology: '*all ideology has the function…of 'constituting' concrete individuals as subjects*'. This works through recognition: '*all ideology hails or interpellates concrete individuals as concrete subjects*' (ibid.: 162). In other words, we live out our lives as authors of our actions in ideology through a process of recognising ourselves in the pre-existing discursive subject positions that interpellate us. And as with the early part of the essay, Hall had mixed feelings: enthusiasm for his definition that 'ideology represents the imaginary relationship of individuals to their real conditions of existence' (ibid.: 153) since it was similar to his own reading of Marx's phenomenal forms ['imaginary relationship']/real relations ['real conditions of existence'] that I discussed earlier. His misgivings centred on the way that the theory of the subject was hived off from the rest of the essay. This led to discursive and psychoanalytic theorising about subjectivity, inspired by Foucault and Lacan (from whom Althusser borrowed the term interpellation), but devoid of any connection to the question of reproduction (Hall 2016: 135).

Re-enter Laclau. In *Politics and Ideology in Marxist Theory*, Laclau (1977: 160) introduces the term 'articulation' in order to rethink 'the class character of an ideological discourse'. Rather than think of it in terms of content—the class content of ideology is determined ultimately by the class-based relations of production—and hence reductively, Laclau proposes a two-step solution. Following Althusser, he suggests that '*what constitutes the unifying principle of an ideological discourse is the "subject" interpellated and thus constituted through this discourse*' (ibid.: 101). But given the diverse elements, including many without a particular class connotation, that go to make up any given ideological discourse, the only way that class can become the 'unifying principle of an ideological discourse' is through '*a process of articulation*' (ibid.: 161). It is, thus, the form in which diverse elements are connected that produces the class character of an ideology (or 'the principle of articulation of its constituent interpellations', ibid.: 160) not the class content of its constituent elements. To demonstrate this, Laclau uses the way the ideology of nationalism, which has no class connotation in itself, has been variously articulated in class terms.

Using much simpler language and the homely example of an articulated truck to demonstrate, Hall (1986/2019: 235) defines articulation as 'the form of the connection that can make a unity of two different elements, under certain conditions'. He emphasises the point that Laclau has demonstrated with his nationalism example, that any discursive unity achieved by one form of articulation can be re-articulated to form another: 'the so-called "unity" of a discourse is, really, the articulation of different, distinct elements which can be re-articulated because they have no necessary "belongingness"' (ibid.). However, he adds a second point about unity, which for him is the crucial one: 'The "unity" which matters is a linkage between that articulated discourse and the social forces with which it can, under certain historical conditions, but need not necessarily, be connected' (ibid.). This, always contingent and never guaranteed, connection, of 'articulated discourse' with 'social forces' is the one that 'matters': the 'unity' of discourse and social relations, not just a unified discourse. Hall goes on to acknowledge Laclau's development of the theory in *Politics and Ideology in Marxist Theory* and the similarity in their thinking.

This way of thinking the unity of discourse and social relations is what *Hegemony and Socialist Strategy* severs when it breaks 'with the discursive/extra-discursive dichotomy' and, in consequence, 'the thought/reality opposition'(Laclau and Mouffe 1985: 110) in its attempt to theorise the specificity of the 'logic of contingency' (ibid.: 3) so central to Laclau's earlier book. While Laclau and Mouffe deny that their argument has anything to do with the existence of a world beyond thought, only that objects can only be constituted discursively (ibid.: 108), the effect is to convert social practice into language. This is what Hall's earlier quoted remark about the book claims. He went on to call this an 'upward' reductionism: 'the fully discursive position is a reductionism upward, rather than a reductionism downward, as economism was' (Hall 1986/2019: 241). In typical Hall fashion, this conclusion follows a fulsome acknowledgement of what the 'discursive perspective', and Laclau and Mouffe's work in particular has achieved:

The discursive perspective has required us to think about reintroducing, reintegrating the subjective dimension in a non-holistic, non-unitary way. From this point of view, one cannot ignore Laclau and Mouffe's seminal work on the constitution of political subjects…The discursive metaphor is…extraordinarily rich and has massive political consequences. For instance, it enabled cultural theorists to realise that what we call "the self" is constituted out of and by difference, and remains contradictory, and that cultural forms are, similarly, in that way, never fully closed or "sutured"…It [their book] is a sustained philosophical effort, really, to conceptualise *all* practices as nothing but discourses, and all historical agents as discursively constituted subjectivities, to talk about positionalities but never positions, and only to look at the way concrete individuals can be interpellated in different subject positionalities. The book is thus a bold attempt to discover what a politics of such a theory might be. All of that I think is important. (ibid.: 239–40)

At that point the critique starts: with Hall expressing his preference for Laclau's earlier book; then noting that their 'critique of reductionism has apparently resulted in the notion of society as a totally open discursive field'; adding the point about thinking 'that the world…is language'; and ending with the 'reductionism upward' point (ibid.: 240–41). He ends his critique by returning to the continuing importance of historical materialism: 'I think the discursive position is often in danger of losing its reference to material practice and historical conditions' (ibid.: 242).

In response to a question about whether Laclau and Mouffe's *Hegemony and Socialist Strategy* is not political enough, Hall's response is that 'their problem isn't politics but history. They have let slip the question of the historical forces which have produced the present, and which continue to function as constraints and determinations on discursive articulation' (ibid.). When asked about whether the issue was the level of abstraction, Hall delivers what I think is the defining point about his approach to theorising. He says that the problem is not the issue of theory as such and that 'they are quite heroic' in their attempt at a 'rigorously articulated general theory'. Although Hall confesses that he does not 'operate well at that level' he does not deny the importance of such work. However, their problem is the failure 'to recognise the constraints of existing historical formations'. The particular problem is this:

when they come down to particular conjunctures, they don't reintegrate other levels of determination into the analysis. Instead, they take the abstractions which have been developed and elaborated, in a very rigorous and conceptual way at a high philosophical level, and insert them into the here and now. You don't see them adding, adding, adding, the different levels of determination; you see them producing the concrete philosophically, and somewhere in there is, I think, the king of analytic slippage I am talking about. (ibid.: 243)

Ultimately, Hall suggests, they failed to submit to the messy discipline of the conjuncture, as all theorising, however rigorous and logical its ambitions, must.

Summary and Conclusion

This chapter has attempted to demonstrate Hall's principled eclectic approach to theorising. It has not attempted to be a comprehensive survey of his theoretical writings, nor an evaluation of them. Rather, it has been a selective, thematic exploration of his use of theory. It has focused on some of the key themes that preoccupied Hall throughout his intellectual/political life in order to show the constancy with which he approached theoretical topics, the principles that continued to guide his thinking, even as the content of his thinking about the topics changed. Interestingly, although Laclau and Mouffe had a different relationship with Marxism than Hall had by the mid-1980s, they all acknowledged their indebtedness to Marx: 'if our intellectual project in this book is *post*-Marxist, it is evidently also post-*Marxist*' (Laclau and Mouffe 1985:4); 'I am a "post-Marxist" only in the sense that I recognise the necessity to move beyond orthodox Marxism...But I still operate somewhere within what I understand to be the discursive limits of a Marxist position' (Hall 1986/2019: 243). Ultimately all theorising fails when it does not keep the conjuncture in mind, whether it replaces that with the functionalist 'logic' of structuralism in the case of Althusser or the philosophically formalist 'logic' of contingency in the case of Laclau and

Mouffe. Although he produced no theory that will forever be associated with his name, Hall's enduring contribution to theorising was never to lose sight of the conjuncture.

References

Althusser, L. 1969. Contradiction and overdetermination. In *For Marx*, L. Althusser, trans. Ben Brewster, pp. 87–128. Harmondsworth: Penguin.
Althusser, L. 1971/1977. Ideology and ideological state apparatuses (notes towards an investigation). In *Lenin and Philosophy and Other Essays*, L. Althusser, trans. Ben Brewster, pp. 121–73. London: New Left Books.
Barthes, R. 1972. *Mythologies*, selected and trans. A. Lavers. London: Jonathan Cape.
Foucault, M. 1972. *The Archeology of Knowledge*. London: Tavistock.
Foucault, M. 1977. *Discipline and Punish*. London: Allen Lane.
Foucault, M. 1980. *Power/Knowledge*. Brighton: Harvester.
Freud, S. 1893/1974. The psychotherapy of hysteria. In Freud and Breuer (1974: 335–93).
Freud, S., and J. Breuer. 1974. *The Pelican Freud Library Volume 3: Studies on Hysteria*, trans. and ed. James and Alex Strachey with editorial assistance by Angela Richards. London: Pelican.
Gramsci, A. 1971. *Selections from the Prison Notebooks*, ed. and trans. Q. Hoare and G.N. Smith. London: Lawrence & Wishart.
Gray, A., J. Campbell, M. Erickson, S. Hanson, and H. Wood (eds.). 2007. *CCCS Selected Papers*, vol. 1. London: Routledge.
Hall, S. 1973/2019. Encoding and decoding in the television discourse. In Morley, ed. (2019: 257–76).
Hall, S. 1977a/2019. Culture, the media, and the "ideological effect". In Morley, ed. (2019: 298–335).
Hall, S. 1977b/2019. Rethinking the "base and superstructure" metaphor. In Morley, ed. (2019: 143–71).
Hall, S. 1977c/2019. The hinterland of science: Ideology and the sociology of knowledge. In Morley, ed. (2019: 111–42).
Hall, S. 1986/2019. On postmodernism and articulation: An interview with Larry Grossberg and others. In Morley, ed. (2019: 222–46).

Hall, S. 1992. The West and the rest: Discourse and power. In Hall and Gieben, eds. (1992: 275–320).
Hall, S. 1997. The work of representation. In Hall, ed. (1997: 13–64).
Hall, S. (ed.). 1997. *Representation: Cultural Representations and Signifying Practices*. London: Sage.
Hall, S. 2007/2019. Richard Hoggart, *The Uses of Literacy*, and the cultural turn. In Morley, ed. (2019: 35–46).
Hall, S. 2016. *Cultural Studies 1983: A Theoretical History*, ed. and with an intro. J.D. Slack and L. Grossberg. Durham and London: Duke University Press.
Hall, S. 2017. *The Fateful Triangle: Race, Ethnicity, Nation*, ed. K. Mercer with a Foreword by H.L. Gates, Jr. Cambridge, MA and London: Harvard University Press.
Hall, S., and B. Gieben (eds.). 1992. *Formations of Modernity*. Cambridge: Polity Press.
Hall, S., and T. Jefferson (eds.). 2006. *Resistance Through Rituals: Youth Subcultures in Post-War Britain*, 2nd ed. London: Routledge.
Hall, S., R. Lumley, and G. McLennan. 1977/2007. Politics and ideology: Gramsci. In Gray et al., eds. (2007: 278–305).
Hall, S., C. Critcher, T. Jefferson, J. Clarke, and B. Roberts. 2013. *Policing the Crisis: Mugging, the State and Law and Order*, 2nd ed. Houndmills, Basingstoke: Palgrave Macmillan.
Hoggart, R. 1957. *The Uses of Literacy*. London: Chatto & Windus.
Laclau, E. 1977. *Politics and Ideology in Marxist Theory: Capitalism—Fascism—Populism*. London: New Left Books.
Laclau, E., and C. Mouffe. 1985. *Hegemony and Socialist Strategy: Towards a Radical Democratic Politics*. London: Verso.
Marx, K. 1852/1968. *The Eighteenth Brumaire of Louis Bonaparte*. In Marx and Engels (1968: 94–179).
Marx, K., and F. Engels. 1968. *Marx and Engels Selected Works in One Volume*. London: Lawrence & Wishart.
Morley, D. (ed.). 2019. *Stuart Hall Essential Essays Vol. 1: Foundations of Cultural Studies*. Durham and London: Duke University Press.
Weber, M. 1930. *The Protestant Ethic and the Spirit of Capitalism*. London: Unwin.

Part III

Conjunctural Analysis Today: Brexit, Trump and the Politics of Difference

7

Race, Immigration and the Politics of Difference

In this chapter, I want to use Hall's later writings on race as a way of contextualising Brexit. Here Hall addresses a series of themes to do with race, ethnicity, nationalism, identity and immigration. Although mostly written nearly thirty years before Brexit, and all before 9/11, these writings seem to me to be remarkably prescient of the Brexit conjuncture. They all, in various ways, address what Hall (2017: 86) had come to see as '*the* problem of the twenty-first century - the problem of living with difference'. Brexit, as I hope to show in the following two chapters, was a good, regional example of this.

New Ethnicities, New Identities

Introducing the special issue of *Cultural Studies* on Stuart Hall and race, Claire Alexander (2009: 458), one of Hall's finest interlocutors on matters of race, starts thus:

© The Author(s), under exclusive license to Springer Nature
Switzerland AG 2021
T. Jefferson, *Stuart Hall, Conjunctural Analysis and Cultural Criminology*,
Palgrave Pioneers in Criminology,
https://doi.org/10.1007/978-3-030-74731-2_7

It is almost impossible to overestimate the significance of Stuart Hall in shaping the field of racial and ethnic studies in the past four decades...From his seminal intervention *Policing the Crisis*...through his work on race and class, and race and the state, to his more recent theorizations around 'new ethnicities' and 'the politics of difference', Hall's writing has redefined the ways in which race research is thought and done.[1]

The later writings that concern us here are the 'recent theorizations' mentioned, the series of essays written principally between the late 1980s and the early 1990s,[2] including the DuBois lectures of 1994 (Hall 2017) that were only published after Alexander's review, and his thinking on multiculturalism (Hall 2000/2019b).

Connecting these to his earlier work, at one level they constitute Hall's attempt to explore the second part of Althusser's Ideological State Apparatuses (ISAs) essay that we looked at in the previous chapter. This is where Althusser introduces the idea that the function of ideology is to interpellate individuals as subjects: to constitute each and every one of us as ideological subjects by 'hailing' us in a way that we recognise that that is who we are. As I briefly noted then, Hall had been critical of how that idea had subsequently been taken up in Foucaultian discursive and Lacanian psychoanalytic theorising because the idea of subjectivity had lost all connection to ideology and the question of reproduction. However, in addressing the issue himself, his concern with subjectivity was not theoretically-driven but, as always, an attempt to intervene politically in what he saw as an emergent problem, in this case the politics of race in the UK: to argue the case that existing theory lagged behind political developments and thus stood in need of correction if it was not to become a regressive drag on the struggle. It was thus a theoretico-political intervention into the conjuncture of Thatcherism from the subjective side of ideology. Just as his writings on Thatcherism proved too radical for some socialists, these proved too radical for some anti-racists.

---

[1] The work on 'race and class and race and the state' is a reference to his work for UNESCO on the Caribbean and on South Africa (Hall 1977 and 1980/2019a), which belong, theoretically, with *Policing the Crisis (PTC)* as part of what I think of as Hall's middle period.
[2] Hall (1988a, b, 1991/2019b, 1992/2019b).

7 Race, Immigration and the Politics of Difference 141

However, this was also the moment when, in self-critical mode, he felt that his analysis of Thatcherism had neglected the international dimension. So, the essays start locally but are international in scope: a sort of broad framing of the global conjuncture. As always, they are historically located, with key terms, like race, ethnicity, nation, identity, diaspora subjected to wide-ranging genealogical analyses. Leavened with everyday examples and punctuated with autobiographical reflections, collectively the essays manage to make some tenaciously difficult ideas about some seemingly intractable problems appear simple, or at least thinkable, once the connections between the global and the local, geographically, historically and in terms of everyday experiences, have been persuasively brought to light. In sum, these essays are politically motivated, historically specified, geographically located, theoretically driven, conjuncturally focused, commonly exemplified and autobiographically punctuated, engaging similar subject matter from different entry points, sometimes repetitively,[3] but with a clear sense of purpose: the problem of living with difference.

The first of these essays, 'Minimal selves' (Hall 1988a), was the result of a talk he had been invited to give at the Institute of Contemporary Arts in London about 'the minimal self'—a reference to the fragmentary sense of identity espoused in postmodern discourse of which he was so critical. At the time, he had no idea how seismic these interventions were to become. He starts with these words: 'A few adjectival thoughts only'. He continues autobiographically, joking about how his migrant status (delivered, no doubt, with his customary chuckle),[4] once a mark of '*difference* from the rest of you' (presumably talking to a largely white audience), is, 'in the postmodern age', no longer a marginal but

---

[3]'Repetitively' here references the fact that these essays were originally delivered as talks, differently focused and to different audiences, but with similar ideas being explored, resulting in some overlapping of explanations and examples. In addition, however, the first two talks (Hall 1988a, b) were effectively amalgamated in a third talk which was published as Hall (1991/2019b). In this case, the repetition is more direct and deliberate.

[4]Hall's ability to make the most intellectually demanding topic accessible, and to deliver it with humour, in a talk or lecture was second to none. And what characterised his delivery was the chuckle with which he would introduce the humour. Gary Whannel's obituary notice, 'Remembering the chuckle' (2014), is a good place to start if you have not been fortunate enough to witness Hall in lecturing action.

a 'centered' experience: 'welcome to migranthood'. It is this thinking about his own sense of identity which made him understand 'something about identity' which had been puzzling him 'in the last three years'. He continues with an everyday observation about black youth:

> I've been puzzled by the fact that young black people in London today are marginalized, disadvantaged and dispersed. And yet they look like they own the territory. Somehow, they too, in spite of everything, are centered, in place: without much material support, it's true, but nevertheless, they occupy a new kind of space at the centre. And I've wondered again and again: what is it about that long discovery-rediscovery of identity among blacks in this migrant situation, which allows them to lay a kind of claim to certain parts of the earth which aren't theirs, with quite that certainty?. I do feel a sense of - dare I say - envy surrounding them. (ibid.: 44)

Contrast this with the 'typical biography' of a black youth who ends up 'mugging', that we outlined in *PTC*. A crude paraphrase includes: fighting white bullies in school; finding employment difficult; rowing with concerned parents; leaving home; drifting with friends; sleeping rough or wherever; questioning by police; fighting with police; dealing with 'nigger taunting'; finally, mugging (Hall et al. 2013: 354). What has changed between these two moments: the 1970s 'moment of the mugger' and the 1980s moment of black youth 'centeredness'? In many ways, black youth in Thatcherite Britain were having a harder time than their 1970s counterparts, given the dramatic rise in unemployment and the tougher policing the regime sanctioned, as evidenced by the period's recurrent, police-triggered rioting. In other words, despite the situation of black youth being much the same or worse, as Hall acknowledged, he noticed a change: a positive cultural shift of some kind. Unravelling the significance, in all its complexity, of that everyday observation of what he came to name a 'new ethnicity' was the task that the essays, variously, set themselves.

This new confidence of black youth on the streets that Hall was puzzling over was the everyday version of a cultural shift taking place in the arts and culture generally with the emergence of black artists of all kinds: 'They are making astonishing cultural work, the most important work in the visual arts. Some of the most important work in film and photography and nearly all of the most important work in popular music' (Hall 1991/2019b: 80). None more so than the film, *My Beautiful Laundrette* with its screenplay by Hanif Kureshi. Of it, Hall said,

> it is the most transgressive text there is. Anybody who is black, who tries to identify with it, runs across the fact that the central characters…are two gay men…one…white and one…brown. Both of them are struggling in Thatcher's Britain. One of them has an uncle who is a Pakistani landlord who is throwing black people out of the window. This is a text that nobody likes. Everybody hates it. You go to it looking for what are called 'positive images', and there are none. (ibid.: 81)

Hall loved it *precisely* because of its lack of positive images, calling it 'one of the most riveting and important films produced by a black writer in recent years' (Hall 1988b: 30). Others agreed, as it won many awards. Understanding why it was important politically was part of what forced Hall to revisit the term 'black'.

Speaking autobiographically, Hall pointed out that the term is not a reference to skin colour, since it was 'never uttered' in the Jamaica of his childhood, where black people were overwhelmingly in the majority. Rather, it is 'a political category', first heard by him 'in the wake of the civil rights movement, in the wake of the decolonisation and nationalistic struggles', and which entered Jamaica in the 1970s: 'for the first time, black people recognised themselves as black. It was the most profound cultural revolution in the Caribbean, much greater than any political revolution they have ever had' (Hall 1991/2019b: 75). This positive re-valorisation of a previously negative term, like the coining of the phrase 'black is beautiful' in the USA in the 1960s, is an example of articulation in practice: of disarticulating it from its previous negative referents and re-articulating it with positive ones. And, in the process, providing the basis for the emergence of a new identity: 'In that very struggle is a change of consciousness, a change of self-recognition, a new process of identification, the emergence into visibility of a new subject' (ibid.). We should never forget the struggle dimension of articulatory work of this kind, its articulation with social forces (against which were ranged powerful, oppositional forces), embracing in this case the whole gamut of black resistance in the USA in the 1960s, from race riots and civil rights marches to the emergence of black nationalism and the Black Panthers: many lives were lost; some murdered by the state.

It was this new notion of 'black' that united the anti-racist struggles in 1970s Britain. Asians, Afro-Caribbeans, Africans, immigrants from a variety of different cultures and continents, began to identify 'politically as black' (ibid.: 76). Then, 'the enemy was ethnicity…what we called "multiculturalism"' (ibid.: 77) because, in reducing the problem of racism to misunderstood cultural differences, it failed to acknowledge the systemic character of racism. This Hall called 'Identity Politics One', the moment of a constructed black identity subsuming the diverse experiences of its constituent ethnic groups. However, there were negative consequences of such a constructed, collective identity since clearly not everyone from such a diversity of ethnic groupings could identify experientially with the proffered identity even when they were committed to it politically: 'it had a certain way of silencing the very specific experience of Asian people' (ibid.). Moreover, in also subsuming other social relations, like gender, it silenced them too: meaning that a masculinist version of 'black' tended to hold sway. *My Beautiful Laundrette* is a transgressive text because it breaks with these silences in many different ways. It certainly 'has a politics' but one 'which is grounded in the complexity of identifications which are at work' (ibid.: 81). Hall called this 'Identity Politics Two', the moment of 'living identity through difference'.

> It is the politics of recognizing that all of us are composed of multiple social identities, not of one. That we are all complexly constructed through different categories, of different antagonisms, and these may have the effect of locating us socially in multiple positions of marginality and subordination, but positions which do not yet operate on us in exactly the same way. (ibid.: 78)

This notion of a shift from Identity Politics One to Identity Politics Two presupposes a particular and unfamiliar conception of identity. When he synthesised the ideas from both of the papers published in 1988 to produce 'Old and new identities, old and new ethnicities', Hall chose to start by outlining the theoretical antecedents of the idea of identity lived through difference (Hall 1991/2019b). Beginning with the traditional 'logic of identity' that presumes a core 'true self', as evidenced in the notion of the 'Cartesian subject' as 'the ground of action' and its modern, psychological equivalent, 'the continuous, self-sufficient, developmental, unfolding, inner dialectic of self-hood' (ibid.: 64), Hall declared that this understanding of identity is 'finished...for a whole range of reasons' (ibid.). Then, in two brief pages he outlined, incisively and amusingly, the successive decenterings of the subject occasioned by the theoretical revolutions of Marx, Freud and Saussure, and the upsets precipitated by 'other enormous historical transformations' that produced 'the relativization of the Western narrative...and...the displacement of the masculine gaze' (ibid.: 66). However, he continued, 'that is not all that has been disturbing the settled logic of identity...there has simultaneously been a fragmentation and erosion of...the great collective social identities of class, race, nation, gender, and the West' (ibid.). Maybe this old conception of identity was never as stable and homogenous as we thought; but now there are 'certain...things it simply will not, or cannot, decipher or explain' (ibid.: 68).

Drawing on the rethinking of identity that had taken place in feminism and psychoanalysis, Hall offered, in the interests of brevity, a programmatic account of the new dimensions of identity. First, 'identities are never completed...they are always...in process'. Second, 'identity means...the process of identification...which...is always constructed through ambivalence...through splitting...Splitting between that which one is and that which is the other. The attempt to expel the other...is always compounded with the relationships of love and desire. This is a different language from the language of...the Others who are completely different from oneself' (ibid.: 69). This was also a completely different language from Althusser's interpellated subjects. The idea of the expelled Other residing inside one as a consequence of the ambivalence of desire, 'the self as it is inscribed in the gaze of the Other', the great 'unspoken silence' of identities, was clearly psychoanalytically inspired as Hall acknowledged. However, as with all Hall's work, this was not some blind theoretical borrowing but a creative appropriation of theory, disciplined as always by concrete, historical examples. In thinking of the 'necessity of the Other to the self' (ibid.: 70), he used first the powerful example he often used, from Fanon's *Black Skin, White Masks*, of Fanon as a young Antillean child knowing who he was 'for the first time' after a white French child's exclamation, 'Look Mama, a black man', simultaneously shattered and violently recomposed his existing sense of self (ibid.).

However, it is the second, more personal example, that brilliantly illustrates the silent Other inside English identity. It is a humorous example, but one suffused, for me, with a suppressed, implacable anger (the silent Other inside Hall's customary chuckle):

> People like me who came to England in the 1950s…symbolically, we have been there for centuries…I am the sugar at the bottom of the English cup of tea. I was coming home. I am the sweet tooth, the sugar plantations that rotted generations of English children's teeth. There are thousands of others beside me that are…the cup of tea itself. Because they don't grow it in Lancashire, you know. Not a single tea plantation exists within the United Kingdom. This is the symbolization of English identity - I mean what does anybody in the world know about an English person except that they cannot get through the day without a cup of tea? Where does it come from? Ceylon/Sri Lanka, India. That is the outside history that is inside the history of the English. There is no English history without that other history. The notion that identity has to do with people who look the same, feel the same, call themselves the same, is nonsense. As a process, as a narrative, as a discourse, it is always told from the position of the Other'. (ibid.)

The idea that identities are composed from 'never completed' differences entailed further theoretical elaboration: a closer look at 'difference'. Enter Derrida and his distinction 'between "difference" and "*différance*", spelt with an "a"' (ibid.: 71). This is a difference that makes a difference. Although, strictly speaking, Derrida's usage encompasses both 'to differ' and 'to defer', it is the latter meaning that opens up new ground, Hall suggests, as it moves the notion of difference beyond that of binary oppositions (male/female). This will prove crucial to the politics of difference and the difference between an absolutist notion of difference and a more open, 'deferred', meaning. Where Saussurian linguistics depends on difference for meaning, Derrida's contribution introduces the prospect of the infinite postponement of meaning: of it being forever deferred.

While better able to encapsulate the complexity of identity, the politics of difference as endless deferral are difficult: too difficult for some, who have settled for deconstructive 'play' instead: sophisticated word games with signifiers that never stop sliding. How to use Derridean deferral of meaning politically? By taking up a position, stopping the slide, breaking the endless deferral: 'You take a bet…on saying something. You have to be positioned somewhere in order to speak…you have to come into language to get out of it. There is no other way. That is the paradox of meaning' (ibid.: 72–73).

So far, I have drawn out from the essays Hall's noticing of a new confidence among black youth on London's streets and its cultural echo in the art world—the mid-1980s conjunctural starting point—and its explanation in terms of the emergence of a new politics of identity lived through difference, in contrast with the all-encompassing 'black' identity of the 1970s that worked politically by erasing ethnic differences. I have also outlined the historical shifts in conceptualising identity that enabled this new politics of identity to be thinkable in this way. Moving on to the social relations 'hidden' behind this shift, in line with Hall's new insistence that the conjuncture needed to be understood internationally, involved situating this British case within its global context. Hall's starting point for this was the moment leading up to the emergence of Identity Politics One: the rise of street racism and 'the passage of clearly racialized immigration laws by the British parliament' that ended any illusions about assimilation. This, 'the end of the assimilationist dream', Hall continued, 'is a watershed moment with global historical significance' (Hall 2017: 87). Quite what he meant by that is a long story that I will try to keep short.

The Multicultural Question and the Politics of Difference

The end of assimilationism was also a moment of multiculturalism. I say 'a' moment not 'the' moment since it was a re-emergence:

> Multicultural societies are not new. Long before the age of European expansion (from the fifteenth century onward) - and with increasing intensity since - the migration and movement of peoples has been the rule rather than the exception, producing societies which are ethnically or culturally "mixed"...The plantation systems of the Western world, the indentured systems of South-east Asia, colonial India, as well as the many nation-states consciously carved out of a more fluid ethnic canvas - in Africa, by the colonising powers, in the Middle East, the Balkans and Central Europe, by the Great Powers - all loosely fit the multicultural description. (Hall 2000/2019b: 98)

Three features of the post-war period, that collectively constituted 'a strategic reconfiguration of social forces and relations across the globe' (ibid.: 99), operated to put the multicultural question 'center stage in the field of political contestation' (ibid.). These features were decolonisation, the ending of the Cold War and globalisation. Decolonisation produced 'many *new* multiethnic and multicultural nation-states' (ibid.). But, they continued to be dogged by the problems of the colonial era, remaining poor, underdeveloped, with weak civil societies and all-but-destroyed indigenous cultures, and neoliberalism served only to compound these problems. The result was that, 'Increasingly, crises...assume a multicultural or ethnicized form' as the old unequal power struggle between colonisers and the colonised were 'restaged and displaced as struggles between indigenous social forces...or between them and the wider global system' (ibid.).

Something similar has been happening after the ending of the Cold War and especially, after 1989, in the regions directly affected by the dismantling of the Soviet Union and its declining influence. Compounded by the attempt of the West, without any attention to cultural or other specificities, to create market economies out of relatively underdeveloped societies, one result has been 'that the unresolved problems of social development have combined with the resurgent traces of older, still unrequited ethnic and religious nationalisms, allowing the tensions to resurface in multicultural form' (ibid.: 100). However, Hall, continued, 'this is no simple revival of archaic ethnicities' but 'older traces are combined with new, emergent forms of "ethnicity", which are often a product of uneven globalization and failed modernization' (ibid.).

7 Race, Immigration and the Politics of Difference   149

Ironically, nationalism figures strongly: these 'revivalist movements...see the nation as an engine of modernization and a guarantor of a place in the new world system, at precisely the moment when globalization is bringing the nation-state-driven phase of capitalist modernity to a hesitant close' (ibid.).

Hall's third factor was globalisation. This was 'not new' since 'European exploration, conquest, and colonisation were early forms of the same historical process...But since the 1970s, the process has assumed new forms while also being intensified' (ibid.: 100–101). The features associated with the new globalisation are by now familiar:

> the rise of new, deregulated financial markets...global capital and currency flows...transnational forms of production and consumption, the exponential growth of the new cultural industries and new information technologies, and the rise of 'the knowledge economy'...time-space compression [i.e. the attempt]...to cohere particular times, places, histories, and markets within a homogeneous, 'global' space-time chronotope...the uneven disembedding of social relations and processes of detraditionalization. (ibid.: 101)

However, its impacts have not been uniform: even though 'Its dominant cultural tendency is homogenization...It has also had extensive *differentiating* effects within and between different societies'. In other words, 'homogenization' is not inevitable but 'a hegemonizing process...a system for *conforming difference* rather than a convenient synonym for the obliteration of difference' (ibid.: 101–102).

Lined up against this 'hegemonizing process' is what Hall called 'the subaltern proliferation of difference': the struggle of the 'locals', when faced with the 'global', to become 'modern'; but on their own terms by indigenising the global. These 'vernacular modernities' break with 'the classic Enlightenment binary between Traditionalism and Modernity' (ibid.: 102). They are not mere left-overs from the past but globalisation's other side: conjuncturally specific and politically labile, as Hall concluded.

> 'The local' has no stable, transhistorical character. It resists universalism's homogenizing sweep with different conjunctural times. It has no fixed

political inscription. It can be either progressive or regressive and fundamentalist - open or closed - in different contexts...Its political thrust is determined not by essential content...but by its articulation with other forces. (ibid.: 103)

Hall saw 'hybridity' as another way of conceptualising these postcolonial vernacular modernities with their mixtures of elements from cultures of origin with elements from Western capitalist modernity. To a greater or lesser extent, all immigrant cultures are like this. Attempting to make sense of their new situation and feel comfortable in it, they will draw on both familiar cultural traditions and elements from their new culture of arrival, like Hall's example of 'the Muslim student who wears baggy, hip-hop, street-style jeans but is never absent from Friday prayers' (ibid.: 115). As 'the margins' emigrate to 'the centre' and multicultural hybridity becomes increasingly the norm, quite what is central and what marginal becomes questionable. Hence Hall's joke about his migrant status and finally feeling 'centered', with which he started his talk on 'Minimal selves': 'welcome to migranthood'.

The political implications of this are far-reaching. Once racism revealed the fundamental contradiction at the heart of the assimilationist approach—become more like 'us'/ your difference prevents you ever becoming fully 'us'—and hybridity revealed a different logic at work—that of difference as against the logic of 'sameness' of assimilation—the debate about the relationship between the universal and the particular was opened up. As Hall expressed it, multiculturalism challenged 'the dominant discourses of Western political theory and the foundations of the liberal state' (ibid.: 115). By this he meant, principally, 'universal citizenship', the idea that all of us as citizens in a given jurisdiction enjoy the same rights, and 'the cultural neutrality of the state' (ibid.: 116), meaning the state guarantees those same rights, such as the freedom of religion, speech, etc., equally, under the rule of law. In the new intellectual climate, however, 'The post-Enlightenment, liberal, rational, humanist universalism of Western culture looks...less *universal* by the minute [and more like]...the culture that won: the particularism which successfully universalized and hegemonized itself across the globe' (ibid.: 115).

7 Race, Immigration and the Politics of Difference

In practice, of course, universal citizenship was always less than fully inclusive and 'the neutrality of the state only works when a broad cultural homogeneity among the governed can be assumed' (ibid.: 116). In the latter case, such a homogeneity has to be 'imagined' or constructed into being, to provide 'the focus of identification and belongingness':

> The discourses of the nation do not…reflect an already-achieved unified state. Their purpose is, rather, to forge or construct a unified form of identification out of the many differences of class, gender, region, religion, and locality which actually crosscut the nation…To achieve this, these discourses must deeply embed and enmesh the so-called culture free 'civic' state in a deep entanglement of cultural meanings, traditions, and values which come to stand for or represent the nation'. (ibid.)

In short, liberal universalism had always been partial or less universal than its ideal and partially the product of invented national traditions. However, multiculturalism posed the issue of particularism even more sharply: 'What…cannot any longer be sustained…is the binary contrast between the particularism of "their" demands for recognition of difference versus the universalism of "our" civic rationality' (ibid.: 117).

It is important to remember here Hall's point about the two meanings of difference: the binary us/them notion, difference as 'restricted, unified, closed, absolutist, defensive, and essentialist', and the 'looser, more permeable, and more porous' (Hall 2017: 134) notion of *différance* as deferral, as constantly mutating. Despite the fact that most modern nation-states are the products of *différance*, 'cultural hybrids…mongrelized and diasporized beyond repair' (ibid.: 143–44), up until the 'crisis of identity' precipitated by post-war migrations from the former colonies, the restricted, essentialist notion of national identity prevailed. After the loss of empire, this eventually hardened into an 'unbridgeable racialized difference between "us" and "them"' (ibid.: 146).

This 'crisis of identity' was not confined to Britain but was happening

> *in all the Western nation-states as a consequence of globalization*…What is precipitating it…is not simply the internationalization of capital…the element that really unfixes a certain conception of homogeneous national cultural identity…is mass migration…the great planned and unplanned

movements of people, roughly from the global South to the global North…a movement from periphery to center that really has no precedent in history since the forced migrations and exodus from eastern Europe at the end of the nineteenth century, and before that the mass transport of millions through the slave trade in the sixteenth to eighteenth centuries. (ibid.: 147–49)

This process was both 'multiculturalizing and hybridizing the closed and homogeneous conceptions of cultural national identity' (ibid.: 149) and being fiercely resisted in 'the defensive restoration of ethnic absolutism in the struggle to cobble together new stories of cultural identity' (ibid.: 150). This could be seen everywhere: 'in the various forms of religious fundamentalism across the globe…in the deep suspicion of Europe that fuels the current "Little Englandism" of the anti-European Union movement…in the revival of racist politics with the so-called New Europe' (ibid.: 150–51).

After many more examples of this 'restoration of ethnic absolutism' drawn from across the globe, Hall concluded that 'the crucial distinction between closed and open constructions of cultural identity [the distinction 'between the politics of difference and the politics of *différance*']…runs right across, and completely disrupts, our conventional alignments of left/right, progressive/regressive, even racist/antiracist…[and] has become, quite literally *the* decisive political frontier of our times' (ibid.: 157).

A similar argument was made about diaspora. There can be a closed or open reading of it. The Jewish diaspora entails a closed reading: attempting to hold on to a strong sense of Jewishness wherever located. An open reading is associated with those contact zones of diasporic formation 'where different cultures not only intersect but are obliged to modify themselves in the face of one another…neither the refusal of difference nor its hardening and fixing, but its constant and on-going negotiation' (ibid.: 166). In this case, 'Diaspora cultures…will always be inevitably syncretized' (ibid.).

What did all this imply for a new politics of difference or multiculturalism? One based not on some imagined nation but the nation as it actually existed, comprised of its many different communities. As Hall put it, 'It would have to address the double political demand, which arises from...[the] interplay between the gross inequalities and injustices arising from the absence of substantive equality and justice, and exclusion and inferiorization arising from the lack of recognition and sensitivity to difference' (Hall 2000/2019b: 120). If, broadly speaking, racism in all its forms, including that embedded in the existing imagined idea of nation, constituted liberalism's consistent failure to get to grips with either the issue of difference or equality for minorities, the issue for cultural pluralists was how to respect differences without essentialising them: how to recognise not the distinct communities of difference of our imaginations but the hybridised, diasporised, migrant communities of *différance* with their 'fragmented traces and broken repertoires of several cultural and ethical languages'. (ibid.: 121)

Once the universal was recast as a particular, as it must be in any multicultural society where there was, by definition, no universal but only many particulars, we needed a new way of thinking the relationship between equality (which is what, in formal terms, is guaranteed by universal citizenship) and difference: 'This is the dilemma, the conundrum - the multicultural question' (ibid.: 123). Having attempted, with the help of Laclau (1996) to resolve the issue philosophically, Hall was forced to conclude that this may not be doable 'in the abstract. But it can be negotiated in practice' (ibid.). What this amounted to, he thought, was constant negotiation between particulars within a broader public space which must remain pluralistic, heterogeneous and respectful of *différance*. This would require 'two further conditions of existence: a deepening expansion and radicalization of democratic practices in our social life, and the unrelenting contestation of every form of racialized and ethnicized exclusionary closure (whether practiced by others on minority communities, or within communities)' (Hall 2000/2019b: 125–26). Hall ended this particular essay by suggesting this was both a 'propitious moment' to raise the question 'because Britishness as a national identity is in a transitional state, beset by problems and up for extensive renovation and renegotiation', and a moment of 'profound danger':

it is seen by many as the straw that broke the camel's back. It points towards the redefinition of what it means to be British, where the unthinkable might come to pass - it might be possible to be black-and-British, or Asian-and-British (or even British-and-gay)! However, the idea that *everyone* should have access to the processes by which such new forms of "Britishness" are defined, coupled with the loss of Empire and decline as a world power, is literally driving some of its citizens crazy. The 'pollution' of Little England - as some see it - is calculated to produce not just a resurgence of the old biological stereotypes but a proliferating lexicon of new exclusionary binaries, grounded in racialized 'cultural difference': a British version of the new racisms which are abroad everywhere and gaining ground. (ibid.: 126)

This essay on 'The multicultural question' was published in the same year as the Parekh (2000) report on multiculturalism: *Commission on the Future of Multi-ethnic Britain*. Hall was a member of that commission and his ideas on multiculturalism were a significant presence. However, the new Labour government chose to reject the idea that Britain needed to acknowledge its racism before progress could be made and, with it, the prospect of any serious governmental attention to the problem. Then came the ultimate multicultural challenge: 9/11 and the subsequent 'war on terror'.

References

Alexander, C. 2009. Stuart Hall and "race". *Cultural Studies* 23 (4): 457–82.
Appignanesi, L. (ed.). 1988. *Identity: The Real Me*. ICA Document 6. London: Institute of Contemporary Arts.
Hall, S. 1977. Pluralism, race and class in Caribbean society. In UNESCO, *Race and Class in Post-Colonial Society: A Study of Ethnic Group Relations in the English-Speaking Caribbean, Bolivia, Chile and Mexico*, pp. 150–84. Paris: UNESCO.
Hall, S. 1980/2019a. Race, articulation and societies structured in dominance. In Morley, ed. (2019a: 172–221).
Hall, S. 1988a. Minimal selves. In Appignanesi, ed. (1988: 44–46).

Hall, S. 1988b. New ethnicities. In Mercer, ed. (1988: 27–31).
Hall, S. 1991/2019b. Old and new identities, old and new ethnicities. In Morley, ed. (2019b: 63–82).
Hall, S. 1992/2019b. What is this "black" in black popular culture. In Morley, ed. (2019b: 83–94).
Hall, S. 2000/2019b. The multicultural question. In Morley, ed. (2019b: 95–133).
Hall, S. 2017. *The Fateful Triangle: Race, Ethnicity, Nation*, ed. K. Mercer with a Foreword by H.L. Gates, Jr. Cambridge, MA and London: Harvard University Press.
Hall, S., C. Critcher, T. Jefferson, J. Clarke, and B. Roberts. 2013. *Policing the Crisis: Mugging, the State and Law and Order*, 2nd ed. Houndmills, Basingstoke: Palgrave Macmillan.
Laclau, E. 1996. *Emancipations*. London: Verso.
Mercer, K. (ed.). 1988. *Black Film, British Cinema*. A Special Issue of ICA Documents 7. London: BFI/ICA.
Morley, D. (ed.). 2019a. *Stuart Hall Essential Essays Vol. 1: Foundations of Cultural Studies*. Durham and London: Duke University Press.
Morley, D. (ed.). 2019b. *Stuart Hall Essential Essays Vol. 2: Identity and Diaspora*. Durham and London: Duke University Press.
Parekh, B. 2000. *Commission on the Future of Multi-ethnic Britain*. London: Runnymede Trust.
Whannel, G. 2014. Remembering the chuckle. *MeCCSA Three-D* Issue 22, July 15.

8

The Brexit Conjuncture Part One: The Referendum Result and How We Got to 9/11

In this chapter and the next, I want to conduct a conjunctural analysis of the moment of Brexit in order to demonstrate the contemporary relevance of this form of analysis. My focus will be on the UK 2016 UK Referendum on whether to leave or remain in the European Union (EU). Having identified the elements of the Referendum result that require explanation, I return to the 1970s, in order to provide the essential backdrop to how we got there. As with the previous chapter, I end with 9/11, leaving the story since then to be concluded in Chapter 9. My analysis will attempt to stay somewhat connected with the themes and concerns of *Policing the Crisis (PTC)*. These connections will act as a reminder of the book's starting point and of the relevance of an analysis of Brexit for criminologists.

It is not my intention to repeat the lengthy discussion of the nature of a conjuncture and its necessary methodological protocols, which formed the subject matter of Chapter 2, but merely to add this rider. In an interview with Les Back towards the end of his life, Hall said his notion of the conjunctural had become less like Gramsci's and more like Marx's attempt to capture 'the concrete in thought'. This entailed absolute fidelity to 'historical specificity' and is achieved by adding more and more 'levels of determination' (Hall 2008/2019: 271). So with Hall's warrant, my analysis will attempt to add more 'levels of determination' in the interests of trying to specify what kind of historical moment Brexit was. Moreover, and again in the spirit of Hall, I will trust what I hope to have learned from him: historically-informed interpretation. Reflecting on how he knew that Thatcherism constituted a break with 'the postwar settlement' and a new 'configuration' (a question he had clearly been asked many times), he said: 'I can't tell them that. It's not a precise methodology; it's not something which I apply outside to it. It's interpretive and historical. I have to feel the kind of accumulation of different things coming together to make a new moment: this is a different rhythm' (ibid.: 272). Here one can hear echoes of Hall's grounding in both literature and sociology: in the interpretive approach to literary texts of F. R. Leavis as well as the 'interpretive understanding of social action' (Weber 1947: 88) of Weber's sociology. But always disciplined by historical specificity.

The 2016 Referendum Results

I need to start with a broad summary of the referendum results because together these supply the 'phenomenon', the victory for the Leave campaign, which requires to be subjected to further analysis to get at the many determinations in play. To do this I am indebted to the 'early reflections from leading UK academics' (52 in all; papers not authors) in a volume edited by Daniel Jackson and colleagues (2016) based on their initial findings about the 'media, voters and the campaign'. Focusing, at this stage, on their findings rather than their interpretative reflections, the following constitutes a brief summary.

It was an intemperate, angry campaign that was unexpectedly won, narrowly, by the Leave campaign whose message was simpler, embracing sovereignty and immigration, and delivered with greater passion than the Remainers more rationally delivered argument about the economic costs of leaving the EU. The press, measured by circulation not titles, were massively pro-Leave, a message that was also more often and more vociferously expressed, although evidence suggested Leavers had decided their position before the press formally took up their positions. Vote Leave, the main Leave campaign group, also had a more active media strategy in terms of press releases and rebutting opposition claims. Leave campaigners used social media more, did so more actively, and, in terms of targeting, more successfully. Generally, public and commercial broadcasters were even-handed in presenting both sides of the debate, although statistical claims and counter-claims were rarely independently interrogated and politicians, experts and campaigners were indiscriminately used to 'balance' viewpoints. Perhaps unsurprisingly in consequence, only a minority felt well-informed when they came to vote. Brexit voters tended to be older, less formally educated Tory voters, although a significant minority of Labour voters in the traditional Labour heartlands also voted to leave. The conventional pollsters all (bar one) failed to predict the result, unlike the 'text mining' polling of social media sites which were largely accurate.

These findings pose several inter-related questions that provide starting points for the gradual deepening of the analysis. Why was the Leave campaign conducted so much more passionately and effectively than that of Remain? How, specifically, did social media influence the outcome? Why was expertise 'balanced' with other viewpoints and not given a special status? Finally, why did Leave win so unexpectedly; or, who were the 52% who voted to leave? Although not evident from these findings, we do know that the success of the Leave campaign was achieved, apparently, against all the odds—the government's recommendation, the view of the majority of parliament and of the great and the good, the consensus of expert advice about the dire economic consequences of leaving, the general expectation that people would, as they usually do in a referendum, opt for the status quo, and even the expectation of many Leave supporters. Witness the surprise, not to say horror, on the faces of Boris Johnson and Michael Gove, key members of the Conservative government as well as the most prominent figures in the Vote Leave campaign, on learning they had won.

As with all conjunctural analyses, we need first to say why existing explanations of the phenomenon are inadequate. To the extent that these have become commonplace, part of our everyday understanding of the result, they constitute part of the current common sense on Brexit. Thus, we need to start by critiquing this.

Critiquing a Common Sense Understanding of Brexit

In *PTC* we started our analysis with a critique of what we called 'the "rising crime rate" equation', the common sense answer to our initial question about why very long sentences were being handed out to boy 'muggers': violent crimes were rising, courts were becoming 'soft' on criminals, hence the need for them to 'get tough' (Hall et al. 2013: 13). The equivalent common sense answer to why Leave won would be a mendacity plus xenophobia equation: a mendacious media and unscrupulous populist politicians between them misled an ignorant public, and incited its xenophobia. There are elements of this equation dotted around the 52 articles analysing the result that I looked at. The following examples offer strong versions of it:

> In 2016 our mainstream media failed spectacularly. Led, inevitably, by the viscerally anti-EU *Mail, Sun, Express* and *Telegraph* papers, most of our national press indulged in little more than a catalogue of distortions, half-truths and outright lies: a ferocious propaganda campaign in which facts and sober analysis were sacrificed to the ideologically driven objectives of editors and their proprietors. (Barnett 2016: 47)

> The Leave campaign and their supporters in the press pushed immigration as the dominant reason for leaving the EU, increasingly framing the issue in intemperate and inflammatory language. That such rhetoric appeared so frequently in utterances of privileged white male campaigners like Nigel Farage and Boris Johnson is deeply problematic, serving to normalise and legitimate openly xenophobic and occasionally racist sentiments. (Harmer 2016: 38)

It is not that either statement is wrong in itself—the right-wing tabloids in particular are notoriously mendacious and immigration and xenophobia were important features of the Leavers' campaign—but they are inadequate as they stand. The former overplays the role of conventional media while the latter underplays pre-existing public anger about immigration. The fact that less than a third of those under 24 read print media, for example (Levy et al. 2016) and over two-thirds of the readers of the tabloids mentioned were already Brexiteers before the media campaign (Freedman 2016),[1] along with the already mentioned greater influence of social media, means, at the very least, that more than media mendacity is needed to explain the vote; and, as we shall see, immigration as an explanation of the vote embraces far more than the intemperate language of politicians.

Building a Better Analysis: Getting Started

The Media and Expertise

Let me start to build a more adequate explanation by first addressing the questions thrown up by the findings summarised above, starting with the role of social media. Broadly speaking, the 'massively pro-Leave' sentiment of the mainstream press was echoed in social media. Whether measured in terms of supporters, activity, visibility or 'likes', Brexit supporters easily outgunned Remainers on Instagram and Twitter (Polonski 2016: 94; Llewellyn and Cram 2016). Whether or not this greater online support for Leave 'acted like a self-fulfilling prophecy' as Polonski (2016: 94) suggested, or greater targeting success produced the Brexit outcome as Mullen (2016: 89) argued, the greater more effective involvement of Brexiteers on social media requires to be unpacked if we are to understand its contribution to our ultimate explanation.

Two features of the Leave campaign—its greater emotional charge and its simpler message—made it a far better 'fit' for social media campaigns, according to Polonski (2016: 94). Simpler messages angrily expressed spread faster than more reasoned, complicated arguments, apparently. If so, we need to explore further both the message and the anger. Take first

---

[1]Although, given the very long history of tabloid antipathy to the EU, the media no doubt played a role in developing that pre-existing Brexit mindset.

the simpler Leave message, which everybody knew at the time since it was endlessly repeated throughout the campaign: 'Take Back Control'. According to Barry (2016: 14), 'The message was effective because easily understood and open to multiple interpretations', in contrast with the Remain camp's lack of an equivalent. I will return later to the issue of it being 'open to multiple interpretations'. But 'easily understood' means anyone can get the message; there is no need for an expert to interpret. This feature is almost definitional of social media, as opposed to conventional media. It bypasses professionalism and expertise: of journalists, politicians, scientists. Anyone and everyone can join in, say their piece, opine: ignorance and informed analysis, common sense and expertise. It's all the same: 'democracy' rules.

Posing the issue of expertise in the form of a question links it to the second feature, that of the greater anger of the Leave campaign: where was this hostility to expertise coming from? Why were the reasoned arguments of professional politicians and economic experts given such short shrift? A purely technocratic explanation would simply blame the near ubiquity of the new social media with its radical democratisation of knowledge. This has produced, overall, so the argument goes, a general dumbing down. However, this fails to address the issue of hostility: why is expertise per se no longer a warrant for having something of relevance to contribute to a debate? Here there is a need to distinguish between hostility to politicians ('experts' in politics) and disdain for, or indifference to, expertise generally. The origins of hostility to the former have a general dimension, the growing sense of distance between parliamentarians and their constituents for which the issue of politicians 'over-claiming' expenses in 2009 has become the defining iconic moment from which they have yet to recover. However, this is better dealt with when the issue of who voted for Brexit is addressed directly.

The origins of indifference to the expertise of any kind, scientific or otherwise, have several dimensions. Longer term, many of these have their origin in the academy itself: the seedbed of expert knowledge. The collapse of Communism as a political alternative to capitalism may not have signalled 'the end of history', as Fukuyama (1992) once thought, but it massively brought into question the Marxist idea of a science of society. Postmodernism was quick to fill the breach. 'Truth' became a modernist relic: relativism ruled. But, 'truth' had been under attack from other quarters for a while. What counted as knowledge in the academy had been largely produced by dead, white males. Feminist, gay, lesbian and post-colonial scholars (to name only the most active) had been busily rewriting the 'grand narratives' of their respective disciplines (just as, a little earlier, Marxists and other radical criminologists had attempted to rewrite the traditional criminological canon). The net result of all these multiple attacks on pre-existing knowledge, even within the academy, has been an undermining of the notion of a singular 'Truth', in favour of multiple or partial 'truths', depending on, to use a term coined within feminism, one's 'standpoint'. It is not difficult to see that such a series of 'interruptions' to existing expertise might begin to destabilise the simplified versions of scientific discourses circulating outside the academy.

Against this general background of the relativisation of knowledge, there are a range of more conjunctural issues. For example, who believed in the expertise of economists after their collective failure to anticipate 2008 (notwithstanding the odd dissenting voice)? Yet Remain relied on these same discredited voices to mount its case. Or, the questioning of medical expertise evidenced by the growing hostility to vaccination by 'anti-vaxxers'. Overall, what seems to have happened is that the genuine hostility towards politicians and elites (which I come to later), in the context of a long-term delegitimation of what counts as knowledge and a series of more conjunctural discreditings, has managed to convert mere disdain for experts, who no longer 'truly' know best, into something more toxic.

In the context of the delegitimation of expertise, common sense grows in importance. According to Gramsci (1971), common sense is key to the battleground of ideas: to the struggle for hegemony. Experts deal in science and philosophy; but the people live their lives, make sense of their experiences, understand their world, not through the rarefied discourses of experts but through their translation—and politicians have a key role here—into everyday language: the language of current common sense. 'Take Back Control' is one such common sense translation. Rather than the difficulties of what that might actually entail, especially 'with public understanding of the EU at the lowest in the EU' (FitzGibbon 2016:

16), it is 'easily understood'. Moreover, being 'open to multiple interpretations' it was also widely understood, a necessary dimension in any ideological struggle. What I am suggesting then is that the combination of the longer term undermining of truth and hence the value of expertise, together with the greater significance of social media which renders all discourses equal,[2] made the issue of common sense more salient than ever. In such a situation, the scales favour the right, who have proved over the years much more adept at adopting and adapting common sense for political purposes.

In order to see why the right were more likely to come up with the killer, common sense slogan, revisiting *PTC* can help. *PTC* attempted to address the common sense about crime underpinning the moral panic about mugging. In the chapter entitled 'Explanations and Ideologies of Crime' (Hall et al. 2013: Chapter 6), we attempted to show how a particular cluster of images—about respectability, work, discipline, family, city and the law—formed the core elements of the, then dominant, cross-class consensus on crime: what we called the 'traditionalist' ideology of crime. Our empirical warrant for this, public and private letters about the Handsworth 'mugging', was, as I noted in Chapter 3, slight (but better than nothing). We also suggested that this traditionalist world view produced and sustained a 'conservative *sense of Englishness*', the roots of which lay in the particular appeal of common sense and personal experience to English conservatism. These roots, we explained, run deep, as Perry Anderson (1964) famously argued: the everyday prejudices and commonplace thinking of 'traditionalism' and 'empiricism', not a systematic ideology, have always formed the basis of the ruling ideology in England. I will return later to the importance to the Leave campaign of a 'conservative sense of Englishness'. For now, I want merely to recall that this concern to understand the role of common sense politically continued to preoccupy Hall right up until his final article (Hall and O'Shea 2015) on 'Common-sense neoliberalism'. What frustrated Hall even more than the successes of Thatcherism was the persistent failure of

---

[2]A slight paradox in this argument about the role of social media is that young people, its greatest users, were more likely to vote remain.

the Left to engage with traditional common sense and attempt to transform it into radical 'good sense'. The concern of the Remain campaign to counter 'Take Back Control' merely with narrowly focused dire predictions of the economic consequences of leaving was symptomatic in this regard; it never saw the need to engage with the register of common sense but remained reliant on discredited experts.

If the Right were more likely to win the battle of ideas where common sense was in command, given the prevailing 'post-truth' intellectual climate, the dominance of an 'anything goes' social media and the historical weight of traditionalism, this only helps explain why Remain lost the online battle of ideas (a battle, as the above data suggests, they barely engaged). How this failure related to losing the battle on the ground requires us to explain who was successfully 'hailed' by the slogan, Take Back Control, and why at this particular time. As we saw earlier, the slogan's openness to multiple interpretations was, along with it being easily understood, regarded as the key to the breadth of its appeal. William Davies (2016) called it 'a piece of political genius…[that] worked on every level between the macroeconomic and the psychoanalytic'. To my mind, that underestimates the specificity of its genius. Because what it does, brilliantly, is unite three crucial elements: passivity, sovereignty and immigration. It converts the passivity of a feeling of having lost control into an active response (TAKE…control), while also offering to reclaim a sovereignty lost to the EU (take BACK) and, finally, to secure the country's borders against immigrants, refugees and terrorists (take…CONTROL).[3] This reading can help explain who was actually hailed by the slogan.

---

[3]Just to be clear, I am not suggesting that Davies (2016) is wrong or that mine is the only possible reading. My readers also suggested additional interesting readings. However, in the interests of economy, I stand by my singular interpretation while acknowledging it cannot be exhaustive.

The Geography and Demography of the Leave Vote

The geographical pattern is difficult to summarise neatly. Most of the country voted to leave: approximately three out of every four parliamentary constituencies in England and Wales. Leave's strongest support (in descending order) came from the Midlands and the north-east, followed by Yorkshire and Humber and Eastern England. Remain was strongest (again, in descending order) in Scotland, London and Northern Ireland.[4] Otherwise, apart from northern cities and towns with large university populations, like Newcastle, Lancaster, Leeds, Liverpool and Manchester, the Remain vote was largely to be found in the south. However, in terms of individuals rather than areas, despite the strength of support for Leave in the north and Remain in the south by geographical area, 'most people who voted leave - by absolute numbers - lived in southern England' (Dorling and Tomlinson 2019: 28). What this demonstrated was that Leave voters came from both sides of the 'prosperity' divide, from more affluent rural and suburban regions of the south as well as from struggling, post-industrial communities.

However, there was some disagreement about the relationship of class and deprivation to the Leave vote. Goodwin and Heath's (2016a: 325) aggregate-level analysis, having overviewed the areas with strongest support for the Leave vote, concluded that these areas tended to be economically disadvantaged, largely white and with low levels of education. Lord Ashcroft's (2016) individual-level exit poll findings appeared generally to be in agreement: those not working, retirees reliant solely on a state pension, council tenants, those with only a secondary school education, those who were white and those from the lowest social classes (using the conventional categories C2, D and E), were all much more likely to have been leave voters. By contrast, Dorling and Tomlinson (2019) claim that the majority (59%) of Leave voters were middle class

---

[4]From Goodwin and Heath's (2016a: 324) aggregate-level analysis of the result.

(using the conventional categories A, B and C1), and that there was practically no correlation between voting leave and 'constituency deprivation indices' (ibid.: 33).[5]

Antonucci and colleagues' (2017) individual level study combined something from both positions in its findings. Agreeing with Dorling and Tomlinson on the importance of the middle-class vote to the leave majority, although in this case class was assigned by respondents themselves, they modified this slightly in finding the importance specifically of the 'squeezed middle'. By this they meant those in what they called the 'intermediate classes' who reported a recent worsening in their financial situation. In educational terms, this cluster was also somewhat intermediate, neither graduates nor early school leavers. We might call these intermediates the downwardly mobile, lower middle classes, although with a different methodology many of these might have been defined as working class.

It was this latter methodological tack that Butcher (2019) took in arbitrating between the positions. Basically, the two 'sides' were asking rather different questions of the data. Those finding that middle-class Brexit voters were the majority were asking, specifically, about the class composition of the Leave vote; those arguing the reverse were asking, effectively, how classes voted. Thus, it was correct to say, along with Dorling and Tomlinson and others, that 59% of Leave voters were middle class *and*, like Lord Ashcroft and others, 'that working class votes went in substantial majority for Leave, and middle class substantially for Remain' (Butcher 2019: 3). However, Butcher added several 'strong caveats' to the idea that the leave vote was secured by a substantial middle-class majority: the middle classes, as defined (ABC1s), were the largest group in society and were more likely to vote. Moreover, and most tellingly, the definition of the middle class used, by including the C1s, who were the UK's largest group, was misleading. The decline of skilled manual workers, or C2s, was accompanied by a growth of

---

[5]This is based on an analysis by Rae (2016). Jump and Mitchell's analysis, 'using the most granular referendum data and the most detailed deprivation data currently available', found that there was a positive association, but that it was 'neither strong nor straightforward' (Jump, R. C. and Mitchell, J. (2020) 'Deprivation and the electoral geography of Brexit'. *Unpublished paper*).

people working in sales, services, administrative, supervisory and secretarial occupations, who tended to be classified C1. Do they belong with the middle classes or was this just a recomposition of the working class? In terms of income there was little in it with the average income of C1s being only marginally higher than that of C2s. Or, as Butcher graphically concluded, such a notion of middle class included 'a very large number of people who are a pay packet or two away from poverty' (ibid.).[6]

Although both Dorling and Tomlinson (2019) and Antonucci and Colleagues (2017) saw their respective analyses as challenging what they saw as the dominant explanation of Brexit as the angry vote of the 'left behinds', as exemplified in Goodwin and Heath's (2016a) account, what Butcher's timely intervention demonstrated was that this was an unnecessary either/or polarity. What these findings collectively showed was the need for a both/and approach, because, in terms of findings rather than explanations, the Brexit vote plainly encompassed (albeit in contestable numbers) all social classes: the affluent middle classes, the squeezed 'intermediate classes' and the struggling, working-class poor. At this stage, that is all I need to establish. Explanations must wait until we have a full picture of the phenomenon.

In terms of ethnicity, the findings were complicated but revealing. According to Goodwin and Heath (2016a), the areas with the fewest EU migrants tended to vote Leave and those with the most Remain. However, for England and Wales (the only areas for which relevant data were available), those areas which had experienced a recent increase in EU migrants, over the last ten years, were more likely to vote Leave. As for areas with large non-white populations, these tended to be less likely to vote leave. As we know from Lord Ashcroft's Poll that substantial majorities of black, Asian and Muslim voters voted to remain and a majority of white voters to leave, the non-white presence in these areas may have accounted for this finding. The Poll also revealed that leave voters were much more likely to identify as English not British and remain voters as British not English.

---

[6]Butcher also reminded us that the categories, ABC1, etc., were never designed to measure social class but are 'National Readership Survey' categories 'intended to measure readership habits by social *grade*' (Butcher 2019: 2).

In political terms, Leave voters were substantially more likely to be Conservative supporters and Remain voters Labour supporters. Since the Labour voters who did support Leave were largely from declining areas in the Midlands and the North, traditionally Labour heartlands, this produced what Cochrane (2020: 168) called a 'strange alliance between those in the Conservative heartlands…and those in the de-industrialized regions'. Unsurprisingly, nearly all UKIP supporters voted to leave. Education was another key division with the 'most educated' areas far more likely to have voted remain and the 'least educated' areas leave (Goodwin and Heath 2016a)[7]; although, as with class, Antonucci and colleagues (2017) found a stronger association of Leave voting with 'intermediate levels of education'. However, in a follow-up study, Goodwin and Heath (2016b) found an interesting interaction effect between education and area, namely, in 'low-skilled' areas even graduates were more likely to vote leave, thus behaving like the lowly educated. As for age, for some it was the most unambiguous division: those over 45 voted to leave, by ever larger majorities as the age group got older; and those under 45 were increasingly likely to vote remain as the age group became younger (Henn and Sharpe 2016; Ashcroft 2016).[8] For others, education had a slightly stronger association with Leave voting (Goodwin and Heath 2016a: 328). The least ambiguous division appears to be sex: as many women voted to Leave as men (52%).

The political views of Leavers and Remainers on key issues were diametrically opposed, as Lord Ashcroft's (2016) Poll revealed: multiculturalism, feminism, the Green movement, globalisation and immigration were all seen as 'forces for good' by 'large majorities' of Remain voters, but as 'a force for ill' by 'even larger majorities' of Leave voters. These differences were echoed in their views about quality of life now and in the future: Leavers tended to think life was worse today [in 2016] than

---

[7]This association was even stronger when London and Scotland were excluded. Outside these areas, the country was 'highly polarised along educational lines' (Goodwin and Heath 2016a: 328).
[8]Once the low turnout of the youngest group was taken into account, the group that most favoured remain were, apparently, the 35–44 age group, according to Dorling and Tomlinson (2019: 24), not the very youngest, 18–24 group.

it was 30 years previously and that it would be even worse for their children; Remainers tended to think the opposite. Finally, their reasons for voting leave were also divergent: for Leavers their 'biggest single reason' was sovereignty, followed by regaining control over immigration; for Remainers it was economic fears about jobs and prices, followed by the benefits of the single market.

Summarising the above is not easy as there is no typical leave voter. But there are visible tendencies. He or she might be middle class and southern or working class and northern, or something in between; but Leave voters will tend to be from suburban or rural rather than urban areas, or if from an urban area one that is suffering the ravages of post-industrialisation. They will tend to be white, regard themselves as English not British, and live in a largely white area with few EU migrants or one where there has been a recent influx of immigrants. They will tend to be older, less educated and to vote Tory, or for further right parties. Where they are labour voters, they will tend to be from the declining, post-industrial areas. They will tend to have illiberal views on a range of issues implicating the politics of difference: feminism, multiculturalism and immigration. They will tend to think that things are bad and getting worse. These issues, then, collectively make up the phenomenon that needs examining for its hidden determinations.

From Phenomenon to Explanation: Beginning the Analysis

In line with my earlier argument that we should start with the more obvious explanations and only proceed beyond these when they fail to satisfy, I want to start with the issue of sovereignty because, as I have just noted, Lord Ashcroft's (2016) Referendum day poll revealed it—'decisions about the UK should be taken in the UK'—to be the most important issue in Leave voters' decision-making about how to vote, more so than immigration, a finding confirmed by a similar YouGov poll (Vasilopoulou 2016: 115). Since, ostensibly, the referendum was about just that, were we 'in' or 'out', and only indirectly about immigration control,[9] this poll finding was perhaps not so surprising. So, a starting point for explaining the Leave vote has to interrogate the simple idea that wanting to leave the EU was the reason for voting to do so.

The evidence for that desire goes back to the very start of the UK's relationship with a united Europe. From the outset it had been dogged with a fluctuating degree of Euroscepticism right across the political divide. It was a Labour government which originally turned down France's invitation to join what was then the European Coal and Steel Community in 1951, apparently because 'the Durham miners…[would] never wear it', according to Labour's then Deputy Prime minister Herbert Morrison (quoted in Goes 2016: 84). In 1967, Harold Wilson's Labour Government presided over a complete about-turn as a huge Commons majority voted in favour of Britain's second application for (what was then) European Economic Community membership. However, many did so reluctantly and 'the Labour cabinet was divided' (Gifford 2016: 15). In the event, the application to join was again unsuccessful and entry was only gained six years later, in 1973, under Edward Heath's Conservative government. The new Labour government of 1974, still led by Harold Wilson, were unhappy with the existing terms and did what was to become an enduring feature of the UK-EU relationship, namely, renegotiate terms, which were then put to the people. The resulting 1975 referendum saw a massive majority for joining. Unsurprisingly, there was also a 'No' campaign that crossed the political divide, with Tony Benn on the Left and Enoch Powell on the Right, both of whom had changed their minds after voting for membership in 1967. And, although the national press was overwhelmingly in favour of membership, the Communist newspaper, the *Morning Star*, provided a Left oppositional voice (Freedman 2016: 48).

The pattern thereafter continued similarly: a commitment to membership focused on the economic benefits; a reluctance to commit fully to the political project. Thatcher's successful renegotiation of the UK's

---

[9]Although membership of the EU means a commitment to 'freedom of movement' and thus implies member states lack direct control of their immigration policies, this is a consequence of membership not integral to membership itself. Thus, I argue, the vote was only 'indirectly, about immigration control'.

financial contribution exemplified the former; staying out of the European Monetary Union (the Euro) and Schengen (a 'borderless' security union that eliminates the use of passports inside the area) the latter. Against this backcloth of an endemic Euroscepticism, historically subject to 'large swings' (Thompson 2016: 111) and where only a very small minority (16%) of Britons regarded 'themselves as strongly European' (Green 2016: 103), it feels less surprising that 'after five decades of skirmishes, Conservative Eurosceptics finally secured victory' (Lynch 2016: 77). In other words, the presence of people wanting out was not new; so, consequently, the vote cannot be seen as entirely unexpected.

Given this, voting Leave does not necessarily require more by way of explanation than does the decision of Europhiles to vote remain. It simply needs addressing in its own terms: sometimes a vote to leave is simply a vote to leave. The same could be said about Eurosceptics generally, of the Left as well as the Right. In the rush to explain what some saw as the angry irrationality of Brexit,[10] it is important to acknowledge the failings of the EU, never more compellingly articulated than by Yanis Varoufakis (2017) of his time as Greece's Finance Minister. His account of his dealings with the Union's brutal imposition of austerity measures on a post-crash, debt-ridden, struggling Greece is both a searing indictment and a call for reform. Although he resigned as Finance Minister rather than submit to the EU's punitive demands, he did not advocate to leave the EU but to remain and fight to democratise existing structures. In a similar way, Slimani (2020) criticises the EU's moral failings, in handling the Greek debt crisis and the later migrant crisis of 2015, without renouncing the entire project. So, some of the Leave vote can be accounted for by longstanding Eurosceptics, many (but not all) of whom would have been Conservatives, given the long-standing contentiousness of 'Europe' within the party.

However this still leaves unanswered the questions of why, by the time of the Referendum, a hard rather than a soft Euroscepticism had become dominant; and why wanting out appealed across classes and political parties. The issue of the growth of a hard Euroscepticism,

---

[10]Although it should not be forgotten that Remain's apparently more 'rational', economics-led campaign was said to be driven by irrational fear, hence the 'Project fear' label given it by Vote Leave.

in brief, is the story of successive Conservative prime ministers, from Thatcher to Cameron, variously attempting to assuage their Eurosceptic wing. Eventually, Cameron, trapped between the threat of UKIP and his own Eurosceptics requiring a hard line on Europe and his pro-European liberal democrat coalition partners, made the fateful decision to promise an in/out referendum banking on his ability to renegotiate terms to satisfy both sides. It was a serious miscalculation of his ability to deliver a deal to satisfy his Eurosceptic wing as well as the increasingly angry political mood of the country (cf: Lynch 2016; Martin 2016). This angry political mood is part of the longer story which follows.

This brings us to the 'strange alliance' of older Tories from the Conservative heartlands, those not accounted for by a simple Euroscepticism as just discussed, and the disgruntled, Labour voters from formerly industrialised regions. Since there was nothing in the voting figures to reveal the emotional state of voters, who among these constituted the angry public remains speculative. However, since most commentary seems to assume those most affected by the financial crash and the subsequent years of austerity had more to be angry about, explanations have tended to focus on the working-class Leave voters from the traditional Labour heartlands, those 'left behind'. In the light of what we have learned about the ethnic dimension of the vote, I should add beforehand that I shall not be talking about *the* working class but specifically about the *white* working-class 'left behinds', an intra-class differentiation that most commentators have tended to overlook, as Bhambra (2017) and Sayer (2017) in particular have forcefully reminded us. So, I will start there too, and return in the next chapter to the nature of middle-class Conservatives' dissatisfaction with the status quo.

Were one to construct a composite explanation for the angry, working-class Leave vote it will usually include some or all of the following elements (or determinations), albeit differently accented with a greater or lesser sense of historical antecedents: angry disaffection with political elites; a sense of abandonment by politicians; the erosion of public and welfare services; economic decline and the growth of poverty; growing inequality; racism and xenophobia; immigration. In short, a catalogue of neo-liberalism's dark side, made darker by the post-crash austerity years, overseen by an uncaring and out of touch political class (cf. Fenton 2016: 57).

One problem with these composite lists is whether all the determinations operate in concert towards the same outcome; another, whether all relevant determinations have been included; and, finally, how they combine or work together. Take, for example, the issue of responsibility for the economic crisis. An analysis of YouGov polling found that Remain supporters believed 'the banks, Conservative-led governments and growing inequality' were to blame 'whilst Leave voters blamed EU regulation, the previous Labour government and immigrants willing to work for lower wages' (Birks 2016: 104). In other words, inequality did not seem to have been one of the determinations of the Leave vote (although it might have been a factor in the Remain vote). Moreover, this also suggested disaffection with political parties was not confined to Leave voters (cf: Lilleker 2016: 106). One crucial element missing from the list, as I intend to show, was masculinity.

Given these issues, we need to proceed more carefully, less generally, in explaining the angry Leave vote and try to understand how the various determinations operated as a whole. One issue which did divide Leave and Remain voters, as we saw earlier in the poll findings about what influenced their voting decisions, was the importance of immigration control. For many (despite the other poll finding about the importance of sovereignty), it was the issue that decided the vote: 'If it was about one thing, the 2016 referendum was about immigration' (Geddes 2016: 18); 'they were convinced that waves of immigrants would soon overwhelm their local communities, take their job, and undermine their way of life' (a Labour MP representing a Northern constituency whose constituents had mostly voted Leave, quoted in Barnett 2016: 47). My purpose in what follows is to show how Brexit is a moment when political disaffection, poverty and the disappearance of work, racism and a crisis of masculinity, elements with their own distinctive histories and trajectories, become expressed through the 'one thing' of immigration; how immigration cannot be reduced to the threats to livelihoods and ways of life, as many thought, even though it was about that too. Like the slogan 'Take Back Control', immigration signified far more than it appeared to.[11]

Deepening the Analysis: How We Got There

To understand how this came about, I want to start in the 1970s, just before the Thatcherite, neo-liberal revolution, with *Learning to Labour*, Paul Willis' (1977) brilliant ethnography of a 'counter-school culture': a group of disaffected white 'lads' transitioning from a single sex secondary modern school to the world of work in an old industrial working-class town in the Midlands. Willis was also a member of the Centre for Contemporary Cultural Studies (CCCS) and was researching and writing up at the same time as the authors of *PTC* were doing the same (often using the same desks, as Willis kindly let John Clarke and me share his office). The book's subtitle, *How working class kids get working class jobs*, rendered problematic what many had taken for granted as a simple example of class socialisation at work: of working-class kids taking up their assigned places in the meritocratic order. The surprising finding was the lads' choice of 'dead end' manual labouring jobs and active rejection of the possibility of middle-class ones involving mental labour. The explanation hinged on their feeling of superiority of their choices over those of their conformist peers—the 'ear'oles'—to aim for office work: jobs 'with a future'. Why? Because of the threat to their masculinity posed by the perceived femininity of the 'pen-pushing' mental labour of office work. By opting for the masculine toughness associated with physical labour and (male) shop floor culture, they were reproducing, simultaneously, capitalism's class relations and patriarchy's gendered ones, while inverting the dominant meritocratic ideology which evaluates mental above manual labour.

Although there were no girls in Willis' 'Hammertown' case study, gender was clearly an issue in the relations between 'lads' and 'ear'oles',

---

[11]Which is not to deny that the historically high levels of immigration from the 1990s onwards had an impact on jobs and wages at the bottom end of the labour market.

with the former arrogating to themselves the masculine label. In other words, a gender politics of difference was in play. They also felt different from and superior to the girls they met outside school, who were predictably divided into 'easy lays' ('whores') and 'girl friends' (who were expected to be 'madonnas'), and to the 'substantial' minority ethnic groups, of Asians and West Indians, within school. Although not a major part of the study, we learn of the lads' racist attitudes, language and occasional violence (and hints of a supportive, mainly white, staff), and their different perceptions of the two groups: Asians come off consistently worse on all fronts; West Indians' cultural similarities over things like opposition to school, masculinity, and music and dancing mitigated somewhat the lads' style envy and the issue of sexual rivalry. Superiority could be retained however with jokes about their 'alleged stupidity' (Willis 1977: 49). Just a few years earlier, in 1969, a *New Society* Poll found that the lads' hostility to 'fuckin' wogs' and 'bastard pakis' was widely shared: 'All social groups…agreed…by an enormous margin, that there were "too many coloured immigrants in the country now"' (Sandbrook 2007: 199). Enoch Powell's 'Rivers of Blood' speech had been delivered just a year before that, in 1968. (The 'lads' would have been aged fifteen in 1974; in 2016, Referendum year, 57.)

Willis' lads had no trouble finding work in 1975 in a range of traditional manual jobs. However, this was soon to change with the advent of Margaret Thatcher to power in 1979 and the mass unemployment that followed her ruthless pursuit of marketisation. When Frank Coffield and colleagues (1986) spent over two years in the early 1980s conducting a study of young working-class women and men in the north-east of England, the job market had virtually collapsed: 'in 1974 80 per cent of all school leavers [in Newcastle] found full-time employment, which nine years later in 1983 was obtained by just 16.6 percent' (ibid.: 85).

According to the young people themselves, their options were 'shit jobs, govvy [government] schemes and the dole' (ibid.: 87). 'Govvy schemes' (with their bewildering variety of acronyms: WEEP, YOP, YTS, TOPs, CP, WOC, MSC) were basically the government's attempts to massage the unemployment figures for young adults. They were regarded by those having to do them as similar to shit jobs but worse in terms of pay, conditions and protections (ibid.: 115). To render these facts and figures more concrete, take 'Max', one of the study's young men: 'in the 40 months since he had left school, Max had experienced five separate periods (amounting to 19 months) of unemployment...had spent 14 months on three different schemes, was about to start a fourth, and had worked for 7 months over two summers on the same "shit job"' (ibid.: 26).

Worried about the generalisability of their findings, the authors consulted other local studies and local professionals and concluded that their findings were typical, not only for the north-east, but also elsewhere in similar areas of the north-west as well as in Northern Ireland, Scotland and Wales (ibid.: 12–13). It is worth adding that the full effects of Thatcher's policies had yet to materialise at the time of their research: the bitter defeats of the miners and then the printers were still to come. The sampled young people, and others like them all over these depressed regions, would have been between 50 and 62 at the time of the Brexit referendum. Though never explicitly stated, all the signs are that it was an all-white sample.

Where cannabis, LSD and amphetamines were the drugs of governmental concern in the 1960s, mass youth unemployment in the 1980s was accompanied by a new concern when a previously little used drug, heroin, seemed to be everywhere. Not large by international standards, the advent of *The New Heroin Users* (Pearson 1987) was something of an epidemic in British terms, perhaps as many as 80,000 users (ibid.: 3). Unsurprisingly, 'where the new heroin problem is most serious', Pearson informed us, 'it will be found huddled together with the most serious poverty of unemployed Britain' (ibid.: 4). It 'largely involved white people' (Pearson et al. 1993: 100), even in deprived areas with high proportions of black people (ibid.: 112).[12] Drugs—dealing them—could be a source of survival income as well as being a way of passing time in unemployed communities and easing, if only temporarily, the pains of idleness.

There were also the 'riots'. Starting, in 1980 in Bristol, just one year after Thatcher first came to power, these punctuated the decade and

---

[12]Although the late 1980s saw a new drug scare, about crack-cocaine, the research evidence suggests this was never an epidemic to rival heroin use (Bean 1993).

beyond. With disaffected black youths in the vanguard, deprived urban areas in cities up and down the country with high unemployment levels became, periodically, sites of angry, violent outbursts and confrontations with police forces widely perceived to be oppressive and discriminatory—a perception amply and consistently confirmed by survey after survey. The event triggering the riots was, invariably, heavy-handed policing, sometimes with lethal consequences. Echoing the angry showdowns on the industrial front during the lengthy strikes that eventuated in the pivotal defeats of steel-workers, then the miners and subsequently the printers, together these confrontations were a reminder that there was nothing inevitable about this. Post-industrialisation was ruthlessly imposed in the teeth of sustained opposition.

By the end of the decade of the 1980s, then, the social costs of Thatcherism had been huge, spanning social dislocation, the dismantling of public support structures, widespread poverty and mass unemployment, the criminalisation of black and Asian youth, growing drug addiction and mental illness and family breakdown. On the other hand, as with all painful transitions, there were winners as well as losers. The new prominence of markets, privatisation, entrepreneurship and self-employment offered opportunities too. It was these developments, in part, that enabled the mainstreaming of black music and style, albeit in a somewhat commodified and depoliticised form, that led to black youth becoming style leaders in British youth cultures and their consequent new confidence that Hall noted as we saw in the last chapter. This was to have a mixed effect on white male youth: some wanted to emulate them; others resented their loss of status. It contributed to what came to be regarded as a key crisis of the 1990s: the crisis of masculinity.

With over 500 books on masculinity produced during the decade (Whitehead and Barrett 2001), choosing one to demonstrate the crisis in a way that continues my narrative was never going to be easy. However, Linda McDowell's study of the transition from school to work of white, working class, low achieving, disaffected early school-leavers, *Redundant Masculinities? Employment Change and White Working Class Youth* published in 2003, ticked all the relevant boxes: empirically-based, historically specific and theoretically sophisticated. It also compared its findings to those of Willis's *Learning to Labour* (although it was not an ethnography but an interview-based study with two groups of young men, one from a school in a poor part of Sheffield, the other from a similarly disadvantaged school in Cambridge). Although McDowell valiantly typologised their transitions, the follow up in 2002, two years on from her study, revealed that their similarities were beginning to override their differences. Although she claimed that her original categorisations had for the most part been confirmed, she was obliged to concede that 'the committed workers had not on the whole fulfilled their prospects' and 'those who had begun some form of further education in Cambridge' tended 'to abandon the course part-way through' (ibid.: 241). Her rather grim assessment seemed a fitting endpoint: 'employed in low-wage, often casualized work with few prospects of advancement', their 'prospects of independent living…are not hopeful' and their 'lives…continue to show how changing economic circumstances have trapped young men with little educational and social capital in poor work' (ibid.: 241–42).

Although the situation of McDowell's young men at the turn of the millennium appeared very similar to those 'growing up at the margins' in the early 1980s with their 'shit jobs, govvy schemes and the dole', things had worsened considerably for young unskilled and unqualified men in a number of ways. The dominance of the service sector, which employed two-thirds of the workforce, meant increased female participation rates in the workforce and reduced male rates. As the numbers without any qualifications declined, so too did the prospects for upward mobility, especially after 1990, while their non-employment rates rose. Income inequality increased markedly under Thatcher when the poorest saw their income fall by nearly a quarter in real terms while the numbers living in poverty increased by 160%. Despite a slight decline in the early 1990s, by 2000 income inequality was the highest it had been for 10 years. Despite New Labour's attempts to deal with extremely low wages, including the introduction of a national minimum wage, the numbers living below the poverty line were up by 178% between 1977 and 2002. At the same time, despite increasing the rates, the real value of state benefits was worth less than the 1977 rates. Moreover, these benefits increasingly came with compulsory requirements tied to labour market needs and not the needs of the unemployed.[13]

For working-class boys, the issue of becoming successfully masculine, working-class men, traditionally entailed getting a job, preferably one requiring physical skills, manual dexterity and strength, earning enough to live independently and ultimately to support a wife and children: the male as provider and protector. We have already seen that appropriately masculine jobs, of the kind that Willis' lads found and many in Coffield and colleagues' sample would have liked, were disappearing. And their replacement, service-type jobs, requiring the kind of interpersonal, relational skills traditionally associated with femininity, disfavoured them and were too poorly paid to support living independently, never mind raising a family. In addition to a labour market that increasingly favoured feminine skills, from some time in the early 1990s, girls began outperforming boys in school-leaving exams generally, but also in the traditionally male subjects of science, maths and technology. Girls were also more likely to continue in education and go on to University. And if Willis's lads could still feel superior to the 'stupidity' of their black peers, even as they envied them their street style and sexuality, by the late 1990s that sense of superiority got harder to sustain. By then, the dominance of black youth culture, in style and music, was unarguable.

Excluded by de-industrialization from their class heritage, denied by the advances of girls and a feminised labour market their traditional patrimonial advantage, and robbed by the all-conquering vibrancy of black youth culture of the traditional compensations of white superiority, things had worsened for McDowell's (2003) young men. If we add to this picture the fact that such boys were also widely seen as troublemakers—new Labour was obsessed with the issue and introduced a raft of new 'measures to deal with youth crime, truancy, antisocial behaviour, graffiti and parental neglect' (ibid.: 65)—then we arrive at the notion of a 'crisis' of masculinity. In the case of our white boys, as we have seen, it had both a class and a race or ethnic dimension: strictly speaking, then, theirs was a triple crisis, of class and race as well as masculinity. I shall return to this idea later. However, this was not how McDowell's boys

---

[13] All figures in this paragraph are based on those quoted in McDowell (2003: 33–38).

saw themselves. Rather, they expected to get jobs and be able to create a family life of their own, assumed that they were superior to girls (being unaware girls were doing better than them at school and beyond), and that they were part of a dominant school culture of 'whiteness'. A combination of subsidised living (all but two of those contactable in 2002 were still living at home), being in work or studying (bar one, although many of those in work were unhappily so) and without family responsibilities, suggested that they were still men-children, not yet fully adult, and thus temporarily shielded from the full impact of the crisis. They were in their mid-thirties at the time of the Referendum.[14]

The most serious examples of youthful trouble in the 1990s and early 2000s (leaving aside the more overtly political poll tax riots of 1990) were the riots of 1991, 1992, 1995 and 2001. By the 1990s, with poverty and unemployment endemic and widespread, the riots spread beyond the inner cities to poor estates and areas in Cardiff, Oxford and Tyneside (1991), Coventry, Bristol and the northern mill towns of Blackburn, Huddersfield, Salford (1992), Burnley (1992 and 2001), Bradford (1995 and 2001) and Oldham (2001). The triggering event was invariably an incident involving the policing of youth. But where in the 1980s it was the aggressive and discriminatory policing of black youth that gave black youth their vanguard role, subsequent riots were led by white youths. The other difference between the two moments was racism. Although the racial motivation behind the targeting of Asian shops in some of the riots was not always clear cut, as Campbell (1993: 88) said of the 1991 riot in Meadowell on Tyneside, in the riots of summer 2001, in Burnley, Bradford and Oldham, race played a central role. They started after attacks by white people on Asian homes and some provocative marches by the National Front and the British National Party. Asians then retaliated. These ugly examples of street racism, one version of a politics of difference, occurred just months before 9/11, which changed everything.

What I hope to have shown in this brief historical look at 'how we got there', basing myself on ethnographic and other empirically-based

---

[14]Not quite old enough to be in the 'more likely to vote Brexit' category of over 45s, although some of them may have voted Leave, but these emasculating labour market processes would have affected older working-class men too.

studies rather than purely theoretical offerings, is how a story that starts as an everyday one of class disadvantage—as Willis's lads followed their fathers into manual occupations—became first a crisis—as Thatcher's destruction of manufacturing industry rendered similarly placed men (and women) 'marginal' (Coffield et al. 1986)—and then an exercise in emasculation—as McDowell's young men faced feminised, poorly paid service work and a struggle to achieve independence. All this took place against a background of growing inequality, endemic racism and, in Hall's terms, a failure to embrace the possibilities of multicultural *différance*. In anticipation of the Brexit moment, I have also reminded readers of their ages, and how old they (or people similarly placed) would have been at the time of the Referendum (assuming they survived the ravages of poverty, unemployment, ill-health, drug addiction, depression and suicide). When I take the story forward in the next chapter, the issue of immigration and with it Hall's 'politics of difference' grows in significance, but always in relation to issues of class and gender.

References

Anderson, P. 1964. Origins of the present Crisis. *New Left Review* 23.

Antonucci, L., L. Horvath, Y. Kutiyski, and A. Krowel. 2017. The malaise of the squeezed middle: Challenging the narrative of the "left behind" Brexiteer. *Competition & Change* 21 (3): 211–229.

Ashcroft, Lord. 2016. How the United Kingdom voted on Thursday…and why. *Lord Ashcroft Polls*. Available at http://lordashcroftpolls.com/2016/06/how-the-united-kingdom-voted-and-why/.

Barnett, S. 2016. How our mainstream media failed democracy. In Jackson et al., eds. (2016: 47).

Barry, M. 2016. Understanding the role of the mass media in the EU Referendum. In Jackson et al., eds. (2016: 14).

Bean, P. 1993. Cocaine and crack: The promotion of an epidemic. In Bean, ed. (1993: 59–75).

Bean, P. (ed.). 1993. *Cocaine and Crack: Supply and Use*. New York: St. Martin's Press.

Birks, J. 2016. Workers rights in the EU and out: Social class and the trade unions' contribution to the debate. In Jackson et al., eds. (2016: 104).

Bhambra, G.K. 2017. Brexit, Trump and methodological whiteness. *British Journal of Sociology* 68 (S1): 5214–32.

Butcher, J. 2019. Brexit: Working class revolt or middle class outlook. *Discover Society*, July 3. https://discoversociety.org/2019/07/03/brexit-working-class-revolt-or-middle-class-outlook/.

Campbell, B. 1993. *Goliath: Britain's Dangerous Places*. London: Methuen.

Cochrane, A. 2020. From Brexit to…the break-up of England? Thinking in and beyond nation. In Guderjan et al., eds. (2020: 161–73).

Coffield, F., C. Borrill, and S. Marshall. 1986. *Growing Up at the Margins: Young Adults in the North East*. Milton Keynes: Open University Press.

Davies, W. 2016. Thoughts on the sociology of Brexit. www.perc.uk/project_posts/thoughts-on-the-sociology-of-Brexit/.

Dorling, D., and S. Tomlinson. 2019. *Rule Britannia: Brexit and the End of Empire*. London: Biteback Publishing.

Fenton, N. 2016. Brexit inequality, the media and the democratic deficit. In Jackson et al., eds. (2016: 57).

FitzGibbon, J. 2016. How the Brexit outcome has changed our understanding of referendums. In Jackson et al., eds. (2016: 16–17).

Freedman, D. 2016. Divided Britain? We were already divided…. In Jackson et al., eds. (2016: 48).

Fukuyama, F. 1992. *The End of History and the Last Man*. London: Penguin.

Geddes, A. 2016. The referendum and Britain's broken immigration politics. In Jackson et al., eds. (2016: 18).

Gifford, C. 2016. Brexit: The destruction of a collective good. In Jackson et al., eds. (2016: 15).

Goodwin, M.J., and O. Heath. 2016a. The 2016 Referendum. Brexit and the left behind: An aggregate-level analysis of the result. *The Political Quarterly* 87 (3): 323–332.

Goodwin, M.J., and O. Heath. 2016b. Brexit vote explained: Poverty, low skills and lack of opportunities. *Joseph Rowntree Foundation*. Available at wwwjrf.org.uk/report/brexit-vote-explained-poverty-low-skills-and-lack-of-opportunities.

Goes, E. 2016. The Durham miners' role in Labour's culture wars. In Jackson et al., eds. (2016: 84).

Gramsci, A. 1971. *Selections From the Prison Notebooks*, ed. and trans. Q. Hoare and G.N. Smith. London: Lawrence & Wishart.

Green, J. 2016. What explains the failure of "Project Fear"? In Jackson et al., eds. (2016: 103).
Guderjan, M., H. MacKay, and G. Stedman (eds.). 2020. *Contested Britain: Brexit, Austerity and Agency*. Bristol: Bristol University Press.
Hall, S. 2008/2019. At home and not at home: Stuart Hall in conversation with Les Back. In Morley, ed. (2019: 263–300).
Hall, S., and A. O'Shea. 2015. Common-sense neoliberalism. In Hall et al., eds. (2015: 52–68).
Hall, S., C. Critcher, T. Jefferson, J. Clarke, and B. Roberts. 2013. *Policing the Crisis: Mugging, the State and Law and Order*, 2nd ed. Houndmills, Basingstoke: Palgrave Macmillan.
Hall, S., D. Massey, and M. Rustin (eds.). 2015. *After Neoliberalism? The Kilburn Manifesto*. London: Lawrence and Wishart.
Harmer, E. 2016. Brexit "mansplained": News coverage of the EU Referendum. In Jackson et al., eds. (2016: 38–39).
Henn, M., and D. Sharpe. 2016. Young people in a changing Europe: British youth and Brexit 2016. In Jackson et al., eds. (2016: 108–9).
Jackson, D., E. Thorsen, and D. Wring (eds.). 2016. *EU Referendum Analysis 2016: Media, Voters and the Campaign: Early Reflections from Leading UK Academics*. Poole, UK: The Centre of the Study of Journalism, Culture and Community, Bournemouth University.
Levy, D., B. Aslan, and D. Bironzo. 2016. The press and the referendum campaign. In Jackson et al., eds. (2016: 33).
Llewellyn, C., and L. Cram. 2016. The results are in and the UK will # Brexit: What did social media tell us about the UK's EU referendum? In Jackson et al., eds. (2016: 90–91).
Lilleker, D.G. 2016. Mixed feelings: How citizens expressed their attitudes towards the EU. In Jackson et al., eds. (2016: 106).
Lynch, P. 2016. The triumph and tribulations of Conservative Euroscepticism. In Jackson et al., eds. (2016: 77).
Martin, T. 2016. Cameron and the Europe question: Could it have ended any other way? In Jackson et al., eds. (2016: 82).
McDowell, L. 2003. *Redundant Masculinities? Employment Change and White Working Class Youth*. Oxford: Blackwell.
Morley, D. (ed.). 2019. *Stuart Hall Essential Essays Vol. 2: Identity and Diaspora*. Durham and London: Duke University Press.
Mullen, A. 2016. Leave versus remain: The digital battle. In Jackson et al., eds. (2016: 89).
Pearson, G. 1987. *The New Heroin Users*. Oxford: Blackwell.

Pearson, G., H.S. Mirza, and S. Phillips. 1993. Cocaine in context: London inner-city drug survey. In Bean, ed. (1993: 99–129).
Polonski, V. 2016. Impact of social media on the outcome of the EU referendum. In Jackson et al., eds. (2016: 94–95).
Rae, A. 2016. What can explain Brexit? *Stats, Maps n Pix blog*, June 25. Available at http://www.statsmapsnpix.com/2016/06/what-can-explain-brexit.html.
Sandbrook, D. 2007. *White Heat: A History of Britain in the Swinging Sixties*. London: Abacus.
Sayer, D. 2017. White riot—Brexit, Trump, and post-factual politics. *Historical Sociology* 30 (1): 92–106.
Slimani, L. 2020. Continental drift. *The Guardian Review*, February 29: 32–34.
Thompson, L. 2016. The "Referendum Bubble": What can we learn from the EU campaign polling. In Jackson et al., eds. (2016: 111).
Varoufakis, Y. 2017. *And The Weak Suffer What They Must? Europe, Austerity and the Threat To Global Stability*. London: Vintage.
Vasilopoulou, S. 2016. Campaign frames in the Brexit referendum. In Jackson et al., eds. (2016: 114–15).
Weber, M. 1947. *The Theory of Social and Economic Organization*, trans. A.M. Henderson and Talcott Parsons. New York: Oxford University Press.
Whitehead, S.M., and F.J. Barrett. 2001. The sociology of masculinity. In Whitehead and Barrett, eds. (2001: 1–26).
Whitehead, S.M., and F.J. Barrett (eds.). 2001. *The Masculinities Reader*. Cambridge: Polity.
Willis, P.E. 1977. *Learning to Labour: How working class kids get working class jobs*. Farnborough, Hants.: Saxon House.

9

The Brexit Conjuncture Part Two: From 9/11 to the 2016 Referendum

In this chapter, I shall be undertaking several tasks. First, I need to reintroduce the middle-class Conservative Brexiteers into the analysis, whose story was postponed from the last chapter. Then, I shall continue the story of 'how we got there', tracing it forward from 9/11 to the Referendum moment. In doing so, the issue of immigration, and hence race, grows in significance. So, another task will be to address how immigration and race are connected by unravelling the notion of race and cognate concepts and their relation to questions of racism and difference. Finally, I will address the issue of quite what kind of moment was the conjuncture of Brexit.

I ended Chapter 7 with Hall outlining the difficulties, at the turn of the millennium, facing his proposal for a new political logic for rethinking multiculturalism: how what was propitious from one vantage point—talk of being black-and-British, for example—was driving others, 'Little Englanders', 'crazy'. After which, I reminded that the essay was published a year before 9/11. As we all know, 9/11 and the subsequent 'war on terror' initiated by the USA has impacted all Western democracies in similar ways: security measures have been ramped up as terrorist incidents multiplied; objections to such measures have been quite limited as the need for a tough response has become the new common sense on terrorism; and anti-Islamic sentiment has added fuel to the 'new racism' of Europe and the UK. Hall's moment of 'profound danger' had indeed come to pass. Given what we have seen in Chapter 8 of young, white, under-educated, unqualified, working-class men living in the de-industrialised, poverty-stricken wastelands of contemporary Britain, growing up 'at the margins', saddled with 'redundant masculinities', caught between the lure of a laddish street life of reckless hedonism fuelled by drugs and crime and an ever-receding prospect of 'domestic respectability' (McDowell 2003), Hall's dangerous moment became multidimensional, implicating issues of class and gender as well as race. In other words, the crisis of class relations brought on by Thatcherism, and the crisis of gender relations resulting from the increasing redundancy of traditional masculinity met up with the crisis of race relations exacerbated by 9/11.

But How Has It Been for the Middle Classes?

The 'remaking of the middle classes', as John Clarke (2020: 123) reminds us, has been as significant as the remaking of the de-industrialised working class. For the purposes of explaining Brexit, there are three dimensions of particular significance: loss of cultural authority; loss of economic authority; and the loss of Empire. Underpinning all three dimensions is the expansion and transformation of the class in the second half of the twentieth century, consequent upon the addition of new middle-class occupations to service and manage capitalism's post-Second World War growth, 'the enormous expansion of the state and public services' (ibid.), and the growth of cultural and communication industries. Collectively these changes produced a huge intra-class challenge to middle-class cultural authority. Where the old, traditional middle classes had tended to be culturally and politically conservative, defending tradition and providing 'the common values and standards of the Tory nation', as Rutherford (2019: 1) expressed it, these new middle classes tended to hold very different views. This was partly because of their different social formation, being children of 'the cultural revolution and university expansion of the 1960s' (ibid.). Socially liberal rather than conservative, this new fraction, Rutherford (2019: 1–2) argues, came to control 'institutions of culture, media and learning', became 'the national arbiter and communicator of aesthetic taste and values' and produced 'a liberal intelligentsia that was cosmopolitan, individualistic and, on the whole, anti-establishment'. Even if this account overdraws the differences between the old and the new elements of the middle classes, and homogenises the diverse strands of middle-class expansion (professional, managerial, public sector, cultural industries, etc.), the challenge to traditional middle-class cultural authority since the 1960s is undeniable.

This cultural struggle was, of course, central to the crisis of hegemony that we outlined in *Policing the Crisis (PTC)*. And, as we saw, the traditionalist backlash produced the 'law and order' response of the new Tory government of 1970 (Hall et al. 2013: 243–76). The battles of the 1970s on so many fronts eventuated in the advent of Thatcherism, with its combination of economic liberalism and attempts to reinstate traditional cultural and social authority, assumed to have been lost in schools and families to the new 'permissiveness' advocated by middle-class radicals. This was Thatcher's 'regressive' attempt at modernisation, as Hall's (1988: 2) 'regressive modernization' phrase compellingly characterised it. In other words, what would come to be called the 'culture wars', partly originated in this transformation of the middle classes. I say 'partly' because we should not overlook how the new spending power of the working-class teenager, and the creation of working-class youth subcultures, was helping to fuel a revolution in popular music. This revolution, spearheaded by rock and roll, became part of a wider cultural assault across the arts and culture: 'a working class [cultural] hero' was 'something to be', as John Lennon sang. The accompanying shifts in sexuality had their working-class dimension in the growing concerns about teenage pregnancies. And the expansion of higher education that provided the personnel for the new middle-class occupations was also the escalator of social mobility that propelled many a working-class 'scholarship' boy or girl into the new middle classes. All these changes, considered collectively, mean that the 'culture wars' involved rather more complex cross-class alignments and realignments than simply an intra-class struggle between old and new middle-class fractions. However, having said that, it is not hard to discern the expression of the frustrations of the traditional middle classes with their lost authority in the Leave vote, given what we have learned about the socially illiberal views of Brexiteers.

The loss of economic authority has been more recent, 'spurred - and blurred - by the spread of self-employment in a variety of forms, from the "gig economy" through the expanding service sector to the creative industries, where more and more people are incited to think themselves as "entrepreneurial"' (Clarke 2020: 123). In short, the post-Thatcher landscape has not been without its middle-class victims. Overall, this has entailed 'a weakening of middle-class economic influence' as 'temporary or unstable work is replacing traditional middle-class jobs' (Rutherford 2019: 2), and many of the 'new' middle classes were never in 'traditional middle class jobs' but in public service-based ones. It particularly impacts the young, who are increasingly saddled with student debt, do jobs for which they are overqualified, find the achievement of financial independence difficult, and face a precarious future, one very different from that of their baby boomer parents and grandparents. This generational descent of middle-class offspring, the new downward mobility, has produced uncertainty and unsettledness into middle-class lives, not only for those children directly affected, but also for parents worried about their childrens' futures. For those in the traditional middle classes, along with their loss of cultural authority, this constitutes a double whammy. We saw in the last chapter that what Antonucci and colleagues (2017) called the 'squeezed middle' were more likely to vote leave, and these, what I called the 'downwardly mobile lower middle classes', would fit the profile of those losing economic influence (although many of these, in the ambiguous C1 category, arguably never had any such influence in the first place).

The loss of Empire, my third relevant dimension, was probably the one most often used by commentators to explain the middle-class Brexiteer, commonly deploying Gilroy's influential idea of 'postimperial melancholia' (Gilroy 2004: 98). Cochrane (2020: 168–69), for example, claimed that for 'Conservative heartlands' Leave voters 'traditional forms of social and political authority were being undermined in the context of "post-imperial melancholy"'. To elaborate: Gilroy borrowed Freud's (1957) notion of melancholia, which Freud regarded as a pathological inability to come to terms with loss as opposed to the normal painfulness of mourning.[1] Gilroy explained Britain's 'pathological' failure to accept the reality of its racism or come to terms with its loss of Empire, in terms of 'postimperial melancholia'. Shorn of the notion that it is a free-floating 'context', rather than something felt by particular individuals, it could probably describe the feelings of a certain kind of traditional, patriotic middle-class Leave voter, for whom absence of patriotism is definitional of the internationalist outlook of the socially liberal and Empire is an important part of the definition of what it means to be British. We know from surveys mentioned earlier that many still believe the Empire was a good idea. Given that, it is not hard to imagine that, for some of these, its loss might be hard to bear. It also fits with the traditionalist idea of a 'conservative sense of Englishness', that I mentioned in the last chapter. For, one of its features, as we noted in *PTC*, was the idea of 'the superiority of the English over all other nations on the face of the globe' (Hall et al. 2013: 145). Losing an Empire need not mean losing superiority if only we could cast off the shackles of the bureaucratic EU and start afresh....

Loss is not something that is necessarily dealt with pathologically rather than through realistic acknowledgement. Whether or not this happens partly depends on the difficulties presented by the prevailing social conditions. As we have seen with working-class lives, pre- and post-Thatcher, times have been difficult. This is also true for the traditional middle classes. The 'culture wars', for example, have not only been an intra-class (and inter-class, as I noted earlier) struggle but have also implicated the crises of gender and race relations, among other things. The loss of heavy industry and the growth of a service economy may not have impacted middle-class men in the way it has working-class men, but the loss of male authority in the context of the growth of 'two career' families presented its own stresses, to say nothing of the

---

[1] Strictly speaking, Gilroy's usage derives from Freud's idea as used by two German psychoanalysts, the Mitscherlichs, to understand the reaction of Germans to the death of Hitler.

many other feminist challenges to traditional patriarchal practices. And race relations, multiculturalism and immigration may not have directly impacted the lives and livelihoods of traditional middle-class communities in predominantly white rural and suburban areas, but as we have seen with the geography of Brexit, this did not stop immigration being seen as problematic. The less direct contact, the more room for 'pathological' fantasies to thrive. Likewise with all the other social problems with which working-class communities have had to contend more directly: strikes, riots, drug 'epidemics', crime, and so on. In other words, even before having to concede political authority to Tony Blair's New Labour government, there was plenty enough 'going wrong' for traditional middle-class Tories to encourage 'unrealistic' responses: or what, talking about working-class youth subcultures in *Resistance through Rituals (RTR)*, we called, following Cohen's (1972) lead, 'magical' solutions.

From New Labour to the Coalition Government, 2010

Generally, the New Labour years presented a mixed face on the multiculturalism with which for some they are associated: the Blair government established the Inquiry into the racist murder of black teenager Stephen Lawrence that found the Metropolitan police guilty of 'institutional racism' (Macpherson 1999); but it rejected the Runnymede Trust's *Report of the Commission on the Future of Multi-Ethnic Britain* (Parekh 2000), which comprehensively exposed Britain's manifold multicultural failings (thanks, in part, to Hall's presence as a Commission member). It also passed the Nationality, Immigration and Asylum Act of 2002, which enabled the state to deprive British born citizens of their citizenship, a legislative shift in favour of security that would be used against the Windrush generation as well as those suspected of Islamic extremism (Shamsie 2018). Its brief flirtation with a multi-cultural 'Cool Britannia' (Hall 1998/2017a: 297) was at odds with its generally punitive approach to various 'outsider' groups: 'anti-social' youths (subjected to the infamous Anti-Social Behaviour Orders or ASBOs); visa-less migrants (rounded up and expelled by private security firms); suspected terrorists (imprisoned without trial) (Hall 2011/2017a: 327–28). The mixed nature of its responses was the corollary of what Hall called 'New Labour's double shuffle': a social democratic government pursuing a neo-liberal programme in a way that maintained its traditional electoral support bases (Hall 2003/2017a): or, Thatcher-lite. Meanwhile, support for the far right British National Party (BNP) had been growing and, in the aftermath of the northern mill town riots of 2001, achieved significant successes in the local council elections of 2003. However, it was the failure to anticipate the responses to opening the door in 2004 to immigration from eight of the new central and east European members of the EU, seven years before necessary (unlike most other member states), that was to prove most directly salient for Brexit. The resulting influx of new immigrants far exceeded the expected modest numbers (Geddes 2016). The following year saw the London bombings, 7/7, carried out by four British-born Islamic terrorists that left 52 murdered and 700 injured. In 2006 Nigel Farage became leader of the United Kingdom Independence Party (UKIP), the far right, populist party concerned about rising immigration and opposed to multiculturalism and the 'Islamification' of Britain.

On the economic front, the world was growing at a phenomenal rate. Between 2000 and 2006 the world's wealth doubled, with China and India averaging growth rates of around 10%. With capitalism unchallenged after the fall of the Berlin Wall and the collapse of the Soviet Union, and finance capital increasingly dominant after Thatcher's abolition of exchange controls and deregulation of financial markets, the stage was set for the biggest of all credit bubbles as bankers competed with each other to find more and more ways to grow their loan books, and thus their size (a bank's assets are predominantly other people's money loaned out to yet other people).[2] Finding more and more ingenious ways to increase their 'leverage' (basically the size of their loan book relative to their equity) and ever riskier loans, returns on banking shares rocketed, as did bonuses. And as the loans got riskier and the rewards consequently greater, they also became more opaque, understood, if at all, only by

---

[2]In 2008, the Royal Bank of Scotland was 'by asset size…the biggest company in the world', worth 1.9 trillion pounds, a figure larger than the 'entire GDP of the United Kingdom [which] is £1.7 trillion' (Lanchester 2010: 22).

the mathematical whizz kids devising the formulae assessing their riskiness. It was a recipe for disaster. The crash came in 2008 and with it the near collapse of the banking system, given its global interconnectedness. Fearful of a complete collapse of the economy, governments in the USA and Europe as well as the UK used billions of tax payers' money to bail them out, nationalising some in the process. No banker was gaoled, but plenty bleated about depressed bonuses; and no meaningful reforms followed. It is not hard to imagine how all this went down, especially in the depressed Labour heartlands where people were still struggling with poverty wages, inadequate benefits and punitive sanctions,[3] since, despite a world visibly awash with new wealth, little of it was 'trickling down' and the gap between the rich and the poor was getting ever wider: to the victors the spoils.

Then, a year later, adding insult to injury, came the Westminster expenses scandal: MPs from all parties over-claiming or claiming for things that people felt didn't belong on a claim form (like the infamous duckhouse), 'flipping' their houses to claim a larger mortgage relief, or claiming relief on a non-existent mortgage. It was a shoddy and humiliating affair, revealing greed, pettiness, dishonesty and, in the worst cases, criminality. Seven ended up in gaol, five of them from the Labour party. Having just witnessed unimaginable sums of money being given to banks because they were 'too big to fail', the people were now glimpsing something of the lifestyles of their governors and the expenses to which they felt they were entitled. The contrast with the stinginess of the poor's wages or benefits could not have been starker. Although the widespread alienation from politics did not originate here (one could point to John Major's 'Back to Basics' campaign to restore traditional values undercut by the various sex and 'cash for questions' scandals of his MPs and Blair's duplicity over the Iraq war as prior alienating moments), this was to prove a defining moment in the emerging political crisis, partly because of its post-crash timing. At the same time, the anti-immigration BNP continued its upward trajectory by winning two seats in the European parliament. Stephen Yaxley-Lennon, otherwise known by the more

---

[3] Which would get worse after the Welfare Reform Act of 2012.

populist-sounding name of Tommy Robinson, once a BNP member, became the de facto leader of the newly established far right, anti-Islamic English Defence League (EDL).

From the Coalition Government to 2016

The expenses scandal was presided over by Gordon Brown's Labour government. But it was his unguarded response to a Labour voter complaining about immigration in Rochdale, calling her 'bigoted' without realising he was still on air, that revealed the extent of the gap between the government and the hard up in depressed areas. The election of May 2010 saw the Conservatives, led by their new, 'modern and compassionate' leader David Cameron (a fan of Tony Blair), returned to power promising to bring immigration figures down to the tens of thousands. Without a majority, he was forced into establishing a coalition government with the Liberal Democrats. And given the post-crash economic recession and the extent of the budget deficit, he felt forced to impose austerity measures. The Tories' first emergency budget imposed spending cuts and tax rises amounting to £40 billion. After the credit-fuelled party that virtually destroyed the world's economy and the hypocrisies of the expenses scandal, it was those barely a pay cheque a way from financial disaster who were going to have to pick up the tab in (more) jobs lost, pay cuts and squeezed benefits. The following summer, 2011, saw more English riots, triggered by a(nother) police killing of a young black man, in Tottenham, a poor part of north London, that spread country-wide and lasted for four days. In October, a petition calling for a referendum on Europe, signed by 100,000, was presented to the prime minister.

In January 2013 Cameron finally gave in to the growing pressure and announced that, if re-elected, there would be an 'In/Out' referendum on Europe based on the renegotiated terms he hoped to secure. Aware of the centrality of immigration to the referendum debate, and their manifesto commitment, the Conservatives had already established a working group within the Home Office tasked with creating a 'hostile environment' for illegal immigrants. 'In the summer of 2013' that initiative took the very public form of vans driving around London warning illegal immigrants to 'Go home or face arrest' (Gentleman 2019: 23). As the Windrush scandal eventually revealed, thanks to Gentleman's journalistic commitment, this operation largely amounted to harassing, threatening and wrongfully deporting[4] Commonwealth-born British immigrants who were here legally, leaving them jobless, homeless and without access to health care, in order to reduce net annual migration to less than 100,000 (ibid.: 29). However, the 'vans' policy appeared to be popular as nearly half of those asked in a YouGov poll approved of it (ibid.: 23).

As if to prove his 'modern, compassionate' credentials, at the same moment as the crackdown on so-called illegal immigration, Cameron enacted a 'same-sex' marriage bill. But many traditional conservative activists thought they were being ignored and the law was only passed with opposition support: more Tory MPs voted against the bill than for it. Cameron proving his socially liberal credentials probably did not go down well among his traditional middle-class supporters in the shires either. Hate crimes, which had been on the rise since 9/11, produced some particularly ugly incidents in 2013, such as the brutal murder of Mohammed Saleen, an 82-year-old man, stabbed from behind in Birmingham, and the murder of Pavlo Lapshyn by a self-confessed ideological racist. During the investigation into the Saleen murder, three bombs exploded in local mosques. Nigel Farage's UKIP party achieved a significant breakthrough in local government elections and in the following year, 2014, an emboldened Farage claimed that Powell's rivers of blood speech had been 'correct' in principle. Powell was sacked for his remarks in 1968; but times had changed and Farage's 'party topped the poll in the European elections later that year' (Younge 2019: 1). There was a further tightening of immigration law: the Home Secretary's powers were extended, enabling her to deprive Britons of their citizenship, so long as the Secretary of State had a 'reasonable belief' that the person could get citizenship elsewhere (Shamsie 2018); and new reporting requirements on public bodies made the environment even more hostile for immigrants. The public, apparently, continued to believe in the goodness of

---

[4] 83 confirmed cases, according to the Home Secretary Sajid Javid, reporting to the Home Affairs Select Committee in 2018 (Shamsie 2018: 8).

Empire: a YouGov poll of 1741 people found 59% believed that the Empire was something to be proud of.

In the general election of 2015, the Conservatives won an outright victory, thus enabling them to rule without Liberal Democratic constraints. In the first budget, the Chancellor George Osbourne slashed welfare in favour of the National Health Service and education and reasserted the Conservative's commitment to a neo-liberal, right-wing agenda, claiming he wanted to move from a low wage, high tax and high welfare economy to a high wage, low tax and low welfare economy. Cameron prepared himself for renegotiating terms with the EU. Unfortunately for him, the EU migrant crisis, with its images of huge numbers fleeing poverty and war attempting to enter a Europe that didn't want them, was the dominant news item in August, at the very moment when he was renegotiating terms. In the event, Cameron's renegotiated deal, limiting some migrants' benefits and exempting Britain from further political integration, proved too little, too late.

The February announcement of the referendum date was followed by six cabinet ministers joining Vote Leave, and then by Boris Johnson doing likewise. A month before referendum day, June 23rd, the immigration figures were released: the net migration figure of 333,000 for 2015 was the second highest on record; and at no time in the six years since 2010 had the government got anywhere near its professed target of 'capping' net migration 'in the tens - rather than hundreds - of thousands' (Geddes 2016: 18). Twisting the knife, Boris Johnson and Michael Gove wrote a 5000 word letter to the *Sunday Times* accusing Cameron of eroding public trust with regard to immigration. A week before the referendum, Labour MP Jo Cox was murdered in her Leeds constituency by a self-radicalised, white, male, far-right extremist.

What I hope the above brief run through of the period since 9/11 demonstrates, if only in barest outline, is a series of unresolved crises continuing unchecked or worsening considerably as the salience of immigration steadily increases. The unchecked economic impact of the neoliberal offensive against the labouring and non-labouring poor dramatically worsened during the post-crash recession of 2008 and the years of austerity that followed (while returns on capital quickly caught up lost ground). The political crisis reached a climactic point in 2009 with the expenses scandal. The far right parties, first the BNP and then UKIP, with their anti-immigration rhetoric, which had been making headway since the 1990s, made significant breakthroughs in local and European elections, and, briefly, nationally during the 2000s. And the anti-Islamic EDL movement offered a more provocative, street-based alternative. Britain's endemic crisis of race or ethnic relations, Hall's 'politics of difference', took a new turn for the worse after 9/11: anti-Islamic sentiments fuelled rises in violent hate crimes; and fear of the terrorist 'other' fuelled the resurgence of a reactionary English nationalism, opposition to immigration and multiculturalism, and the growth of far right populism. The crisis of masculinity was closely entwined with all these crises, as we saw earlier with McDowell's study of 'redundant masculinity'. A full consideration of this crisis would take me too far afield here, but would include the often hidden problems of male mental health, depression, drug addiction and suicide and violence against women. However, I shall have more to say on this in the Coda (Chapter 11). The reason immigration became more and more salient has to do with its ambiguity. Like the slogan 'Take Back Control', the ambiguity of the term immigration is why it provides the key to understanding the angry Leave Labour voters (post the 2019 election, often former Labour voters) and the angry middle-class voter: it can be articulated to a variety of diverse, seemingly incompatible discourses and thus mean different things to different audiences. The source of this ambiguity needs further elucidation.

Immigration, Racism and Xenophobia

A key to understanding the capaciousness of these terms is captured in the title of the first of Hall's 1994 Du Bois lectures, 'Race - the sliding signifier', meaning, that 'race is a cultural and historical, not biological, fact…a discursive construct, a sliding signifier' (2017b: 32). This is also true of its cultural equivalent, ethnicity, as we saw earlier with Hall's discussion of the many meanings of multiculturalism, and, concomitantly, the idea of a national culture informing nationalism. In other words, 'race', 'ethnicity' and 'nation' are all 'sliding', 'floating' or 'empty' signifiers, discursive constructs whose meanings are not fixed, but are the result of the state of play of the ever-ongoing politics of difference: competing discourses of difference whose dominance or subordination at any given moment will depend on their articulations with existing power relations. In Chapter 7 we saw Hall's historical and spatial exploration of this politics, ending on the eve of 9/11 with the 'moment of great danger', poised between an absolutist, essentialising politics of difference variously embraced by the far right and a Derridean, *différance*-based one embracing a hybrid, diasporic multiculturalism variously supported by those embracing diversity.

Further complicating the picture and thus expanding the terms' discursive meanings is the role of the unconscious. As we saw with Hall's discussion of identification, the self is always partly composed of the disavowed 'Other': the ambivalence masking the desire that manifests discursively as prejudice, hostility or hatred. Although Hall does not expand on this idea, there is more to be said about the role of the unconscious in racism. Without taking the lengthy detour that unpacking that notion requires, suffice to say for present purposes that different unconscious processes underpin different kinds of 'racism', what elsewhere (Jefferson 2015) I have divided into three types: racial hatred, racial prejudice and 'othering' (in addition to institutional or structural racism that lay outside my concerns in that article).[5] In other words, not only is racism a historically specific discursive construct meaning different things at different times, but at any given moment its meaning is not fixed. It covers a variety of different things from the mildly ethnocentric to hate-motivated violence as well as structural discrimination. These differences have their origin in confusions in the theoretical literature that have fed into popular (and populist) confusions generally in discussions of the topic (Jefferson 2014) and, relatedly, into the fear of entering discussions of anything to do with race or ethnicity in case one is misunderstood and labelled a 'racist'. This fear has bedevilled the contemporary debate about immigration.

Jeremy Seabrook's *City Close-up*, published in 1973, captured the idea of prejudice against immigrants being the conscious expression of

---

[5] I will have more to say on the unconscious in the Coda (Chapter 11).

something unconscious, 'inexpressible fears' that have 'no outlet'; of immigrants being used to legitimate other feelings:

> The immigrants act as a perverse legitimation of inexpressible fears and anguish. What is taking place is only secondarily an expression of prejudice. It is first and foremost a therapeutic psychodrama, in which the emotional release of its protagonists takes precedence over what is actually being said...It is an expression of their pain and powerlessness confronted by the decay and dereliction, not only of the familiar environment, but of their own lives, too - an expression for which our society provides no outlet. Certainly it is something more complex and deep-rooted than what the metropolitan liberal evasively and easily dismisses as prejudice. (Seabrook 1973: 57)

In *PTC* we used this quotation to illustrate the grounding of prejudice in people's everyday lives and experiences as well as to argue for a connection between this 'pain and powerlessness' and social anxiety (Hall et al. 2013: 158–59).

A more recent, post 9/11, study of racism in Stoke-on-Trent (a poor, de-industrialised, strongly Leave-voting area with both historical and contemporary far right connections) found something similar (Gadd et al. 2005). However, adding to the pain was the fear of being branded a racist if they spoke against the transformations of their neighbourhoods. What was particularly revealing was that these sentiments were commonly held, by those interviewees convicted of racially aggravated crimes (a sample of 'racists', most of whom rejected the label) as well as the focus group participants (a sample of 'ordinary' people from North Staffordshire):

> Almost everyone - old, young or middle aged, men and women - felt that the present was unsettling and the future uncertain. Few of them would have been happy to be described as 'racists' - on the contrary, many saw themselves as victims of discrimination - yet almost all of them associated immigration and the descendants of immigration with everything that was wrong with their lives - from crime to unemployment, inadequate healthcare to sub-standard housing...Most, but not all, of our sample of perpetrators had very similar views. (ibid.: 9)

Published around the same time, the update to Young and Willmot's classic *Family and Kinship in East London* (1957), *The New East End* (Dench et al. 2006), was obliged to add a focus on 'race', given the impact on community relations of the influx of Bangladeshis, who, by 2001 in Tower Hamlets, had become 'the largest concentration of a single minority group in any borough in Britain' (ibid.: 227). Talking specifically of 'hostility to new communities', Dench and colleagues (2006: 171–72) found much inter-communal hostility, but also complexity in the attitudes of their sample,[6] a finding introducing an element of contingency into the picture:

> One of the most revealing…features of the findings lay in the complexity of people's feeling. Most white subjects, including some among the most explicitly hostile to Bangladeshis, admitted that while they resented the immigrants and what they felt their presence was doing to the area, they somehow managed to get on with them, or even to like them.

The list of complaints included everything from cooking ('malodorous' smells) and cleanliness (personal and public) to lifestyle and culture (taking over the locality and 'wanting to impose their lifestyle or culture on everyone else') based on an admixture of experience, 'wild hearsay and popular myth' (ibid.: 173–77). A familiar litany. However, 'the largest number of complaints' introduced an element, the issue of entitlement, that was the most significant issue for the authors and is, I contend, a crucial (but usually missing) element in understanding the significance of immigration for Brexit.

> By far the largest number of complaints arose…in relation to Bangladeshi claims on the welfare state. A majority of white respondents questioned Bangladeshi rights and entitlements, or expressed resentment at the level of demands which they place on the system. Listening to these litanies, it became obvious that a large number of the accusations were thoroughly implausible, or involved serious ignorance about how welfare procedures operated…But in many such cases the facts of the matter were probably

---

[6]This comprised 8,370 people, including 799, aged 18 to 94, who were subjected to 'full interviews' (Dench et al. 2006: 14).

irrelevant. Opposition was categorical. Many whites were objecting not to specific abuses of the welfare system, but to the more fundamental fact that Bangladeshis had any right to benefits at all. (ibid.: 177)

To what is the newcomer among us entitled? How should scarce resources be allocated as between the native-born and the immigrant? Who decides the question of scarcity? What principle of justice or fairness—need, contribution, equality or something else entirely—should be used? These, and other questions, seem to be essential elements in any discussion of immigration. They are not easy issues. Moreover, the question of 'entitlements' cannot be resolved in the abstract since it has no necessarily negative or positive connotation: everything depends on what it is being articulated with, and the state of play of existing power relations. Hall's discussion of equality in our post-enlightenment, particularistic world (see Chapter 7) showed something of the theoretical dilemmas. *The New East End* study showed the practical difficulties, given that such discussions are always implicated in the particularities of a local politics with its specific history. The discussion will never escape existing power relations. However, without such a discussion, not only will the negative, 'racist' framing of the debate continue to dominate (an issue in the local politics of the Dench et al. study too), but one of the biggest points of contention between the native-born and immigrants, as was evident in *The New East End* study and in other London-based studies (Back and Keith 1999; Hewitt 1996, 1997), will remain unaddressed.[7]

My final example, taken from Winlow and colleagues' (2017) ethnographically-based study of the far right EDL, emphasised the importance of underlying social relations. However, in its focus on the importance of class it failed to see the significance of gender relations, and, specifically, the role of masculinity in explaining EDL supporters' attitudes, beliefs and behaviour. Describing the League in general, the authors called it 'a misguided attempt to respond politically to the enduring sense of diminishment and lack…[it] attempts to restore what

---

[7]None of this is to suggest agreement with either the framing or the politics of the argument conducted in The New East End Study which have occasioned criticism along many dimensions, especially perhaps the narrowness of its focus (cf. Keith 2008). My concern, however, has been with the study's empirical findings and the issue of entitlement these threw up.

has been lost and defend what remains'. Without a system of formal membership, it was seen as a fragile institution with a sporadic existence whose principal form of politics was a passionately exercised street politics but without a concrete agenda for change. Its core principles, based on dissatisfaction with immigration and hostility towards the spread of the 'alien culture' of radical Islamism, were fuelled by an anger towards the metropolitan elite who had allowed this to happen and had failed to protect 'the economic and cultural entitlements of the white working class'.

Here, then, if anywhere, you would have expected to find hard-core racists, those full of not just prejudice but racial hatred. However, that is not how EDL supporters, overwhelmingly men 'from Britain's old, white working class' in deprived areas, saw themselves, believing that reserving their antagonism for Muslims, or other qualifications to their animosity, excused them from the general charge of racism: 'We're not against blacks or anything else. We're not against any other race. We're just saying...they're taking over, they're not blending in'; 'I'm not bothered by blacks, Muslims, none of that. As long as everyone stays in his own patch there's no bother so far as I'm concerned'; 'I'm not racist...I'm just fucking sick of the immigration'; 'They say we have to become multicultural, but why, why is that a good thing?...its bollocks to think that mixing in is always good. Why? I don't get it'.

The explanation for what the authors call the men's 'inarticulate anger' (rather than hatred) is said to be the devastating effects of the neo-liberal assault on working-class lives and livelihoods combined with a failure of the left to address this in a fundamental fashion, opting instead for the fragmented and reformist cultural politics of identity. By this they meant feminism, anti-racism, the politics of sexuality, etc. Although the authors' characterisation of the impact of neoliberalism was powerful, angry and passionate, and they did not overlook the unconscious dimension (Muslims were said to be scapegoats for fears of economic insecurity), in dismissing the politics of identity *tout court* the authors managed to blind themselves to gender relations: the threat posed to a sense of themselves as men; their masculinity. Interestingly, the 'scapegoats' for this were not Muslims but a group they hated even more: 'their deepest hatred was reserved for mainstream politicians'. The interviews were punctuated with revealing examples of this masculinist animosity: politicians had 'capitulated' to the EU and had made the social security system a 'soft touch'; [supporters] 'spoke at length of their hatred for soft, do-gooding hippies, liberals and multiculturalists'; they 'saw Jeremy Corbyn [whose class politics are as radical as anything on offer] as a do-gooding, weak-as-piss, hippy pacifist…They hated him'; 'Time and time again we were told that the EDL's cause was to protect the cultural and economic interests of England's forgotten white working class'. Men who hated 'softness' wherever they spotted it and who were barely able to protect their jobs, much less their ever-degrading neighbourhoods and prospects, were still committed to the masculinist idea of protection, even if only in their imagination. And, as anyone who has witnessed such men in protest action will know, they are usually raring for that ultimate test of manhood: a fight—with their 'soft', liberal metropolitan opponents, the cops, or whoever. It matters little, the fight's the thing. Not for nothing were their origins in old football hooligan fighting 'firms' (Pilkington 2016: 38).

What I hope the above has established are further factors complicating any discussion of racism, ethnicity, xenophobia and immigration. They have manifold meanings both historically and currently; their manifest discursive meanings obscure unconscious, unexpressed desires and fears. Even those convicted of racist offences or with extreme views on immigration and cultural and religious differences, like EDL supporters, do not regard themselves as racists; they also implicate other discourses like the fairness of entitlements; and their meanings are never innocent of relations of power (and powerlessness).

If we return to the post 9/11 moment with these understandings in mind, several things become clearer. The war on terror and the coming home of that war in the form of Islamic fundamentalist bomb attacks made it less and less possible to have a rational, nuanced conversation about race and immigration even as growing numbers of immigrants made such a conversation more necessary. The growth of hate-motivated racism, in the form of terrorist attacks and the resulting surge in hate crimes, increased the toxicity of the label and thus compounded the difficulty of an open conversation. The further attacks on welfare and the social services in already impoverished areas in the post-crash years of imposed austerity made the issue of entitlement to scarce resources more salient in immigration-receiving areas, even as it became less easy to discuss outwith the twin shadows of racism and terrorism. The closing of the discursive space in which to talk openly about race and immigration, to move it on from a common sense to a good sense discussion, was not helped by governments that, instead of taking a lead, were hopelessly adopting the people's common sense for fear of being overtaken by far right populists who were actively promoting the discourse. Over time, populist common sense on the issue began to feel unchallengeable. Governments, whether Labour or Conservative, became obsessed by numbers and traded in simplifications. Under New Labour in 2002, 'David Blunkett talked of British schools being "swamped" by non-English speaking immigrants' and 'in 2007, Gordon Brown promised to train '"British workers for British jobs"' (Goes 2016: 84). Cameron's obsession with numbers led to promises he couldn't keep and, in a vain attempt to do so, created the cruel inhumanity of the 'hostile environment' with its hounding of British immigrants who just happened to be black. Pandering to the people's common sense on racism and immigration produced racist outcomes, though offending politicians would all strenuously deny the racist label. Such are the dangers of expecting you can address issues of difference without also attending to matters of equality.

The Brexit Conjuncture: What Kind of 'Moment'?

In thinking about what kind of moment was the financial crash of 2008–2009 and how it might be thought conjuncturally, my fellow *PTC* co-author, John Clarke, returned to Hall's words for guidance. Since my purpose here has been to attempt a Hallian conjunctural analysis of Brexit, Hall's words, taken from a conversation with Doreen Massey about the conjuncture of 2008–2009, will serve as a guide for my conclusion too.

the current crisis seems to start in the economy. But any serious analysis of the crisis must take into account its other 'conditions of existence'. For example, the ideological - the way market fundamentalism has become the economic common sense, not only of the west but globally; politically - the way New Labour has been disconnected from its political roots and evolved as the second party of capital, transforming the political terrain; socially - the way that class and other social relations have been so reconfigured under consumer capitalism that they fragment, undermining the potential social constituencies or agencies for change. We can't ignore the way the financial sector has asserted its dominance over the economy as a whole, or indeed its centrality to the new forms of global capitalism. But we must address the complexity of the crisis as a whole. Different levels of society, the economy, politics, ideology, common sense, etc., come together or 'fuse'. The definition of a conjunctural crisis is when these 'relatively autonomous' sites - which have different origins, are driven by different contradictions, and develop according to their own temporalities - are nevertheless 'convened' or condensed in the same moment.... (Hall and Massey 2010: 38, quoted in Clarke 2010: 339)

Starting with the economy is to remind that, on this front, the Brexit narrative started in the 1970s with the crisis of the social democratic variant of capitalism. Developing into the more general crisis of hegemony that *PTC* charted, Thatcher's neo-liberal economic revolution of the 1980s effectively de-industrialised Britain, destroyed the associated unions, broke working-class resistance and thus enabled the development of the present casualised, low waged, non-unionised and precarious service economy. I charted this through the lives of young men from Willis's 'lads' onwards. Capitalism has successfully transferred the crisis and its costs onto working-class shoulders, including those not working, where it has remained ever since. By that I mean simply that aside from the brief recessions following the bursting of the dot.com bubble at the turn of the century and for the year or so following the 2008–2009 crash, overall these have been boom years for owners of capital.

Politically, the crisis has several dimensions. Hall (above) mentioned the disconnect from New Labour, to which I must add the subsequent disconnect from all mainstream political parties and the consequent support for a series of far right populist alternatives, the only ones who seemed able to 'hear' them, especially on immigration. However, there is a further dimension, the education disconnect, that has been steadily increasing. It is not just the decline of working-class MPs that is the problem, but the decline of working-class MPs without any experience of higher education. EDL hostility to cosmopolitan liberals, echoing Goodhart's (2017) distinction between nationalistic 'somewheres' and cosmopolitan 'anywheres', hinges partly on education: the differences between those with little education and the highly educated. For every meritocratic success story that has enabled some of the 'brightest and best' of the working classes—scholarship boys and girls—to become socially mobile, there are many 'left behind', undervalued. Michael Young's satirical essay, *The Rise of the Meritocracy* (1958), presciently predicted long ago that the present basis of social mobility, the selection of an educated elite based on a narrow version of 'merit', would become the dominant educational ideology. Nearly 60 years later, Goodhart (2017) confirms this prediction: 'The promotion of social mobility, as opposed to more equal incomes, as the main highway of social justice in rich democracies is now one of the least contentious issues in British politics'. Leave voters generally were less well educated than Remain voters. Young also predicted the meritocratic elite would become self perpetuating and social mobility would decline in practice. As noted earlier, it has.

If the riots of the 1980s were symptomatic of the crisis of class relations, then those of the 1990s were symptomatic of the crisis of gender relations; more specifically the crisis of masculinity that I exemplified through McDowell's study of the redundant masculinities of her white, male school-leavers in poor areas. This is probably the most overlooked dimension of the Brexit conjuncture. Some of these young men, or others like them, might have become EDL supporters, thus finding an outlet for their anger at their redundancy as (white) men, as in the Winlow et al. (2017) study of EDL 'hatred' for 'soft' (unmasculine) politicians as well as immigration and Muslims. In *PTC*, in talking about the relationship between black labour and class, we argued that 'race is the modality in which class is lived' (Hall et al. 2013: 386). Coming at the end of a long argument, we claimed this as a 'theoretical' point. Although I cannot make a comparable theoretical argument here, I am beginning to think that for white, working class, 'left behind' men with little education (a core element of the Brexit vote) gender is the modality through which class is lived. Their class redundancy is unalterable; but the 'control' dimension of traditional masculinity can still be, and too often still is, reasserted, inappropriately and illegally, in abusive and violent behaviour towards those weaker and more vulnerable. Or in a whole host of anti-social or criminal behaviour, from gang-related 'turf wars' and 'respect'-related fighting to joy-riding. And in pyrrhic victories, like Brexit.[8]

What about the women, some might ask: they were as liable to vote Leave as men and, according to Pilkington's (2016) ethnographic study of the EDL, there were also female supporters, albeit in a minority. To ask the question is to misunderstand how masculinity is a product of gender not sex. In other words, to talk about masculinity is also to talk about femininity, since they always exist in relation to one another; and together, how they relate to each other at any given moment, defines the state of gender relations. A long time ago now, although still much in use, the Australian sociologist Connell (1987) creatively applied Gramsci's concept of hegemony to the notion of masculinity. Thus hegemonic masculinity referred to that form of masculinity that had achieved widespread ascendancy, largely non-coercively, in relation to other masculinities and in relation to femininity. He adds: 'there is likely to be a kind of "fit" between hegemonic masculinity and emphasized femininity' (ibid.: 185). What he meant by that is that where masculinity dominates femininity successfully, hegemonically, there is a degree of 'fit', or widespread acceptance, 'of practices that institutionalize men's dominance over women' (ibid.). If we return to Pilkington's EDL women with this idea in mind, what was clear in her interviews with women supporters was that, while they personally tended not to be in favour of street confrontations with their strong likelihood of violence,

---

[8]Although I am summarising here the role of traditional masculinity specifically in relation to white, working class, male, Brexit voters, its role as a force in global, populist politics is not confined to working-class men, as Freedland's *Guardian* article attests. Using several examples from high status males, including Trump and the supreme court Judge, Brett Kavanaugh, he calls it 'toxic masculinity': 'a sense of male entitlement so extreme it resents any restraint' (Freedland 2018: 3).

they did not challenge the masculinist ethos underpinning the practice either. Hence, in Connell's terms, they were exemplifying 'emphasized femininity'. I think the same argument can be made of Brexit women generally: they did not challenge the angry, rhetorical violence of the campaign but were in lockstep with its hegemonic masculinity.

As for race relations, these have been 'in crisis', more or less visibly, at least since the arrival of the Windrush generation from the late 1940s onwards. The British Nationality Act of 1948, which granted British citizenship to all citizens of the Commonwealth and UK Colonies, was never intended to usher in an era of permanent, black immigration. The result has been successive government's scrambling to undo the Act's unintended consequences with increasingly restrictive immigration and citizenship laws, while attempting to hold in check their more xenophobic colleagues, but failing miserably to eliminate endemic, low level, everyday racism, continuing systemic, institutional racism, the criminalisation of black youth, occasional race riots, etc. Such national leadership led to the whole gamut of disadvantage, discrimination, unthinking prejudice and hate-motivated violence that says, sometimes *sotto voce*, occasionally in a loud scream: BAME lives matter less than white lives. Given that, it may seem presumptuous to pick out the most crisis-ridden moments. 9/11 marked a step change insofar as it introduced a new scapegoat, Muslims, who, in addition to the usual issues of jobs and cultural strangeness, were also seen as a threat to security: as potential 'terrorists'. While Muslims as a security threat were a new scapegoat, the Windrush scandal revealed that old scapegoats, even long-settled British nationals, had not been superseded in the process. And as that new threat occasionally materialised, as it did in the London bombings of 2005, 7/7, committed by British-born Islamic militants, it bolstered anti-immigration sentiment, drove up the hate-crime statistics and increased support for far right parties, including promoting the formation of the EDL, whose sole *raison d'être*, as we saw, was Islamophobia.

Finally, ideology. Was this in crisis? This is trickier to answer. In some ways it wasn't. As Hall says (above) 'market fundamentalism has become the economic common sense, not only of the west but globally'.[9] That is an example of Thatcher's ideological success: 'there is no alternative'. She was not wrong in claiming Tony Blair as her biggest achievement, when subsequent administrations, including Blair's New Labour, never challenged market fundamentalism. It is also the case that the other side of her inheritance, a strong state (or, what we In *PTC* called the 'exceptional state'), has also never seriously been challenged since. In other words, the expansion of state powers in the areas of security, control, criminalisation and public order that *PTC* regarded as exceptional have become, effectively, normalised, part of the new common sense on law and order (cf. Clarke 2010; Coleman et al., eds. 2009). One recent newspaper announcement neatly encapsulated the change: in a tiny insert in *Metro*, the free newspaper, we were told that stop and searches in London had increased by 423% in a year (5 June 2019: 5). There was no reply to the police comment that 'we use it far more assertively than before'. No outrage.[10] The Brixton riots of 1981 were triggered by an 'assertive' stop and search campaign, indecorously named 'Operation Swamp' (Jefferson and Grimshaw 1984: 101).

If the exceptional state constituted the authoritarian dimension of Thatcher's authoritarian populism, her reactionary traditionalism constituted the populist dimension: the regressive element in her apparently contradictory project of what, as we saw earlier, Hall called 'regressive modernization'. This dimension of the project survived less well, questions of nationalism, race and law and order notwithstanding, and despite John Major's short-lived 'Back to Basics' campaign attempting a traditionalist revival. New Labour's liberal cosmopolitanism offered a very different ideological version of modernisation, without breaking with either neoliberal common sense or an authoritarian approach to law and order: 'tough on crime, tough on the causes of crime'. The relationship between traditionalism and cosmopolitanism has been a continuous bone of ideological contention, at least since the so-called culture wars

---

[9] Despite the fact that both the economic crisis of 2008–2009 and the current pandemic-induced one precipitated the suspension of market fundamentalism and the injection of massive amounts of public money and other forms of state intervention.

[10] Now, in the wake of the murder of George Floyd and the Black Lives Matter campaign going global, issues of stop and search and police violence are becoming more visible once again.

of the 1960s, and has played out variously in more recent political struggles over identity, often in the same political party. David Cameron's legalising of same-sex marriage in the teeth of opposition from his own traditionalists was a case in point. In broad terms, it was seen as the key ideological difference between the (traditionalist) 'Somewheres' and the (cosmopolitan) 'Anywheres': between Leavers and Remainers (Goodhart 2017). Overall, then, despite Thatcherism being a hegemonic project in that it was attempting a thoroughgoing restructuring of society across all dimensions, it never quite achieved ideological hegemony despite the Brexit victory and the many now seemingly irreversible changes she did inaugurate.

In sum, these multiple, long-running crises, economic, political, ideological, and of masculinity, race and ethnicity, mostly taking the form of a gently simmering disaffection, occasionally reaching angry boiling points, with their diverse origins, temporalities and tempos and regional specificities, begin to become more intertwined after 2001. It had a new enemy that everyone could agree upon—the Muslim fundamentalist terrorist. It had new political voices to articulate dissatisfactions via new, or newly revived, political parties. It had an increasingly prominent issue, immigration, that addressed multiple concerns including lost jobs and deteriorating public services to upsetting neighbourhood changes and security (cf. Vasilopoulou 2016). Eventually, and serendipitously, it had a unifying cause: Brexit. All that was needed was an inclusive slogan that could condense these diverse disaffections: articulate them in a way that overrode differences. 'Take Back Control' became that slogan and the Referendum result duly marked the moment of a conjunctural crisis. Not, I hasten to add, a new crisis of hegemony such as we fortuitously stumbled across in *PTC* and that ushered in Thatcherism (and Reaganism in the USA) and the neoliberalism that is still the overarching capitalist framework globally, but a new moment in the still ongoing crisis of hegemony that the project of Thatcherism attempted to address. Brexit (along with the election of Trump in the same year) are both, like Thatcherism, populist, hegemonic projects aiming for the wholesale transformation of society rather than simply electoral reversal. In terms of Hall's politics of difference, with which I ended Chapter 7, they are both attempts to reinstate an absolutist version of difference as against a multicultural, hybrid version. Hall's feared 'dangerous moment' has indeed come to pass. Whether or not all such supporters are racist, Derek Sayer's (2017) detailed analysis of both the Brexit and Trump voters demonstrated clearly that they were overwhelmingly white, and English in the case of Brexit. His conclusion that this was 'the electoral equivalent of a white riot' certainly fits with my argument about the centrality of immigration.

References

Antonucci, L., L. Horvath, Y. Kutiyski, and A. Krowei. 2017. The malaise of the squeezed middle: Challenging the narrative of the "left behind" Brexiteer. *Competition & Change* 21 (3): 211–29.

Back, L., and M. Keith. 1999. "Rights and wrongs": Youth, community and narratives of racial violence. In Cohen, ed. (1999: 131–62).

Chancer, L., and J. Andrews (eds.). 2014. *The Unhappy Divorce of Sociology and Psychoanalysis: Diverse Perspectives on the Psychosocial*. Houndmills, Basingstoke: Palgrave Macmillan.

Clarke, J. 2010. Of crises and conjunctures: The problem of the present. *Journal of Communication Inquiry* 34 (4): 337–54.

Clarke, J. 2020. Building the "Boris" bloc: Angry politics in turbulent times. *Soundings* 74: 118–35.

Cochrane, A. 2020. From Brexit to…the break-up of England? Thinking in and beyond nation. In Guderjan et al., eds. (2020: 161–73).

Cohen, P. 1972. Subcultural conflict and working class community. *WPCS* 2: 5–51.

Cohen, P. (ed.). 1999. *New Ethnicities, Old Racisms?*. London: Zed Books.

Coleman, R., J. Sim, S. Tombs, and D. Whyte (eds.). 2009. *State, Power, Crime*. London: Sage.

Connell, R.W. 1987. *Gender and Power: Society, the Person and Sexual Politics*. Cambridge: Polity.

Dench, G., K. Gavron, and M. Young. 2006. *The New East End: Kinship, Race and Conflict*. London: Profile Books.

Freedland, J. 2018. The insidious force in global politics? Toxic masculinity. *The Guardian Opinion*, September 29: 3.

Freud, S. 1957. Mourning and melancholia. In *The Standard Edition of the Complete Psychological Works of Sigmund Freud*, vol. XIV. London: Hogarth Press.

Gadd, D., B. Dixon, and T. Jefferson. 2005. *Why Do They Do It? Racial Harassment in North Staffordshire: Key Findings*. Keele: Centre for Criminological Research, Keele University.

Geddes, A. 2016. The referendum and Britain's broken immigration politic'. In Jackson et al., eds. (2016: 18).

Gentleman, A. 2019. In the eye of the storm. *The Guardian Weekend*, September 14: 22–29.

Gilroy, P. 2004. *After Empire: Melancholia or Convivial Culture?*. London: Routledge.

Goes, E. 2016. The Durham miners' role in Labour's culture wars. In Jackson et al., eds. (2016: 84).

Goodhart, D. 2017. *The Road to Somewhere: The Populist Revolt and the Future of Politics*. London: Hurst & Co. ebook.

Grayson, R., and J. Rutherford (eds.). 2010. *After the Crash: Re-inventing the Left in Britain*. Soundings in collaboration with the Social Liberal Forum and Compass. London: Lawrence and Wishart e-book.

Hall, S. 1988. Introduction. In *The Hard Road to Renewal: Thatcherism and the Crisis of the Left*, S. Hall. London: Verso.

Hall, S. 1998/2017a. The great moving nowhere show. In Hall (2017a: 283–300).

Hall, S. 2003/2017a. New Labour's double-shuffle. In Hall (2017a: 301–16).

Hall, S. 2011/2017a. The neoliberal revolution. In Hall (2017a: 317–35).

Hall, S. 2017a. *Selected Political Writings: The Great Moving Right Show and Other Essays*, ed. with an intro. S. Davison, D. Featherstone, M. Rustin, and B. Schwarz. London: Lawrence and Wishart.

Hall, S. 2017b. *The Fateful Triangle: Race, Ethnicity, Nation*, ed. K. Mercer with a Foreword by H.L. Gates, Jr. Cambridge, MA and London: Harvard University Press.

Hall, S., and T. Jefferson (eds.). 2006. *Resistance Through Rituals: Youth Subcultures in Post-War Britain*, 2nd ed. London: Routledge.

Hall, S., and D. Massey. 2010. Interpreting the Crisis. In Grayson and Rutherford, eds. (2010: 37–46).

Hall, S., C. Critcher, T. Jefferson, J. Clarke, and B. Roberts. 2013. *Policing the Crisis: Mugging, the State and Law and Order*, 2nd ed. Houndmills, Basingstoke: Palgrave Macmillan.

Hewitt, R. 1996. *Routes of Racism: The Social Basis of Racist Action*. London: Trentham Books.

Hewitt, R. 1997. *Routes of Racism: The Manual*. London: Greenwich Council's Central Race Equality Unit and Greenwich Education Service.

Jackson, D., E. Thorsen, and D. Wring (eds.). 2016. *EU Referendum Analysis 2016: Media, Voters and the Campaign: Early Reflections from Leading UK*

Academics. Poole, UK: The Centre of the Study of Journalism, Culture and Community, Bournemouth University.

Jefferson, T. 2014. Racial hatred and racial prejudice: A difference that makes a difference. In Chancer and Andrews, eds. (2014: 359–79).

Jefferson, T. 2015. What is racism? Othering, prejudice and hate-motivated violence. *International Journal for Crime, Justice and Social Democracy* 4 (4): 120–35.

Jefferson, T., and R. Grimshaw. 1984. *Controlling the Constable: Police Accountability in England and Wales*. London: Frederick Muller/The Cobden Trust.

Keith, M.J. 2008. Between being and becoming? Rights, responsibilities and the politics of multiculture in the new East End. *Sociological Research Online* 13 (5): 11. Available at http://www.socresonline.org.uk/13/5/11.html.

Lanchester, J. 2010. *Whoops! Why Everyone Owes Everyone and No One Can Pay*. London: Penguin.

Macpherson, W. 1999. *The Stephen Lawrence Inquiry: Report of an Inquiry by Sir William Macpherson of Cluny*. London: Stationery Office.

McDowell, L. 2003. *Redundant Masculinities? Employment Change and White Working Class Youth*. Oxford: Blackwell.

Parekh, B. 2000. *Commission on the Future of Multi-ethnic Britain*. London: Runnymede Trust.

Pilkington, H. 2016. *Loud and Proud: Passion and Politics in the English Defence League*. Manchester: Manchester University Press.

Rutherford, J. 2019. From Woodstock to Brexit: The tragedy of the liberal middle class. *New Statesman*, December 19: 1–10. https://www.newstatesman.com/politics/brexit/2019/12/woodstock-brexit.

Sayer, D. 2017. White riot—Brexit, Trump, and post-factual politics. *Historical Sociology* 30 (1): 92–106.

Seabrook, J. 1973. *City Close-Up*. Harmondsworth: Penguin.

Shamsie, K. 2018. Citizen of nowhere. *The Guardian Review* November 17.

Vasilopoulou, S. 2016. Campaign frames in the Brexit referendum. In Jackson et al., eds. (2016: 114–15).

Winlow, S., Steve Hall, and J. Treadwell. 2017. *The Rise of the Right: English Nationalism and the Transformation of Working Class Politics*. Bristol: Policy Press.

Young, M. 1958. *The Rise of the Meritocracy 1870–2033: An Essay on Education and Equality*. London: Thames & Hudson.

Young, M., and P. Willmott. 1957. *Family and Kinship in East London*. London: Routledge & Kegan Paul.

Younge, G. 2019. Given Britain's history it's no surprise racism infects politics. *The Guardian Journal*, November 29: 1–2.

10

Conclusion: From *Policing the Crisis* to Trump, and Beyond

I started the book with several questions. Given the existing, vast literature on Hall and his work, I asked: 'why another volume? Why now? And, why should criminologists be interested?' The book, I went on to say, would 'attempt to answer these questions'. Let me offer here a brief summary answer to all three questions. My starting point was a dual recognition: that despite Hall's reputation within criminology, the existing literature about him largely concerned cultural studies and was not written by criminologists; and that what had been written about him by criminologists, which tended to centre on *Policing the Crisis (PTC)*, somewhat misunderstood what that book was attempting. Generally speaking, neither issue might have warranted an intervention since Hall's primary contribution has indeed been to cultural studies and all of us who have put pen to paper have experienced being misunderstood. But, the additional element in this instance was the emergence of a body of work specifically calling itself cultural criminology and claiming Hall as one of its father figures. If even those calling themselves cultural criminologists misunderstood what *PTC* was attempting, then another volume could be justified.

However, another volume would not have materialised had I not been asked to write about the contribution to criminology of a person from a list of names provided by the publisher. Hall was on that list. Had he not been, I would probably have declined the invitation. Such is the way contingency works. So, one answer to 'why now?' is because I was asked. I remember Hall once responding similarly to a question about the origins of his writings. Mostly in response to invitations, he said. But, 'why now?' also has a political dimension, the importance of which grew along with the book. If reading is a voyage of discovery for the reader, writing is a voyage of discovery for the author. I write, Juliet Mitchell once said somewhere, to discover what I don't know. Any creative act is the same. The endpoint can never be entirely predicted. In my case, what I thought of at the outset as merely exemplary, namely the moment of Brexit to demonstrate the continuing relevance of conjunctural analysis, ballooned into three chapters (if you count Chapter 7 devoted to Hall's 'politics of difference'). In other words, the process of engaging with Hall's work over the period of writing this book has heightened the significance for me of conjunctural analysis, the book's core concern. Hall said towards the end of his life that 'I think conjuncturally about politics now'. Me too.

Hall had a special talent for conjuncture and conjunctural analysis. The book argues that this was evident from his earliest writings and that it achieved its finest flowering in *PTC* and his subsequent writings on Thatcherism. This is why the book should be of interest to criminologists. In the first place because its absence from the writings of cultural criminologists is what renders their work theory-driven, hence ultimately abstract rather than concrete. And, secondly, conjunctural analysis is inherently political. Cultural studies was nothing if not political; unfortunately 'not political' is what it became in some postmodern iterations, much to Hall's chagrin. For cultural criminology to take the apolitical, postmodern path is something to be resisted because criminology too is nothing if not political. How can it not be, engaging, as it must, with state power in all its various forms and guises? So, criminologists *should* be interested in conjunctural analysis, which is not to say that this is the only possible intellectual/political engagement, as Hall recognised.

It would be tempting to end here. This has been a long and demanding road and the book is already much longer than originally envisaged. However, as I write these words, the story which continues to hold the world's attention, briefly overshadowing even pandemic news, is the American election and Trump: when will he concede and what then? This global interest in the fate of America is partly a function of America's significance as a world power; but it is also driven by the fact that Trump is one among many populist world leaders and his particular fate, we think, can help us understand something more broadly about this present moment of populism, especially whether the populist tide is now turning. Given that the specific object of attention of conjunctural analysis is the present moment, it seemed odd, and politically irresponsible, to end without briefly addressing this question. Hall would certainly have done so.

Three other considerations assisted my decision. First, my prior analysis of Brexit, which almost coincided with Trump's election victory of 2016, provides a readymade comparative dimension of two different but similar populist social formations. Second, there was the fortuitous appearance of two contrasting, Gramscian-inspired analyses of the Trump moment (Fraser 2019; Hart 2020). Between them, together with an earlier Hart (2019) essay, these presented me with an economical way of structuring theoretical and political points about conjunctural analysis that I thought a conclusion might usefully highlight. Finally, Gillian Hart's work, which is centred on the idea of a global conjuncture and what this means theoretically, empirically and politically (Hart 2019, 2020), offered not just the chance to think about the global dimension of populism, but also to develop Hall's efforts to provide an international framework for his 'politics of difference' that we encountered in Chapter 7. Hart copiously cites Hall and *PTC* as the inspiration for her work. However, her innovative use of the ideas that inspired her has now enabled me to think anew about the global dimension of any conjuncture. In so doing, she has become an inspiration for this conclusion and a fitting follow up to Hall.

Using the work of Hart and Fraser to structure what follows essentially involves three key issues: the politics of populism; the role of the state;

and the centrality of multiple, interacting contradictions in conjunctural theorising. Although both of their analyses are inspired by Gramsci, their differences are more significant. Politically, the key difference is about the nature of authoritarian populism and its relationship to 'left' or 'progressive' populism. This connects with whether or not the state has a significant place in their respective analyses. As for their theoretical differences, how the relationships among multiple contradictions are dealt with is central. Is the complexity of these interrelationships recognised as befits a conjunctural analysis? After addressing these issues using Hart and Fraser's analyses of the accession of Trump, I end with my own brief analysis of where his failure to be re-elected leaves Trumpism. However, I start with Hart's 2019 article which addresses the politics of populism and, specifically, whether a left populism is possible.

The Politics of Populism: Is a Left Populism Possible?

The first of Hart's two articles, 'From authoritarian to left populism? Reframing debates' (2019), is essentially a discussion of the concept 'authoritarian populism' and its relationship to the idea of 'left populism'. Her purpose is to reframe the debate currently 'cast in terms of whether or not left populisms can defeat right-wing forms of populism' to ask '*how* to produce deeper critical understandings of the forces generating intensifying nationalisms, racisms, and populist politics in the neoliberal era, in not only Europe but also many regions of the world beyond Euro-America' (ibid.: 310). Global conjunctural analysis is her answer, which is thus implicitly set against those advocating a left populism. Effectively then, Hart argues that a global conjunctural approach renders redundant the debate between left and right populism—whether the former can defeat the latter.

Hart recognised Hall as the original author 'of the concept of authoritarian populism as part of his critical analysis of popular support for Thatcherism' (ibid.: 308), and Hall's usage of it in understanding Thatcherism is central to the arguments of many of those whose work is cited: like Fassin (2018), who sees populism as 'a weapon' in the service of neoliberalism. This usage, in which populism is intrinsically connected to authoritarianism and the political emergence of Thatcher's neoliberal project, is contrasted with those liberal writers who regard authoritarian populism as opposed to neoliberalism and with those on the left who think that discursively constructing a left populism is the pressing political task. This left-populist approach, associated especially with the post-marxist work of Laclau and Mouffe (Laclau and Mouffe 1985; Laclau 2005; Mouffe 2018), essentially entails attempting to reorientate the discourse of the right in a progressive direction through providing new articulations emphasising equality and social justice. The goal? A new Gramscian 'common will' connecting working class and new social movement demands through a 'chain of equivalences' (Mouffe 2018).

In the second of her two articles, Hart specifically links the work of Fraser (2019) with that of Mouffe (2018): they both 'see the rise of the right as a senile disorder of late neoliberalism that calls for a dose of good electoral politics to steer it in a more progressive direction' (Hart 2020: 240). I think this criticism is a little harsh. Mouffe is aware of the importance of authoritarian populism to Thatcherism, of the role of the state as an oppressive institution, of the need to radically democratise existing representative institutions, and of the importance of the affective dimension in politics, and Fraser might repudiate the connection to Mouffe's discursive approach given her opposite tendency of a latent economism. Nonetheless, Hart is onto something. The real problem with both, in what Hart (ibid.) calls their 'distinctive though related ways', is, ultimately, the failure to take conjunctural analysis seriously enough. That requires, as Hall insisted in his criticism of Laclau and Mouffe as we saw in Chapter 6, attending to the linkage between discourse and social forces. That is the articulation that matters and not simply the articulation between discursive elements. It is not that Mouffe and Fraser are unaware of the importance of social forces; but that, as we shall see in the case of Fraser, the connections made are general rather than conjunctural and thus end up losing sight of significant connections. Crucially, for present purposes, this affects how she understands the relationship between authoritarian populism and the state, and the relationships among contradictions, which become subordinated to her schematic, ideal typical model.

Authoritarian Populism and the Authoritarian State: Complementary Poles

If we fast forward to Hart's final section of her earlier paper, 'toward a global conjunctural analysis', by which time Poulantzas has been introduced into the debate, she seeks to build on the complementary differences between Poulantzas's (1978) concept of 'authoritarian statism' and Hall's responding 'concept of authoritarian populism' (Hart 2019: 319). Starting with Hall, Hart returns to the importance of *PTC*:

> Apropos Hall, instead of starting with authoritarian populism I have found it more useful to go back to the coauthored volume *Policing the Crisis* (1978) - a fully dialectical analysis of the simultaneous economic and political crises of the 1970s, which makes it vividly clear how race and class are profoundly imbricated in ways that paved the way for Thatcherism - and which also dramatizes the authoritarian tendencies linked to moral panics over crime and race that preceded Thatcherism and enabled it to gain traction. Rereading the book for me has also made it clear how it was Hall's dialectical reworking of Laclau's (1977) concept of articulation that enabled his profoundly important intervention in the South African race versus class debate in 1980 - which represents, more broadly, a demonstration of Marx's method with vitally important political stakes. This dimension of Hall's work has been sidelined in the debate over authoritarian populism - and constitutes, in my view, a far more significant contribution. (ibid.: 320)

What I think Hart is emphasising here is the importance of starting with specific moments, conjunctures, rather than the concept of authoritarian populism, as contributors to the populism debate tend to. It was this that led Hall to notice the 'authoritarian tendencies linked to moral panics over crime and race'. This 'paved the way' for Thatcherism, enabling it to 'gain traction'. The reference to Hall's intervention in the South African race versus class debate is a reference to his paper 'Race, articulation, and Societies structured in dominance' (Hall 1980a/2019), the second of two papers originally prepared for UNESCO on race, class and colonialism (see Hall 1978 for the first of these). As Morley (2019: 106) argues it, the 'declared aim' of the essay 'is to develop an analysis of the historically specific forms of racism and its effects and of the different ways in which racist ideologies have operated in specific historical and empirical conjunctures'. In doing this, 'in working through…theoretical and methodological questions as carefully as [he does, the essay]… makes a major contribution' (ibid.) to how to understand the articulation of race and class. I shall return to this question below. But, first a word on Poulantzas and 'authoritarian statism', the concept to which Hall's 'authoritarian populism' was 'a response'.

As we have seen, the key figures Hall tended to cite in terms of influences, apart from Marx, were Althusser, Gramsci and Laclau in his Marxist phase. However, we members of the Centre for Contemporary Cultural Studies (CCCS) also spent a lot of time in the 1970s reading, discussing and debating the enormous output of Poulantzas (five major books in a decade, before his untimely death aged 43), whose writings, although much influenced by Althusser, were also highly original. The admiration between Hall and Poulantzas was mutual: Poulantzas was a great admirer of *PTC*—an 'excellent book' that he found 'extremely stimulating' having 'read it cautiously and annotated nearly every page' (letter to Hall, 29/4/79)—and Hall's review of Poulantzas's last book, *State, Power, Socialism (SPS)*, (which unfortunately had also to serve as an obituary notice) called him 'a theoretician of exceptional and original stature' who 'set his distinctive mark on some of the most advanced and intractable debates within Marxist theory' (Hall 1980b: 60, 61). As always with Hall, generous acknowledgement was tempered with critical assessment. In Poulantzas's case, as with Althusser, Hall commented on the 'tension…between "structure" and "practice"…which continued to haunt his…work' and a 'tendency towards a *formalism* of exposition' (ibid.). Hall's overall assessment of the book is paradigmatic of his critical generosity. The book is 'profoundly unsettled' with 'a real theoretical unevenness…Yet, this…also constitutes…its generative openness…in many ways [it is]…clearly coming apart at the seams…It is strikingly *unfinished*. It offers us a picture of one of the most able and fluent of "orthodox" Marxist-structuralist thinkers putting himself and his ideas at risk. This is Poulantzas adventuring…The example it leaves to us - above all, in its determination, at the end, to address questions of the utmost and immediate political relevance - is, in a very special way, exemplary' (ibid.: 68–69).

While it is appropriate to remind readers of the influence of Poulantzas (one of my readers thought I might have underplayed his influence on Hall), it is their different takes on authoritarianism that concern us here. Although Hall thought 'authoritarian statism' was 'an important formulation, which nets certain critical features of Western European capitalist states in a period of crisis, and usefully distinguishes it from "fascism"' (ibid.: 68), he did not think Poulantzas took enough note of the issue of popular support: 'how…progress towards "authoritarian statism" has been secured at the base by a complementary shift in popular consent-to-authority - the product of a remarkable and intensive ideological struggle, of which "Thatcherism" is a symptomatic example'. This is why Hall had proceeded elsewhere 'to argue that the thesis of "authoritarian statism" needs to be complemented by a theory of "authoritarian populism"' (ibid.).[1]

Once again, it is the importance of conjunctural specificity that requires the two terms, authoritarian statism and authoritarian populism, be thought in tandem. In true Hallian fashion, Hart wants the best of both. In addition to *PTC*'s focus on the everyday world of British life, she wants *SPS*'s attention to the novel form of authoritarian state emerging in Europe and America: more controlling, less democratic and with 'draconian' attacks on civil liberties. It should not be forgotten, however, that the notion of the 'exceptional' state in *PTC* is not dissimilar: our focus on popular consent was not at the expense of noticing changes in the form of the state; they were, as Hall noted, complementary. These complementarities underpin Hart's own 'current efforts to bring resurgent nationalisms and populist politics in South Africa, India, and the United States into the same spatiohistorical frame of analysis' (Hart 2019: 321): her own effort to reframe the debates.

Hart ends by suggesting that if you bring 'the United States into the same frame as South Africa and India', the question becomes why it took so long for Trump to achieve power, 'given the long histories

---

[1] The anti-statism dimension of the popular support for Thatcherism survives in the Brexiteers hostility to the overarching EU state dictating 'our' laws and culture.

of racism, right-wing nationalism, and populist politics in the United States; the ravages of neoliberal forms of capitalism; and the abandonment of the working class by the Democratic Party' (ibid.). Her second article begins to answer this question; but first we need to see how Fraser explains Trump and whether or not this is compatible with a conjunctural analysis.

Ideal Types or Conjunctural Analysis: The Importance of Contradictions

The title of Nancy Fraser's short book, *The Old is Dying and the New Cannot be Born*, is a quote from Gramsci that suggests she might be attempting a conjunctural analysis. However, despite that, and the liberal use of the concept hegemony, her actual approach suggests otherwise. She starts with the assumption of a 'global political crisis' evidenced by Trump's election victory and the similar triumphs of racist, anti-immigrant and authoritarian regimes around the world. This crisis, a consequence of the widespread collapse of belief in established political authority and its accompanying common sense view of the world, is, she claims, Gramsci's 'crisis of hegemony'. Hegemonic worldviews are sustained by a ruling class-led alliance of social forces, 'the *hegemonic bloc*', which always embody a set of beliefs about justice and right, or normative assumptions about distribution (how goods and income should be distributed; broadly the economic structure and class) and recognition (how is respect and esteem ordered; broadly, a society's status hierarchies). Challenges to existing hegemonies come from the dominated classes forming a counter-hegemonic bloc and constructing an alternative, '*counterhegemony*' based on a different set of normative assumptions. As we shall see, these assumptions can be either 'progressive' or 'reactionary'. These then are the key terms—hegemony/counterhegemony; distribution/recognition; progressive/reactionary—together with neoliberalism/populism with which Fraser explains 'what made Trump and Trumpism possible', namely, 'the breakup of a previous hegemonic bloc - and the discrediting of its distinctive nexus of distribution and recognition' (Fraser 2019: 11).

Essentially, the explanation is in terms of a see-sawing between reactionary and progressive versions of neoliberalism which are finally upended by the successful emergence of Trump's reactionary populist alternative to either form of neoliberalism. Thus, Bill Clinton's Democratic victory in the early 1990s was the result of successfully combining a regressive politics of distribution—one 'that fostered a vast upward redistribution of wealth and income' (Fraser 2019: 15)—with a progressive politics of recognition—one that supported feminists, anti-racists, environmentalists and other progressive forces which established the hegemony of 'progressive neoliberalism'. Achieving this entailed breaking with the older Democratic alliance (who remain unlabelled as either progressive or reactionary) and defeating the 'reactionary neoliberalism' of the preceding Republican dominated years which, as the name implies, combined a regressive politics of distribution with a regressive politics of recognition, one 'with an exclusionary vision of a just social order: ethnonational, anti-immigrant, and pro-Christian, if not overtly racist, patriarchal, and homophobic' (ibid.: 16). (The British comparison would be Blair's 'cosmopolitan' new Labour neoliberalism defeating the regressive traditionalist version of neoliberalism that was Thatcher's legacy.)

However, this new hegemonic bloc of progressive neoliberalism left many behind, as neoliberalism let 'uncompetitive' manufacturing industries decay and the cosmopolitan progressives looked down on the old-fashioned, parochial and paternalistic cultures of the left-behind working classes. The situation worsened as de-industrialisation accelerated, casual, low-wage jobs proliferated, and living standards declined. The election of Obama, who expanded Medicaid and adopted the rhetoric of Occupy Wall Street, nonetheless continued with progressive neoliberalism 'despite its declining popularity' (ibid.: 20). (Interestingly, the Republican years of George W. Bush, 2001–2008, between Clinton and Obama are passed over in silence: were these also *progressive* neoliberal years?) Things came to a head in the 2015–2016 election season when two outsiders, Bernie Sanders and Donald Trump, attempted to put together radical alternatives to the status quo. Sanders' alternative was a '*progressive populism*' consisting of an inclusive politics of recognition combined with a progressive, socialist politics of distribution; Trump's was a '*reactionary populism*' consisting of a populist politics of distribution premised on large-scale infrastructural projects combined with 'a hyperreactionary politics of recognition' (ibid.: 23): exclusionary, nationalist, racist, misogynistic and homophobic. Thereafter, the progressive populist option disappeared with the selection of Hillary Clinton rather than Sanders as the Democratic candidate, thus reinstating the status quo option of progressive neoliberalism. Trump, after winning the election on his reactionary populist option, abandoned 'the populist distributive policies' and 'proceeded to double down on the reactionary politics of recognition, hugely intensified and ever more vicious' (ibid.: 24–25).

The result was, according to Fraser, 'not reactionary populism, but hyperreactionary neoliberalism'. However, this 'does not constitute a new hegemonic bloc…It is, on the contrary, chaotic, unstable, and fragile' (ibid.: 26). This is the nature of the current political crisis in the USA: 'In this situation, the words of Gramsci ring true, "The old is dying and the new cannot be born; in this interregnum a great variety of morbid symptoms appear"' (ibid.: 29). Although Fraser does not downplay the scale of the problem in practice, what is needed (in theory) to produce a new, progressive hegemonic bloc is a progressive populism that combines 'egalitarian redistribution', thus effectively aligning 'working class supporters of Trump and of Sanders', and 'nonhierarchical recognition', thus effectively making the alliance of progressive forces more class aware and the left-behind working class communities less beholden to 'militarism, xenophobia and ethnonationalism' (ibid.: 32).[2]

Despite its somewhat schematic distinctions (politics of distribution/politics of recognition) and use of simple labels (progressive/regressive), can this charting of shifts between moments nevertheless pass muster as a conjunctural analysis, broadly defined? Or, should it be seen as a model: a set of ideal types to capture certain features of

---

[2]Although, earlier, I said that Fraser might repudiate Hart's bracketing her with Mouffe (2018), the idea of attempting to reduce the appeal of working-class xenophobia does resemble Mouffe's ideas about disarticulation/rearticulation: the need to disarticulate xenophobic discourse from its regressive, right populist version of democratic demands by entering into a 'chain of equivalences' with other democratic demands that thus create, through this rearticulation, a progressive or left populist version of democratic demands.

the period under investigation? Despite her use of historical exemplification, which in many ways exceed her rather too narrowly conceived model/types, I think the omissions and related problems are too many to warrant describing it as a conjunctural analysis. Take the moment of reactionary neoliberalism, the moment of Reaganism that equated with British Thatcherism. As we know with Thatcherism, this was also a populist moment, one that required constructing popular support for its new neoliberal agenda as well as an authoritarian state to aggressively impose it against fierce opposition. But authoritarian populism gets no mention, nor any convincing replacement idea of how a reactionary politics of recognition built support for its neoliberal politics of distribution. Thatcher's authoritarian state lived on through succeeding administrations, including the years of New Labour's Blairism. Yet there is no mention of the state at all in Fraser's discussion of progressive neoliberalism, despite the fact that Fraser is well aware of the mass incarceration of poor, young black men for minor drug offences during the Clinton administration (ibid.: 34). The subsequent George W. Bush years (about which nothing at all is said) were dominated by 9/11, the war on terror and a host of new, repressive state measures. It is difficult to see how locking up large numbers of young black men, largely for being poor, is compatible with a *progressive* politics of recognition (which embraced antiracism and multiculturalism), nor how a repressive, authoritarian state can be deemed hegemonic, but both have somehow to be incorporated in Fraser's 'hegemonic bloc of progressive neoliberalism' which lasts right up until the interruption of Trump's reactionary populism. Expressed differently, the term progressive neoliberalism is simply too restrictive and static a concept to embrace the multiplicity of contradictions—economic, political, ideological, cultural—with their different origins and temporalities, promoted by the collapse of the old social democratic hegemony and the painfully protracted attempt to install a neoliberal alternative, which, despite being the economic common sense of the age, has never become hegemonic politically.

Hart's analysis of the moment of Trump, or 'Trump-Bannonism', is differently focused, on the global rather than the domestic nature of the conjuncture, and framed by a novel question: hence the article's intriguing title, 'Why did it take so long? Trump-Bannonism in a global conjunctural frame' (2020). Being, in my terms, properly conjunctural, it has a very different feel to Fraser's book. For a start, in contrast to Fraser's assumption of a global political crisis based simply on the worldwide appearance of reactionary populist regimes, Hart provides a definition of the phenomenon she is dealing with: 'global conjunctural moments [are]…major turning points when interconnected forces at play at multiple levels and spatial scales in different regions of the world have come together to create new conditions with worldwide implications and reverberations' (Hart 2020: 242). Although this seems to reintroduce the notion of crisis ('major turning points') into the definition of conjuncture that I thought (in Chapter 2) was only definitional of certain conjunctures, it feels enlightening here.

She mentions three such 'major turning points': 'the end of the Cold War' [the 1990s], the moment that signalled 'the widely presumed and celebrated global triumph of neoliberal capitalism combined with secular liberal democracy'; 'the late 1940s [the moment of the emergence of the Cold War Era] and the late 1960s/early 1970s' [the moment that birthed neo-liberalism] (ibid.). To understand the present moment of 'resurgent nationalisms, racisms and populist politics in many regions', she says, we will have to revisit these earlier 'global conjunctural moments' but also 'the *longue durée* processes of racial capitalism, settler colonialism, and imperialism…through which South Africa, India and the US were formed as nation-states' (ibid.). A tall order; too tall for present purposes. However, it is worth emphasising why she thinks this global approach important and why, in particular, South Africa and India have been chosen to help illuminate 'Trump-Bannonism'. First, she thinks advocates of left populism, like Mouffe and Fraser, 'radically underestimate the analytical and political challenges of the current conjuncture', which for her entail 'deeper spatio-historical understandings' (ibid.: 240, 241). As for the choice of South Africa and India, these are secular liberal democracies where 'neoliberal projects only took hold in the 1990s' (ibid.: 241) and where populist forces have captured state power. In other words, core similarities offer the prospect of each helping illuminate her 'global frame of analysis' (ibid.).

However, our concerns mean that we must leave behind her discussion of her global conjunctural frame and how focusing on 'major turning points' helps illuminate South Africa, India and the USA, 'as variously connected yet historically specific nodes in globally interconnected historical geographies - and as sites in the *production* of global processes' (ibid.). It is, in ambition and execution, an impressive achievement that bodes well for the book she is writing, for which this essay is 'a prolegomenon'. Instead, we turn to why, in global conjunctural terms, Trumpism was a late entrant to the populist 'club'. Even here, in the interests of space, we must forsake her detailed argument for her six-point summary. Although it does her less than justice, it will suffice to make my argument.

She starts with point (a), the global conjunctural moment of the 1960s and 1970s, and mentions the intense struggles between left and right of the 1960s, the intensified capitalist crisis of the 1970s, and the 'mounting political crises associated with the Vietnam War…revolutions in Iran and Nicaragua, and the Soviet invasion of Afghanistan' (ibid.: 251). Here, then, is our eminently recognisable 'crisis of hegemony', with the conflict in Northern Ireland, we suggested in *PTC*, our 'own backyard "Vietnam"' (Hall et al. 2013: 255). This is followed in point (b) by Reaganism: 'Reagan's accession to power in 1981 represented the dismantling of Fordist hegemony, the consolidation of a project grounded in a new right-wing coalition [neoliberalism], and the emergence of new forms of U.S. imperialism driven both by global financial restructuring and…Proxy Wars…in which the fiercely anti-communist Christian Right that coalesced in the 1970s…played a central role' (ibid.). In British terms, we had Thatcherism, the Falklands war (that got Thatcher re-elected with a huge majority after the unpopularity of her early reforms), elements of a new Right and an emergent nationalism but no precise equivalent of the 'fiercely, anti-communist Christian Right'. Christian values do survive, despite declining church attendance, but these tend to work indirectly, through their association with 'Britishness' on state occasions and in key celebratory moments, for example, rather than as a political lobby group (although Mary Whitehouse's religiously-inspired, anti-permissiveness campaigns of the 1960s were a lobbying group).

The next step in her argument, point (c), moves to 'the end of the Cold War' [the 1990s] when 'there was a sharp rupture in the right-wing coalition between the Christian Right and the neo-conservatives that swept Reagan to power' (Hart 2020: 251). This, again, has no British equivalent; nor is it mentioned as part of the move from reactionary to progressive neoliberalism which Fraser (2019: 35) glosses purely in articulatory terms: 'the Clintonite wing of the Democratic Party quietly disarticulated that older alliance'. Hart (2020: 251) adds that 'tensions within the Christian Right further undermined Patrick Buchanan's bid for state power on a populist ticket'. Here, then, is one reason for why it took so long for Trumpism to emerge: Buchanan's defeat, on an 'America First' platform that Trump would later steal, demonstrated that the necessary alignment of conjunctural forces was still but a possibility. What also delayed Trumpism, and point (d) in Hart's argument, was that most people were 'caught up in a frenzy of consumerism and spiraling debt', made possible 'by financial deregulation under Reagan and Clinton, asset price inflation, massive foreign capital inflows that lowered the cost of debt, and enabled…by the tsunami of cheap consumer goods from China and Chinese purchasing of Treasury Bonds'. In offsetting 'shrinking employment, stagnant incomes, and escalating inequality', this mass consumerism managed to hold in check 'resurgent right-wing populist movements' (ibid.). Here, the consumerist 'upside' of Thatcherism's brutal 'downside' is recognisable.

Point (e), 'The 9/11 attacks…took the wind out of the sails of isolationist nationalist movements like Buchanan's by unleashing waves of militant patriotism combined with Islamophobia' (ibid.): a further reason for the delayed moment of Trump's nationalist populism. Additionally, 'the Bush II' years witnessed 'the Christian Right …[becoming] deeply embedded in the White House' and, as a result of the wars in Iraq and Afghanistan, valorisation of the military became part of common sense understanding. Finally, point (f), the billions of dollars used to bail out the banks in 2008 following the financial crash exposed the hypocrisy of neoliberalism's free-market ideology. This '*also* exposed the fragility of a consumer debt dynamic that is peculiar to the U.S. because of its imperial position. *In addition* this was the moment when Obama assumed power, *and* when the wars in Iraq and Afghanistan had been thoroughly discredited' (ibid.: 252). In other words, some of the things that served to delay the Trump moment, like debt-driven consumerism and militaristic common sense, were now being questioned.

In sum: 'The confluence of these contradictions created a conjunctural moment in which Buchananesque articulations of racist nationalism and nativism could take root and metastasise over the Obama years - a process driven not only by Trump, but the much wider global networks of right-wing white Christian nationalism in which Stephen Bannon remains situated' (ibid.). Why all this remains properly conjunctural, even in the brief and truncated version presented here, and not schematic in the ideal-typical way that we saw in the Fraser analysis, is because in Hart's argument multiple contradictions do not simply line up in either a reactionary or progressive direction but are riven with internal conflicts, like when the coalition of the right gets split between the Christian Right and mainstream neoconservatives, and are constantly being contingently reassembled, like when the failure of the wars in Iraq and Afghanistan enable the nativist ideology of patriotism to gain strength. It is only in understanding the complexity of these contingently assembled multiple forces can we 'shed light on the slippages, openings, and contradictions where pressure might be applied, as well as connections and alliances from which new possibilities might emerge' (ibid.: 241) and construct an appropriate, conjunctural politics. If Hart's question was why it took so long for Trumpist populism to achieve state power, it remains to ask whether the defeat of Trump signals a global shift of some kind. In the light of this defeat, how might a conjunctural framework evaluate the present balance of forces?

After Trump: Climate Change, the Refugee Crisis, Black Lives Matter and the Covid Pandemic

Let us start with the US election result: a win for Joe Biden. Does the defeat of Trump signal the defeat of Trumpism? Two things at least suggest not. Firstly, the narrowness of the democratic victory and, secondly, the fact that Biden represents a return to the Democratic status quo that was unsuccessful in 2016 rather than something more radical. In other words, the conversion of the narrow Trump victory of 2016 into a narrow Biden victory in 2020 indicates that we are still witnessing a political stalemate: the old is dying and the new cannot be born.[3] However, the fact that the Democrats were able this time, not only to win the popular vote (again) but also the crucial electoral college vote in some of Trump's rust belt states, is a change that signals something. Let me briefly explore what that might be.

Since becoming President in 2016, Trump faced at least four challenges that, collectively, have become crucial to understanding the global conjuncture: climate change; the refugee crisis; Black Lives Matter (BLM); and the Covid pandemic. On all four counts he has failed miserably—but not according to him and his core supporters: his base. So, it is important to say how his failures affected the 2020 result. Take climate change. Here, despite overwhelming evidence to the contrary including an extraordinary level of destruction resulting from fires, flooding and extreme weather events, his strategy has been, at best, denial. Through his commitment to the extractive industries like oil, shale gas and coal, he has actively promoted climate change. His continuing support (the second biggest popular vote ever) suggests that this denial coupled with promotion strategy is something his core supporters share. This is assisted by the fact that many of these will also be evangelical Christians, for whom climate catastrophes can readily be interpreted, and often are, as 'God's will' (a noticeable response among Hochschild's (2016) evangelical Tea Party interviewees too in response to local manmade environmental disasters that had often seriously compromised their health and livelihoods). Trump's courting of the Christian Right fits a reading of this kind.

However, beyond his committed base, things looked different. More mainstream Republicans and progressive capitalists are mindful of the

---

[3] Some might regard a lead of 7 million in the popular vote and 74 in the electoral college votes as a fairly comprehensive victory, as indeed it was eventually. However, since many of the votes in the 'flipped' states were close, it is also accurate to call the resulting victory narrow: comprehensive but narrowly so. This is important if we are to draw a realistic picture of what lies ahead politically, which is my concern here.

growing economic as well as environmental costs of denial. Disinvestment threats to fossil fuels along with the emergence of green energy are partially remaking the capitalist landscape: not quickly enough for committed activists but happening nevertheless. So, whatever the precise balance of capitalist forces supporting Trump (do business friendly taxes and reduced regulation compensate for the market volatility that came with his chaotic presidency?), the ground is shifting away from denialism. Trump's regressive pledges on bringing back dying, dirty industries, despite licensing lots of extractive industries on public land, have largely been unfulfilled. Faced with the green challenge, not just from activists but from capital's more progressive wing, this was never likely to happen. Moreover, Trump's withdrawal of the USA from the Paris Climate Accord would have pleased only the more reactionary capitalists. And the changing demographic in the South and some of the other swing states—younger, better educated and more diverse—is not a climate denial demographic. All of these factors suggest that Trump's denial of the reality of climate change would have worked against him among all those not already convinced Republicans.

Trump's stated strategy on immigration and the refugee crisis was to 'build the wall', make Mexico pay for it and crack down on 'illegals'. Lacking the power to enforce the Democrat-controlled House of Representatives or the Mexican President to produce the necessary billions of dollars to finance the wall's construction, he doubled down on the 'crackdown', which proved to be racist in language and discriminatory and inhumane in practice. This may have gone down well with his increasingly fanatical base, but less well with the large Latino communities and black and Asian people in the border states. This cost him, dearly. Of the four States bordering Mexico, only Texas still has a Republican majority. Neighbouring New Mexico and Arizona, both Republican wins in 2016, have now been flipped. California, unsurprisingly, retained its Democratic majority. Changing demographics also played their part. Young people voted in much greater numbers than in 2016, especially in the fiercely contested states, and these were mostly Biden voters, even more so in the case of black, Asian and Latino youth. So, again, his chosen strategy on immigration was counter-productive electorally with those beyond the already persuaded.

In order to understand the increased visibility and global spread of BLM in 2016 after the police killing of George Floyd, we need to remind ourselves of its origins in 2014, during the Obama administration, in the aftermath of the police killing of Michael Brown in Ferguson (Lowery 2017).[4] This, too, had a pre-history since police killings of unarmed black people and resulting protests did not start with Michel Brown, but are part of the long-standing, contentious and troubled relations between black communities and the police. For example, almost all the riots since the 1930 were sparked by a policing incident (ibid.). However, what changed under the Obama administration was rising expectations among the black community about the possibilities of change and, concomitantly, increased fear and anger among sections of the white community that this might indeed come to pass. The right wing, Republican Tea Party movement, forerunners of what would become Trump's base, formed in 2009, the year after Obama's first election victory. Instead of the racial reconciliation or 'post-racial' unity that some thought the Obama election presaged, the racial divide hardened: police killings of black men produced not only BLM but, on two separate occasions in 2016, in Dallas and Baton Rouge, the retributive shooting of police officers by lone gunmen, killing three and injuring others; and nine black Americans were killed in a church in Charleston, South Carolina in 2015 by a young white supremacist hoping to start a race war. Charleston was also where the race issue widened into a battle over the legitimacy of the confederate flag. BLM, partly formed by young black Obama activists disillusioned with how little had changed on the racial front, became the key focal point of the racial divide: for young black activists as well as for the angry white backlash that equated, in time-honoured fashion, black protest with riots, looting and criminality.

What changed in 2016 was that BLM became a global phenomenon. It is worth reminding of the scale of the problem. A *Washington Post* investigation after the 2014 Brown killing revealed that an unarmed black person was being shot and killed by police every 10 days, with mental illness a factor in nearly a third of these cases (ibid.). This

---

[4]This was the moment when the movement went national. The hashtag #BlackLivesMatter was first used after the acquittal, in July 2013, of George Zimmerman, who was not a police officer, for the vigilante killing the African-American teenager Trayvon Martin.

continued. Despite global protests and the eyes of the world watching, new cases emerged, regularly, relentlessly, right through the election campaign. Where Obama's sympathy with the families of those killed by police angered white supremacists, Trump's racist dog whistling and tacit support simply emboldened them. This was the backdrop to the extraordinarily cruel and heartless killing of George Floyd, with every gruelling detail captured on video, that was to make BLM a global symbol of police oppression and systemic racism.

Trump's response to the BLM protests, which were mostly peaceful, was denial, like his response to climate change: in this case, that there was a problem with policing that was endemic and systemic, hence that BLM protests were legitimate and justified. Instead, he chose to present the protestors as a law and order problem. Ironically, but not untypically, it was only after heavy-handed policing responses to minor disorders, including using the National Guard, that more serious disorder ensued, thus justifying further aggressive policing: the authoritarian paradox. But, for Trump, it seemed to offer a political lifeline. With the pandemic playing havoc with the economy, and thus with what he saw as his route to a second term, casting himself as the guarantor of law and order, in contrast to his 'anarchistic', 'defund-the-police-supporting', Democratic opponents, he doubled down on the hardline rhetoric, hoping to galvanise his base and scare the undecided. (The use of law and order to galvanise the right and the Republican party is, of course, a well-worn tactic: it brought Nixon to power in 1969 and provided the rhetoric for the mugging panic as we outlined in *PTC*.) While Trump's hardline, white supporters seemed to welcome the opportunity it seemed to present of bearing arms in public, and some suburbanites may have been persuaded, young people, especially black, Asian and Latino youth, were not wearing it. As we have seen, they voted massively for Biden, in larger numbers than usual, especially in key swing states. These were the BLM constituency whose vote was probably as much anti-Trump as pro-Biden. Once again, Trump's chosen strategy of playing only to his base probably hindered rather than helped his campaign beyond that.

As for the pandemic, what started out as denial, Trump's routine approach to inconvenient problems, morphed into a chaotic mixture of minimisation (Covid was no worse than a common flu), blaming others (the Chinese, inept state governors, etc.), changing tack (wear a mask; masks are for sissies) and, when all else fails, simply lying (the pandemic is fake news: a hoax). The result of this appallingly inept failure of leadership was the highest number of deaths anywhere, currently (January 6, 2021) 365,000+, with infection rates to match: overall, 21.5 million, which is approximately a quarter of all cases worldwide.[5] This carnage, much of it avoidable, combined with his failure to acknowledge the level of suffering this caused to the families and friends of the dead as well as the countless others who survived but perhaps with long-term health effects, will have cost him electorally. Because, as we now know, Covid disproportionately impacts older people and poorer communities and thus some of the very people that propelled him into the White House in the first place on the promise of bringing back lost jobs and generally improving their lives. Its disproportionate impact on Black people can only have strengthened the Democratic vote.

Which brings us to the elephant in the room: the economy. If there was a guiding thread through Trump's chaotic, zig-zagging handling of the pandemic it was this: the attempt to keep the economy on track, which increasingly tended to mean a rising rather than falling stock market, not jobs. The distinction between the 'real' economy of jobs, wages and unemployment and the stock market is important because they are not necessarily in lockstep. Stock market returns to investors, in the form of dividends and capital appreciation, can be (and usually have been) rising while jobs are disappearing or wages are being cut. This disjunction, which is a function of the neoliberal deregulation of the financial markets in the 1980s and the subsequent dominance of financialised capitalism, speaks to the different interests of fractions of capital, as well as the toxic combination of a booming (finance-based) economy and the devastation of old industrial regions. It was the promise of jobs in the devastated 'left behind' regions, provided by creating

---

[5] Although, it should be added, that the US all time deaths per million figure is only the 12th worst in the world. Belgium heads that list, with the UK also ahead of the USA. All figures from Statista.com. It should not need adding that the reliability of coronavirus statistics varies between countries and different agencies produce slightly different sets of figures. China, for example, had recorded only 4,634 deaths, apparently, by January 6, 2021.

big, new infrastructural projects and reviving heavy industries, accompanied by tax reforms favouring working- and middle-class people that was the economic dimension of his original populist appeal. Trump made many boasts about what he was doing to foster jobs and reduce unemployment but the infrastructural projects never happened, tax cuts benefitted only the already rich, changes on the jobs front were ad hoc, cosmetic or symbolic, and the trade wars with China did not improve the lot of farmers (farm bankruptcies continued to rise, up 20% in 2019). Although Trump thought at the beginning of 2020 that selective economic 'good news' statistics might be enough to win him a second term, the pandemic ensured that if he was going to win it would have to be by doubling down on his reactionary rhetoric and policies and threatening of worse to come under a Biden administration: the collapse of law and order, socialism, communism, etc. In other words, by attempting to project the aggressive, divisive chaotic instability of his own administration onto a future Democratic one. In the event, it failed. But not by much. So where does this leave the incoming Biden administration?

Let us start with the economy, in order to remind ourselves that neoliberalism was never in play in the election. So, the market will continue to set the parameters for economic operations. However, the massive state handouts prompted by the pandemic, on top of those following the financial crash of 2008, might rekindle the ideological flames produced by Occupy Wall Street. The outcome of experiments with a Universal Basic Income taking place around the world may also be usable in this regard. Overall, capitalists will be somewhat split over the election outcome: Trump's massive business tax cuts will be a thing of the past but so too will be his chaotic unpredictability. Biden will bring back capitalism's desire for a predictable and stable legislative and trading environment, even if the regulatory regime is strengthened somewhat.

Politically, the loss of jobs and the closure of businesses as a result of the pandemic will require a huge stimulus from government, as will reinstating a climate change agenda. Whether Biden's proposed $1.7 trillion dollar green deal investment can cover both sets of priorities remains unclear, since they may point in opposite directions: rebooting the suffering airline industry is not what climate change activists will be looking for. On top of which will be the continuing Republican ability to thwart progressive legislation in the Senate, despite the Democrats managing to flip Georgia in the January 2021 runoffs, since a simple majority, as Obama quickly found in his new presidency of 2009, is not enough to guarantee the three-fifths majority needed for legislation with substantial financial implications. Some more progressive Republicans may well be sympathetic to stimulating a green economy, but others, and not just die-hard Trump supporters, are likely to be more obstructive: congressmen from oil-rich Texas spring to mind here. Much may depend on Democratic extra-congressional activity, which is likely to be ramped up, given a Democratic President and House of Representatives. It also depends on where the Democratic base of Biden's presidency might move to, in terms of action. Even more may depend on what Trump's base, having lost the election, 'fraudulently' according to their leader, does with its anger and frustration in the probable absence of its leader. It will probably move further right, according to Richard Sennett's (2020) pre-election analysis. Rejoining the Paris Climate Accord will help to maintain international pressure.

The ideological struggle will, I think, be the crucial arena. Trump will be gone; but Trumpism remains. By that I mean those whose support for Trump the person, since he has no consistent ideology, is a form of unconditional love or blind belief that whatever he says or does is, without question, for the best. His lies become truth because it is he, their maverick, beholden-to-nobody 'outsider' messiah, who utters them. This feeds his narcissism in a vicious spiral of malign reciprocity. This Trumpist core does not include those whose support was more pragmatic (to keep out the socialist/Communist Biden) or habitual (we've always voted Republican). But, whatever the precise figures, his base remains substantial. And, in the wake of his defeat, and his refusal to accept the legitimacy of Biden's victory, it remains angry, disaffected and dangerously worked up. (Trump's base supporters include many mainly white, mainly older, mainly non-Metropolitan working and middle-class people, probably not college-educated, with strong authoritarian and nativist leanings, similar to the UK's Brexit voters, who are not the unconditional fans that I am focusing on here.)

In thinking about these core supporters, and listening to Cleveland's white, working-class Proud Boys in a television vox pop, armed and apparently raring for a confrontation, returns me to Hart's 2019 article and how she drew upon Laclau's analysis of Peronism to think about the contemporary politics of South Africa, specifically the dangers of a populist appeal 'to the masses to develop their antagonism towards the state' and how this can set things off that become uncontrollable (Laclau quoted in Hart 2019: 318). Like much ultra-masculinist behaviour, it is always difficult to separate rhetoric from reality since so much of it is the bluff and counter-bluff of working-class male street talk, especially if the interviewer happens to be a middle-class 'softie'. However, it should not be forgotten that the far right is now America's biggest terrorist threat, thanks partly to Trump's refusal to condemn, and subsequent blatant support for, white supremacism. It is also increasingly armed.

In other words, the most fractious ideological divide will continue to be around race. And here I want, again, to refer back to Hart's essay in which the relationship between race and class, in *PTC* and Hall's later essay on South Africa, was crucial. In discussing this, I used Morley's summary of the aim of the South African essay to remind us of the importance of historical specificity in understanding the articulation of race and class. I also reiterated Hall's point about the importance of seeing articulations, not in purely discursive terms but in relation always to social forces. In other words, what matters most is not the simple disarticulation of racist ideology in favour of a progressive, non-racist rearticulation (especially with the widespread disagreement about what is and is not racist), but the articulation between race (including racist ideology) and class: what are the social forces sustaining or challenging particular racist discourses?

Let me demonstrate using the contrasting slogans 'Black Lives Matter'/'All Lives Matter', for this, in summary, gets to the core of the contemporary divide between black and white America. Remember what I quoted from Hall at the end of Chapter 7 about the need for 'a new way of thinking the relationship between equality…and difference' once you accept multiculturalism: the idea that there is no longer a universal/particular divide but only competing particulars; the multi-cultural dilemma. Having concluded that this could not be achieved in the abstract, as Laclau was attempting to do, but could be accomplished in practice, Hall went on to discuss the political conditions necessary to ensure equality, highlighting the 'constant negotiation between particulars' that is required. However, I wish to return to the universality/particular question, not with the philosophical guidance of Laclau but with the more concrete guidance of Ghassan Hage (2010) in his discussion of Franz Fanon and 'the affective politics of racial mis-interpellation'. Using, as Hall also did, Fanon's 'Look, a negro' quote,[6] Hage explored it in terms of a particularly painful experience of racism: what he called 'mis-interpellation' or mis-recognising how you were being hailed. Until that point, Fanon experienced himself as a universal subject, equal to all his fellow citizens of the French Republic. What the young boy's remark did, effectively, was to expel Fanon from the universal citizenship he thought he possessed and re-situate him within a colour-defined particularity. Moreover, this was also experienced as a negative particularity since the child became afraid. The shock of having prior expectations unexpectedly breached was what made mis-interpellation so hurtful an experience.

Fast forward to the multicultural moment that produced BLM. For black (and progressive white) Americans, BLM is the latest incarnation of centuries of struggle against black oppression in America, since slavery, that centres on continuing police brutality and the systemic racism which, despite the civil rights movement of the 1960s that created a black middle class, continues to discriminate, keeping black people poorer and more disadvantaged than their white counterparts. In other words, having never been granted the equality formally guaranteed by universal citizenship, theirs is a demand that their lives as black people, their particularity, be made to matter and not routinely subjected to lethal police violence, and other forms of discriminatory treatment. Or, in Hall's terms, this was a multi-cultural demand that their difference be made equal to all other differences. 'Defund the police', a shorthand call for the radical overhaul of how law and order is upheld (rather than the abolition of policing as some have chosen to interpret it) is one of the political conditions seen as necessary for its achievement.

---

[6]Hall recalls the quote as 'Look Mama, a black man'. Both 'black man' and 'negro' are used in the text, the former when Fanon is writing in his own voice, the latter when he is quoting the white gaze.

'All Lives Matter' is a white-led response that cannot work as a discursive strategy, hence its practical ineffectiveness. To be an equivalent particularity, the slogan would have to be 'white lives matter'. But that would immediately be seen as racist; as *further* denial that black lives matter.[7] Hence the reversion to the universalistic, all lives matter; making the claim that including the lives of everyone cannot be deemed racist. But this simply reverts to the status quo. And, in an already racist society, reasserting universalistic claims merely reproduces white dominance and black subordination; in this instance, by silencing the particularity of the lethally oppressive policing of black people.

However, BLM can leave disgruntled, frustrated and alienated white people without much control of their lives, who feel that nobody in authority cares about them, without a way of articulating, in a non-racist way, that their lives matter too. This seems to me to be the slogan's 'unsayable' rational kernel, even if many using it are aware of its racist implications. (Interestingly, 'Flint Lives Matter' was adopted as a slogan by those protesting the lethal contamination of the Flint water supply in 2015. However, as another particularity, it can work alongside, and not in competition with, BLM (helped by the fact that many Flint residents are black).) Hage's use of the notion 'mis-interpellation' can, I think, help us make sense of whites feeling slogan-less when it comes to expressing dissatisfaction with their lives. In their case the issue is not mis-interpellation but non-interpellation: not mis-recognition but non-recognition. More accurately, a perception of not being recognised, since in a racially unequal society like the USA, being a member of the dominant white group is to be automatically hailed: whiteness in a white-dominated society is the universal standard by which things are measured and people are interpellated. However, in a society stratified by class as well as race, it is the dominant class, by virtue of its dominance, that set these standard measures and interpellations. It is this 'doubleness' of interpellation, where people can be hailed by whiteness but subordinated

---

[7]There is, I learn, a 'White Lives Matter' movement and it is regarded as a racist, white supremacist movement.

by class, that can leave the feeling of not being recognised or addressed at all.[8]

This is especially the case where claiming a distinctive, alternative particularity to the universal standard that appears not to recognise you becomes difficult. Black people have, of necessity, always possessed such an alternative particularity since their subordinate status precluded them, in all manner of racist ways, from access to the 'universal'. And working-class people have, historically, had access to their own, particular, subordinate culture. But, de-industrialisation and the destruction of traditional working-class occupations and communities has also destroyed much of traditional working-class culture too. It is this feeling that you lack a distinctive particularity that speaks to (and for) you that may well heighten the racist appeal of white supremacy since it is a particularity that recognises and valorises your white life.

We miss the point if we see this difference between the slogans as something to be addressed with facts, namely, that objectively, as a group, white people, including working-class whites, are better off than black people, including working-class blacks, on every conceivable dimension. A factual response constitutes, in effect, a purely discursive effort at disarticulation/rearticulation. Thus, we are failing to address the specificity of the emergence of the slogan: what it means at this point in time, especially to poor whites living in the ravaged and devastated wastelands of contemporary working-class America. That is what we need to understand. That is what Trump managed to tap into, in his 'fumbling, clumsy, crass way', as Grayson Perry put it after meeting various Trump supporters in Wisconsin, one of the whitest of American states, on his Big American Road Trip documentary for Channel 4. By tapping into their feelings of pride in being American ('Proud Boys' is no

---

[8] It could be argued that middle-class white supporters of the 'All Lives Matter' slogan, being part of the dominant class as well as the dominant ethnicity, can hardly complain about not being recognised. But this would be to overlook the cultural divide between the traditional and the 'new' middle classes that I noted in the last chapter when I discussed middle-class discontent and Brexit in the UK context. Despite the four-year political ascendancy of Trump, the 'backward', rural or suburban 'small town' outlook of the traditional middle classes has long played second fiddle to the cultural dominance of the urban cosmopolitanism of the new middle classes. In combination with feeling mis-recognised on racial grounds ('we are not racists'), there is plenty of evidence, among middle-class as well as working-class white Trump supporters, of not feeling recognised.

accidental naming) and their traditional and politically incorrect views 'these people feel, at last, seen' (meaning, they feel recognised as a social group/force).[9] The left's preoccupation with facts misses this emotional dimension of identity and thus the connection between what people believe (discursively) and who they are (socially). Hillary Clinton's depiction of Trump supporters as 'deplorables' constituted a similar failure: in reducing people to discursive constructs ('deplorables') we have no hope of understanding them as social forces.

It is this desire to be seen, recognised, known for who we are in all our complex contradictoriness, that is the core of the matter. Even Fraser's 'progressive populism', combining 'egalitarian redistribution' with 'nonhierarchical recognition', fails to get this. 'The trick is', she suggests, 'to convince them that the forces promoting militarism, xenophobia, and ethnonationalism cannot and will not provide them with the essential material prerequisites for good lives, whereas a progressive-populist bloc just might' (Fraser 2019: 32). Persuading them out of their beliefs on economic grounds both mis-recognises their current ideological positioning, which makes it feel condescending, and makes the classic mistake of the left that, ultimately, in the last instance, the 'material prerequisites for good lives' is the decisive factor. Arlie Hochschild's (2016) ethnography of Tea Party members recognises the scale of the cultural divide, even though her sample appeared to be more middle class than working class. Her idea of attempting to build 'empathy bridges' through grassroots cross-party conversations can at least be a much-needed listening and learning exercise. However, unless combined with other kinds of political action, such conversations would suffer all the problems of a purely discursive approach to politics.

It will be no easy task to handle BLM in a way that addresses the core concern of police brutality ('defund the police') but that also recognises the concerns of white and black communities to feel safely policed. Obama never managed it and periodic police reform following scandalous revelations has been an endemic feature of American policing since its inception. But, using BLM as the lens through which to

---

[9] Although Perry chose Wisconsin because it voted for Trump in 2016, it was one of the states that secured Biden's victory in 2020.

approach the other problems might be a fruitful strategy since all the global conjunctural issues discussed disproportionately affect working-class black (and other ethnic) communities. The over-representation of black men killed by police is connected, albeit in mediated ways, to their always-potentially-suspect criminal status, to the aggressive over-policing of black communities, to the role of drug possession in black over-representation in prisons, to the mental health crisis, to the poverty that makes drug-selling an economic lifeline in poor communities, to the systemic inequalities that drastically reduce options other than risky street life.

Fortuitously then, we return, via the issue of race, class and criminalisation, to criminology, and to Hall's 'politics of difference'. Can an inclusive rather than Trump's exclusive version of such politics be initiated in post-Trump America? Can black lives be made to matter without also exacerbating racial divisions? We are back to Hall's multicultural question which ended Chapter 7: how can we think about equality in a world where diversity and difference have replaced the idea of universality? Despite the US Democratic victory, matters remain on a knife edge. We are likely to continue to see 'a great variety of morbid symptoms', as Fraser warned we would, while the old continues to die and the new is finding a way to be born. That is where Gramsci's 'pessimism of the intellect' delivers us. But it is the youthful courage and energy fuelling both climate change activism and BLM on the global stage that enables me to end on a note of hope, Gramsci's 'optimism of the will'.

Coming to an End, for the Moment

By working with and subtly adapting the originally Marxist idea of conjunctural analysis, over and over again and in various ways, Hall showed how it is an indispensable methodological tool for those, which must include criminologists, with a theoretical interest in understanding, and a political interest in changing, aspects of any present moment bearing on questions of justice and equality. This was, in a nutshell, Hall's enduring contribution to criminology. It is the continuing relevance of this idea that I have tried to emphasise in moving from *PTC* to Brexit and Trumpism: the moment has changed but the conjunctural approach remains robust. It is this, too, that I think explains why Hall's work does not date, but is rediscovered by new generations. Serendipitously, as I was writing this conclusion, I got an email from someone who had just finished reading *PTC*. The person 'thought it was a fantastic book. Rich and nuanced, and combining theory with concrete empirical detail without ignoring their mediated relation'. That last sentence seems to me to be an excellent brief summary of the methodology and an endorsement of its continuing relevance.

References

Fassin, E. 2018. Left-wing populism: A legacy of defeat. *Radical Philosophy*, June. www.radicalphilosophy.com/article/left-wing-populism.

Fraser, N. 2019. *The Old is Dying and the New Cannot be Born: From Progressive Neoliberalism to Trump and Beyond*. London: Verso.

Hage, G. 2010. The affective politics of racial mis-interpellation. *Theory, Culture and Society* 27 (7/8): 112–29.

Hall, S. 1978. Pluralism, race and class in Caribbean society. In UNESCO, ed. (1978: 150–84 and 457–58).

Hall, S. 1980a/2019. Race, articulation and societies structured in dominance. In Morley, ed. (2019: 172–221).

Hall, S. 1980b. Nicos Poulantzas: State, power, socialism. *New Left Review* 119: 60–69.

Hall, S., C. Critcher, T. Jefferson, J. Clarke, and B. Roberts. 1978. *Policing the Crisis: Mugging, the State and Law & Order*. Houndmills, Basingstoke: Macmillan.

Hall, S., C. Critcher, T. Jefferson, J. Clarke, and B. Roberts. 2013. *Policing the Crisis: Mugging, the State and Law & Order*, 2nd ed. Houndmills, Basingstoke: Palgrave Macmillan.

Hart, G. 2019. From authoritarian to left populism?: Reframing Debates. *The South Atlantic Quarterly* 118: 2, April: 307–23. https://doi.org/10.1215/00382876-7381158.

Hart, G. 2020. Why did it take so long? Trump-Bannonism in a global conjunctural frame. *Geografiska Annaler: Series B, Human Geography* 102 (3): 239–66. https://doi.org/10.1080/04353684.2020.1780791.

Hochschild, A.R. 2016. *Strangers in their Own Land: Anger and Mourning on the American Right*. New York: The New Press.

Laclau, E. 1977. *Politics and Ideology in Marxist Theory: Capitalism—Fascism—Populism*. London: New Left Books.

Laclau, E. 2005. *On Populist Reason*. London: Verso.

Laclau, E., and C. Mouffe. 1985. *Hegemony and Socialist Strategy: Towards a Radical Democratic Politics*, trans. W. Moore and P. Cammack. London: Verso.

Lowery, W. 2017. *They Can't Kill Us All: The Story of Black Lives Matter*. Harmondsworth: Penguin.

Morley, D. 2019. Theoretical and methodological principles: Class, race, and articulation. In Morley, ed. (2019: 101–10).

Morley, D. (ed.). 2019. *Stuart Hall Essential Essays Vol. 1: Foundations of Cultural Studies*. Durham and London: Duke University Press.

Mouffe, C. 2018. *For a Left Populism*. London: Verso.

Poulantzas, N. 1978. *State, Power, Socialism*, trans. P. Camiller. London: New Left Books.

Sennett, R. 2020. Even if Donald Trump loses the election, the US isn't going to heal any time soon. *The Guardian*, November 2.

UNESCO (ed.). 1978. *Race and Class in Post-Colonial Society: A Study of Ethnic Group Relations in the English-Speaking Caribbean, Bolivia, Chile and Mexico*. Paris: UNESCO.

Part IV
Coda

11

Hall, Psychoanalysis and the Problem of Populist Anger

As we saw in Chapter 8, vote Leave was conducted with greater passion than the Remain campaign and anger was the particular passion most often mentioned by commentators. It is also cited more generally as part of what is fuelling the new populism generally: in the UK, in the USA, across Europe. Yet, apart from references to the intemperate, angry language used in debating Brexit on social media, in some *vox pop* interviews or in the limited ethnographic material relating to Brexit, we do not really know who was or was not an angry leave voter (as opposed to fearful, frustrated, resigned or whatever) because we have no easy way of evidencing it. Whatever the inadequacies of the ABCDE classifications used to measure social class, they provided some base-line evidence for calculating the relationship between class and voting behaviour. Because we do not know who were the angry, the issue of anger cannot be simply incorporated into a conjunctural analysis. Yet because it played into the result in some way, it cannot be ignored. Hence the need for this coda, which will examine the difficulties in thinking about anger in relation to the conjuncture. In this way, it will exemplify the question of the role of a psychology, more particularly a psychoanalysis, in conjunctural analysis. Although Hall never addressed the issue directly, I will use some of his general remarks about psychoanalysis to orientate my thinking. An attempt to explore Brexit anger psychosocially will be used to explore the theoretical problems. Finally, some examples of psychoanalytic thinking that offer a way forward will be identified.

Why Is It Difficult to Think About Anger in Relation to the Conjuncture?

The simple answer is because they are operating at two different levels: anger is an individual level phenomenon, whereas conjunctural analysis is conducted at the social level. More precisely, anger has both an individual and a social component. It is a product of an individual's biography as well as a response to external, social circumstances. When a car driver gets angry because the car behind has been tailgating it for miles, the social circumstance 'causing' the anger seems clear and obvious. However, when a car driver is angry with other drivers for little apparent reason, then we are right to conclude that there is also some internal, biographical reason fuelling the anger. Perhaps he or she is still angry from an earlier argument, with a spouse or whoever, and is now inappropriately 'blaming' all and sundry. In this instance, the real, internal reason for the driver's anger is no mystery and is easily accessible to consciousness. But sometimes the internal, biographical trigger for anger is completely inaccessible to consciousness: with people who are constantly angry, for example, or who 'fly off the handle' on the slightest provocation or for no apparent reason. Here, the mismatch between triggering event, internal or external, and the resulting anger suggests something more going on, of which the angry person is unaware. Which is another way of saying that anger, like all emotions, consists of a conscious and an unconscious dimension. Understanding this unconscious dimension of emotional life is the undisputed province of psychoanalysis. In broad terms, a psychoanalytic explanation would suggest that being 'angry for no reason' is symptomatic of some underlying hurt that is too painful to confront directly, so has become repressed. The connection between the apparent triggers and the unconscious hurt has thus become 'hidden'. Bringing these hidden connections to light is what analysis attempts.

Relating this to Brexit, it is quite clear that there was plenty to be angry about. Any Leave voter, and no doubt many a Remain voter, would be able to offer a catalogue of things they were consciously angry about. These social reasons for Brexit anger have been manifest throughout my account. However, the point of raising the issue of the individual dimension of anger is to suggest that a purely social account of anger is necessarily reductive since it will fail to account for the hidden dimensions of anger lurking behind the apparent reasons. And this may seriously skew our understanding of what is really being expressed in the anger. Commentators were not unaware of this when, for example, they decided that 'postimperial melancholia' was the 'real' reason for some of the middle-class anger.

George Cavalletto (2007) approached the problem of levels of analysis by examining how four major thinkers, namely Freud, Weber, Adorno and Elias, had each managed to combine psychic and social factors in producing their respective psychosocial analyses. In his conclusion, he summarised his findings in what he called 'a paradigm of paradigms' (Cavalletto 2007: 260). This intended to show the four principles that they all shared. It is the fourth principle that summarises our problem. It states that '*a reciprocal alignment of sociological and psychological analyses requires that they occur at similar levels of abstraction*' (ibid.: 265). What this is saying is that only by aligning the level of abstraction can the analyses work. An individual level analysis is incompatible with a social one: only when the individual has been reconstructed as a social type, for example, as in the Weberian notion of an 'ideal-type', can a psychosocial analysis work. But, this somewhat contradicts Cavalletto's second principle that '*the psyche dynamically alters that which society imposes upon it*' (ibid.: 262). How can both principles be true: that the psyche has effectivity in relation to the social and is not a simple reproduction of societal impositions, yet can only work in tandem with the social when aligned (meaning one level has had to sacrifice its effectivity and be reduced to the other)? This is a conundrum to which I will return. But first, let us see what assistance Hall's approach to psychoanalysis and the psychosocial might provide, despite his pessimism about working politically with psychoanalysis.

Why Did Hall Find Psychoanalysis and the Psychosocial Difficult to Work with?

Hall was well aware of the importance of psychoanalysis to cultural studies generally and, as we have already seen, he used it specifically in his own work on identity. He also understood that this implied a need to approach cultural studies psychosocially. However, he never interrogated Freud and psychoanalysis in the in-depth way he did Marxism. At least, not in publicly available documents. The only one of Hall's many publications that specifically addresses psychoanalysis is a short lecture he gave in 1987 at the Institute for Contemporary Arts in London on 'Psychoanalysis and cultural studies'. It remained unpublished until after his death when Larry Grossberg tidied it up for publication in the journal *Cultural Studies* in 2018. It is, by Hall's high standards, slight and largely underdeveloped. It is a purely theoretical piece, lacking any concrete exemplification, that discusses the relationship between psychoanalysis and cultural studies. His conclusion, that he did not see how to work politically with psychoanalysis, is in line with my argument about the incompatibility between the individual dimension of anger and the social nature of conjunctural analyses and would seem to close off further discussion. Hall never returned to the matter. However, the essay made a few observations that, underdeveloped as they are, may help take the matter forward.

In talking about the kind of psychoanalysis that had intervened in cultural studies, Hall first dismissed those 'largely unsuccessful' attempts at producing 'a socially or culturally-based general theory' (Hall 2018: 889), in favour of those remaining rigorously psychoanalytic: 'it is only when psychoanalysis apparently focuses on its own object in its own ways, in its own process, that it throws an important, piercing but uneven light on the question which Cultural Studies has tried to pose itself' (ibid.: 890). Specifically, he credits post-Lacanian psychoanalysis and feminism with introducing the importance of the unconscious to cultural studies, after which 'it is not possible any longer to accept a sociological or cultural anthropological account of how the inside gets outside and how the outside gets inside' (ibid.: 891). Melanie Klein's approach is deemed, without theoretical justification, unsuitable, despite offering 'enormous insights'. The preference for a Lacanian psychoanalytic approach has, it seems, to do with the importance it attributes to language, something it shares with cultural studies. However, he also raises a series of criticisms of Lacanian theory that left me wondering why Lacan not Klein is seen as the only possible starting point. For example, the Lacanian idea that 'subjectivity is formed, sexual difference is instituted, language commences, and the law of culture is entered by the subject' all at the same time 'as a consequence of the same process' is criticised for its reductiveness (Hall 2018: 894). He further criticises the Lacanian tendency to theoretical certainty and its difficulties with conceptualising the social and how change takes place. We need both, he continues—'a study of the unconscious and its specific mechanisms' and 'a fully constituted theory of the social'—and 'they cannot be reduced to one another. But all the forms of correspondence or relationship between them which we have of them are inadequate' (ibid.: 896). Here, restated slightly differently, is Cavalletto's conundrum: how can the psyche, with its 'specific mechanisms' be brought into 'correspondence' with the social without being 'reduced to one another'?

For Hall, ultimately, it is the psychic dimension that proves to be the political sticking point:

> But when you put yourself on the terrain of the necessary otherness of the psychical, of the never completeness of subjectivity, of the impossibility of a finished sexuality, it is extremely difficult to know how, from that, you get to any forms of cultural struggle or politics at all.
>
> What is a politics in which you are already complicit with the violence which you are trying to struggle against? Isn't that what psychoanalysis tells us? It's a very radical insight: that psychic life itself is aggressive and violent (ibid.: 896).

His endpoint, about psychic life being aggressive and violent, is a reminder of the psychic inevitability of anger. And, although his pessimistic conclusion is right to point to the difficulties of working politically with psychoanalysis, I want to return to his observations—that psychoanalytic attempts at general theorising have not worked; that psychoanalysis needs to remain 'rigorously psychoanalytic'; and that Melanie Klein's work offers 'enormous insights'—to see if I can offer a more positive take on the political potential of psychoanalysis. This will involve identifying the biographical and socio-cultural conditions needed to contain aggressive anger. But, I shall start with what hasn't worked, and why, demonstrating the point with a recent attempt to offer a psychosocial account of Brexit.

Why Have Psychoanalytic Attempts at a General Theory Been 'Largely Unsuccessful'?

In talking of psychoanalytically-inspired general theories, Hall had in mind all those attempts to understand culture or society that have their origin in Freud's attempts to do so. *Civilization and its Discontents* (1929) is the paradigm example. Ironically, Freud was not very impressed with his own effort. Written in a matter of weeks, without recourse to a library, as a project to pass the time, he thought it 'very superfluous', an exercise in rediscovering 'the most banal truths' (quoted in Jones 1964: 594). In a nutshell, Freud's core 'banal truth' was that, given man's instinctual aggression, civilisation only became possible once this aggression had been repressed through the actions of the super-ego (or conscience) and replaced, consciously, as a sense of guilt. In Freud's own words, again quoted in Jones, 'the price of progress in civilisation is paid by forfeiting happiness through the heightening of the sense of guilt' (ibid.: 597). The Hobbesian problematic of the war of all against all is here resolved psychologically as Hobbes' state, acting in the general interest, becomes Freud's similarly charged super-ego.

Not surprisingly given its origin, this is a reductive account, as Freud's own judgement, along with most others, seems to accept. It is universalistic, valid for all civilisations, and hence historically reductive, and psychologistic, hence sociologically reductive. Given Freud's view that sociology 'can be nothing other than applied psychology' (ibid.: 594) this comes as no surprise. However, this reduction of sociology to psychology is a manifestation of a broader problem, one that besets all attempts to think how society and the psyche are connected, namely, how to conceptualise the psychosocial in a way that recognises the specific effectivities of both the psyche and the social without reducing the social to the psychic, as Freud does—civilisation is built upon the renunciation of instincts—or the psychic to the social, as do later efforts in this same tradition such as those of the Frankfurt school (cf. Adorno et al. 1950). This issue is at the heart of the theoretical problem that undergirds Hall's frustration at the political impasse it seems to introduce. As we saw earlier, Cavalletto regards this reductive alignment of levels as a requirement of psychosocial research—'*a reciprocal alignment of sociological and psychological analyses requires that they occur at similar levels of abstraction*'—even as it contradicts the notion that the psychic and the social are *different* levels of abstraction. It certainly continues to bedevil psychosocial research, as is demonstrated by Barry Richards' attempt to offer a psychosocial explanation of the populist anger that produced Brexit (Richards 2019).

Barry Richards' Psychosocial Approach to Populist Anger

Richards starts by looking separately at the 'societal' and 'psychological' dimensions of populist anger, in their 'monocular' particularities, thus echoing my distinction between the social and individual/biographical dimensions of anger. The societal dimension provoking people's anger is what he calls the 'familiar…explanations' of multiple perceived losses: 'of material security…national sovereignty and…indigenous community' (ibid.: 171). The psychological dimension deploys the less familiar psychoanalytic notion of narcissism to argue that, at the individual level, the anger constitutes 'a narcissistic rage against the "otherness" of authority' (ibid.). Richards then attempts to unite these into a 'binocular' or 'psychosocial' approach. And here, in conformity with Cavalletto's strictures about the need for levels to be in alignment in psychosocial theorising, the psychic level gets aligned with the social; or, in my terminology, gets reduced to the social. Basically, the developments of modernity have not only grown 'a primitive and diffuse anger…in particular segments of most national publics' but these 'have somehow interacted with the intrinsically narcissistic tendencies of the human mind, *with the result of intensifying the narcissistic complex*' (ibid.: 180; my emphases).

Let me be absolutely clear here about how I read his and why I think it fails to uphold the specificity of the psychic level. The first part of the statement talks of the social origins of 'a primitive and diffuse anger' in the 'developments of modernity'. However, it immediately qualifies this by saying 'in particular segments of most national publics'. In other words, only some particular individuals, those comprising 'particular segments', are susceptible to these anger-promoting social developments. This qualification is crucial since it suggests, rightly, that some individuals will be less prone to anger than others. Given that he is talking about the origins of anger in narcissistic rage, we can say that individuals will differ in their likelihood of being afflicted with such rageful tendencies, depending on their already existing narcissistic complex and the antecedents of these. So, when the statement concludes with these social developments 'somehow' interacting with the mind's 'narcissistic tendencies' in a way that intensifies narcissism, it should also add 'in particular segments/individuals'. By not doing so, Richards has aligned the levels, but at the cost of losing the individual level. Thus, effectively, it reads as if he is saying that social developments have produced psychological change, by 'intensifying the narcissistic complex', at the individual level. Since each individual's 'narcissistic complex' is a unique constellation, the effect of intensification will vary and thus the tendency to become angry.

Richards' final section addresses how these social developments 'somehow' interact with the mind to intensify narcissism. He uses Lasch's argument (in *The Culture of Narcissism* 1979) about the growth of narcissism consequent upon a series of changes undermining parental authority, to suggest 'that *part* of the anger underlying the current successes of populism is fuelled by a narcissistic rage that in turn is a product of an erosion of basic trust' (ibid.: 182). And things are apparently getting worse: 'this reduction in our emotional capital is increasing over time' (ibid.). Or, the culture may currently be asking too much of us, emotionally. At this point, the social has developed a psyche of its own: given the new emotional pressures (to be more empathic, civic minded and generous, tolerate uncertainty and complexity), these pressures may 'irritate that part of the collective psyche that recoils from any requirements to give up a measure of our phantasied freedom in the service of the whole' (ibid.).

It should not be forgotten that his analysis is dotted with qualifications. The impact of the culture of narcissism is not monolithic but variable such that 'some people seem to embody the malaise of the time much more than others, and some not at all' (ibid.: 181). And, the argument about narcissistic rage does not account for all but only '*part* of the anger'. Moreover, when addressed in their monocularity, there is much with which to agree with his societal and psychological level explanations. However, the take home argument has not found a way to incorporate these qualifications into the analysis with the result that the psychological dimension of anger, the result of an individual's unique biographical journey, has become subsumed within the social to become, for all practical purposes, a socially generated anger: the social moment of 'intensification' rather than the individual susceptibility to such intensification.

So, in line with Cavalletto's psychosocial principles, the psychological level has been aligned with the social but, in so doing, the psychological particularities of individuals have disappeared, to be replaced by a social 'collective psyche'. The question of which 'particular segments' of which 'national publics' are displaying 'a primitive and diffuse anger' gets sidelined. This is particularly ironic given that the monocular societal level explanations are deemed inadequate precisely for their failure to 'account for the variations amongst Leave-supporting individuals in the intensity of their anger with the "establishment"' (ibid.: 171). Instead, anger loses all conjunctural specificity and becomes a general, cultural phenomenon:

a product of the 'age' or epoch. In short, there has been a double reduction: from the psychological level to the social; and from the specificity of the conjuncture to the general characteristics of the epoch (see Clarke 2010).

It is time to turn from what doesn't work to what might, if we remain 'rigorously psychoanalytic', as this is the only way, Hall suggests, psychoanalysis can shed light on cultural questions. If we want to understand the politics of populist anger, we will need to take anger seriously in its own terms, and not reductively.

How Might Psychoanalysis Focusing 'on Its Own Object' Provide a Way Forward?

Here I must part company with Hall since his preference was to take a Lacanian route. Or, so it seemed. On the other hand, he was highly critical of Lacan and thought Klein's work displayed 'enormous insights'. So, with the warrant of Hall's ambivalence over Lacan and acknowledgement of Klein's achievements, which echo my own view of their respective merits, I am going to focus, first, on the potential of Melanie Klein's thinking to be rendered politically useful. After, I look briefly at Jessica Benjamin's work. These are intended to exemplify the potential of psychoanalysis to assist conjunctural politics. Their contributions have proved their worth in the way that they have been taken up beyond the clinic, as we shall see.

Melanie Klein, Object Relations and Anxiety

Klein's theoretical innovations hinged on the importance she attached to our relations to others and to the central role of anxiety in managing these. These made her the founder of what came to be called the 'object relations' approach within psychoanalysis in which the management of anxiety came to replace repression as the key to understanding subjective life. Moreover, it was the largely neglected early infant-mother relations that provided the basis of this re-theorising, with anxiety at its core.

Although she retained a conventional belief in the instincts as the basis of life, it was how these and the resulting anxiety were managed relationally that mattered more. Thus, although she argued that the 'first form of anxiety' is a result of 'the working of the death instinct within' (Klein 1952: 202), it was the consequent development by the early ego of the three defence mechanisms of 'splitting', 'projection' and 'introjection' to deal with early persecutory anxiety that were central to her theorising. Splitting off the bad feelings and then projecting them into another object were, she argued, the principal forms of dispersing and deflecting the danger and thus reducing anxiety; and 'introjection', or the taking in of objects, could assist the process where the object taken in was one experienced as good.

Concretely, the first external object the infant uses into which to project its bad feelings is the mother's breast when it fails to satisfy or arrive on time. Since the same breast also gratifies, it is also the first object introjected as a good object. Hence, in phantasy, the mother's breast has been split into a good, gratifying breast and a bad, frustrating breast. Further defence mechanisms are developed in order to maintain this split: idealisation of the good breast to keep it safe from the feared bad breast; omnipotent denial of the bad breast's existence; and 'projective identification', which basically entails identifying with the feeling that has been projected into an object. Where the feeling projected is one of hatred, this becomes the 'prototype of an aggressive object relation' (Klein 1946: 183) since identifying with the projected hated parts of the self increases the feeling of hatred towards the object. Klein called this early period, dominated by feelings of persecution and annihilation and defensive splitting, the paranoid-schizoid position. Despite its name, it is entirely normal.

Once the infant can take in the mother as whole object and not just as part-object, the breast, it begins to see that good and bad exist in the same person and do not need to be defensively kept apart. As Klein (1946: 189) expressed it:

> With the introjection of the complete object in about the second quarter of the first year marked steps in integration are made…The loved and hated aspects of the mother are no longer felt to be so widely separated,

and the result is an increased fear of loss, states akin to mourning and a strong feeling of guilt, because the aggressive impulses are felt to be directed against the loved object. The depressive position has come to the fore.

This depressive position is a developmental achievement. But both positions remain as part of us. Which is dominant will be, according to Klein, partly a constitutional matter dependent on the relative strengths of the life and death instincts, and partly a matter of 'external circumstances. For instance, a difficult birth and unsatisfactory feeding - and possibly even unpleasant experiences in the pre-natal state - undoubtedly intensify destructive impulses, persecutory anxiety, greed and envy' (Klein 1956: 212). Crucial to these 'external circumstances' for the infant's development will be the quality of its relationship to the mother and other carers, not just in terms of feeding, but generally.

What that means for a carer, practically, during the paranoid-schizoid phase is being able to hold or contain a child's rage and hateful projections in order to detoxify them rather than retaliate: recognising that you are the adult in the room. Clearly, the ability to do this will be variable, partly dependent on the mother's capacity to contain her own anger and disappointments. Assuming she manages this containment function sufficiently well, if her mothering is 'good enough', over time the child will become more able to be its own container and live with the resulting ambivalent feelings—of love and hate towards the mother—rather than constantly needing to expel the hateful ones. At this point, the infant is capable of operating from the depressive position.

However, whether a child, or adult, operates from the depressive position, or reverts to the paranoid-schizoid position, is context dependent. We are all constantly oscillating between these two positions. Everything is dependent on how containing, or otherwise, are our everyday lives: in our interactions with others including the talk we share, in the institutions we encounter, our jobs, etc. Expressed at its broadest, social conditions can function to promote or inhibit paranoid-schizoid thinking and acting. Whether society is 'good enough' at containing paranoid-schizoid thinking and acting has profound implications for the kind of society that results. Splitting off and projecting into others the hatred that cannot be contained within is one definition of Othering: of failing to live with difference. The racist, the misogynist, the homophobe can all be seen psychoanalytically as operating from the paranoid-schizoid rather than the depressive position. Examples of work using these Kleinian ideas as part of an explanation of racism include Rustin (2000), Clarke (2003), Gadd and Dixon (2011), and my own work (cf. Jefferson 2013). The following is a brief example taken from my 2013 article, a case study of 'Darren', one of the interviewees in the study of racism in Stoke-on-Trent conducted by David Gadd (Gadd et al. 2005). An abbreviated outline of Darren's life taken from two interviews reads thus:

> Darren is a 32-year-old troubled man, unemployed and with few prospects of work, whose life is 'crap'. He has a furious temper, is a serial abuser of his partner, constantly shouts and screams at her children for not doing as they are told, no longer sees two of his own children, drives without license or insurance despite convictions for dangerous driving, and gets angrily abusive when talking about immigrants and 'Pakis'. He hated his drunken, wife-beating father and has fallen out with his only sister for interfering in his own abusive relationship. Misbehaviour as a child, which included arson and shoplifting, eventuated in multiple suspensions from school and being sent to a residential school for unruly children. (Jefferson 2013: 5)

Here is an example of someone whose anger outstrips any purely social explanation; which demands some kind of account of the turmoil of his inner world. A truncated psychoanalytic understanding of this (leaving out other relevant notions such as his narcissism as well as any engagement with the social) included the following:

> Darren's difficult and frightening early life experiences of a violent father and abused mother would have made it more likely that the primitive defences of splitting and projective identification characteristic of Klein's paranoid-schizoid position would become characteristic responses to anxiety-invoking situations. With parents too unreliable as containers or points of identification, paranoid splitting of the world into good and bad is the result, as is the replacement of anxiety by aggression. Examples

of this paranoid world-view were taken from many parts of the interviews with Darren. (ibid.: 10)

A society full of Darrens would be a dangerous place indeed. As it happens, Darren's hate-motivated violence was not simply racially-motivated, but general. However, it was primarily directed at his partner. Domestic abuse is a crime largely carried out by men on their women partners. Within criminology, this violence against women has begun to be regarded as having much to do with masculinity. Psychoanalytically, this returns us to Freud and the Oedipus complex, the processes whereby bisexual infants become aware of sexual difference, sometime between the ages of three and five. Klein cannot help us here since her theoretical innovations pertain to the pre-Oedipal moment. Of all the subsequent revisions, the work of Jessica Benjamin has been the most fruitful. Hence it is to her innovations I now turn.

Jessica Benjamin, the Oedipal Complex and Masculinity

Benjamin's theoretical achievement was to break decisively with the exclusionary, binary logic of conventional accounts—of how boys become masculine and girls feminine—and to point the way towards greater toleration of gender ambiguity. Conventionally, the dissolution of the Oedipal complex emphasises giving up incestuous longings for the mother in exchange for identifications with the father and all that he represents—exchanging object love (desire for) for identificatory love (desire to be like)—and thus acquiring the gendered identity appropriate to one's sex: becoming masculine in the case of our boy child. Benjamin's first step was to focus on the child's identifications with the pre-Oedipal father. In doing so, she came to re-define this moment, one where the child identifies with both parents, as 'overinclusive' (Benjamin 1998: 60), a term she borrowed from Fast (1984, 1990). The issue of how the Oedipal conflict is subsequently resolved comes down to how this overinclusive bisexuality is relinquished: by repudiation or renunciation. In the former case, defensive repudiation, it gets replaced by the mutual exclusivity of conventional gender difference where masculinity is the valued term and femininity the denigrated one. In the case of boys, 'the identification with the mother is repudiated, and the elements associated with his own babyhood are projected onto the girl, the daughter' (Benjamin 1998: xvii). But, it is possible for the boy child to give up his identifications with his mother in a less defensive way: to renounce them, meaning realistically recognising he can never be completely like her, rather than repudiate them through defensive splitting. This does not mean that gender categories can ever be completely abolished, since they rely on the processes of identification and splitting that are part of who we are, psychically. This leaves the question of gender polarity and how to prevent this becoming 'reified, congealed in massive cultural formations, perceived as the Law' (ibid.: 75).

One example exploring the implications of Benjamin's re-theorising in a particular field of enquiry is Wendy Hollway's discussion of gender and care, in her book *The Capacity to Care* (2006). Here she argues that Benjamin's distinction between renunciation and repudiation as different ways of giving up his identifications with his mother, en route to becoming a boy, impact his capacity to care. Realistic renunciation will enable him to retain those aspects of her, like her capacity to care, that he can emulate. Defensive repudiation of everything feminine means also rejecting her caring capacity, since it is, conventionally, associated with the feminine. I have also used Benjamin's ideas in thinking about masculinity in a criminological context (Jefferson 2002). To the extent that conventional masculinity is defined by its opposition to femininity, it is synonymous with repudiation and not renunciation of the feminine. And masculinity based on repudiation not renunciation would seem to be implicated in a host of crimes: what we might call the capacity to couldn't care less, the inverse of the capacity to care. Although neither repudiation nor renunciation are absolute nor unchanging positions, depending on changing circumstances through the life course, it should not be difficult to see how gendered differences in the capacity to care can play into issues of domestic violence and misogynistic attitudes towards women generally. Our earlier look at 'Darren' would seem to be a case in point. The capacity to care is thus deeply implicated in the politics of gender difference.

So, Where Does All This Leave Us, Politically?

Hall was aware of the need for a psychosocial approach. But, so far, all existing psychosocial attempts have been found wanting because, in line with Cavalletto's strictures about the need for an alignment of levels, they have ended up over-riding the particularity of one of the levels, by reducing the social to the psychic, or vice versa. What this boils down to politically is this: only if each side of the psychosocial focuses on its own particular object in its full complexity can it contribute to a broader political project. Otherwise we do end up reducing reality to one level or the other. What is needed then, to put it most forcefully, is a conjunctural politics of the social that includes a conjunctural politics of the psychic.

Let me be clear. People are psychosocial subjects, possessing unique biographies and phantasy lives that affect how they experience their social world as well as sharing common conditions of existence that affect how they experience themselves as individuals. Peopled with such psychosocial subjects, the world is, similarly, a psychosocial product. However, in order to give each dimension, the psychic and the social, its proper due, political action needs to respect the specificity of each, and not in a reductive way. Take racism, for example. Mike Rustin's statement that 'The tendency to see racism as a system of ideological false beliefs, to be banished by anti-racist teaching and propaganda'—still much in evidence among those commenting upon the police atrocities that produced Black Lives Matter (BLM) campaigns—'fails to see that its main power lies at an unconscious level' (Rustin 2000: 191). In other words, we must attend seriously to the unconscious dimension in its own terms—as Rustin's Kleinian approach does—as well as to how ideological, political and economic processes get articulated to such unconscious phantasies in particular historical moments.

Expressed from the dimension of the conjuncture, the question becomes, how does the conjuncture promote, or impede, paranoid-schizoid thinking (to use Klein's psychoanalytic thinking) or the repudiation of femininity (to use Benjamin's psychoanalytic contribution) and thus contribute to racist, sexist, homophobic and other forms of 'Othering'? What are the institutional, social and cultural arrangements that work to trigger or contain anger? Calling an 'in/out' referendum and the existence of social media as a major vehicle of public communication are both conditions more likely to promote than impede angry, paranoid thinking since both sacrifice nuance and ambiguity for binary thinking. And social media are nothing if not vehicles for 'sounding off' and expressing feelings. Which then get amplified by 'like'-minded followers. Trump's obsessive tweeting—'Build the wall'; It's fake news'; 'Lock her up'—exemplifies all three features: simplistic thoughts, angrily expressed, intended to fire up his like-minded supporters. Add in a public already alienated politically, divided culturally and struggling economically, plus a defining issue, immigration, that has long been the object of all manner of projections, and it is hard to imagine a situation more designed to encourage paranoid-schizoid responses and to trigger rather than contain anger.

Another way of thinking about the social conditions promoting or impeding paranoid-schizoid thinking is to return to the ideas of Menzies Lyth (1960/2000). Basically, she was interested in how organisations work to sustain or reduce anxiety. Her most famous study was an attempt to understand the high levels of anxiety among student nurses on hospital placements and how this might be reduced. She drew parallels between the stressful nature of the nursing experience and early phantasy life and accompanying anxieties, and saw how features of the job could re-activate some of these early phantasies and anxieties. She then looked at the various forms of 'socially structured defense mechanisms' the organisation had developed, not always consciously, to cope with these high levels of anxiety (e.g. restricting the nurse/patient relationship by splitting up the contacts with any particular patient; depersonalising the relationship with patients, eliminating decision-making by standardising the performance of tasks). Although these attempts to defend against anxiety did not, apparently, reduce anxiety nor were they particularly efficient, the notion of social defence mechanisms remains useful, so long as we retain its specificity as a social level construct. Menzies Lyth was insistent on this:

> I wish to make it clear that I do not imply that the nursing service *as an institution* operates the defenses. Defenses are, and can be, operated only

by individuals. Their behaviour is the link between psychic defenses and the institution. (ibid.: 178)

To return to my insistence on the specificity of each dimension of the psychosocial, individuals, not organisations, get anxious, angry, fearful, etc. Organisations, by the way they are structured alleviate or exacerbate, but do not originate, these emotions.

In terms of who is more or less likely to be angry, we can look at the statistics that variously implicate mental health issues. Psychoanalysis, a theory of desire and pleasure, in practice is usually about trying to understand the various ways we develop to deal with the other side of pleasure, namely, pain and frustration. Anger is one such, but may manifest indirectly, symptomatically, in anything from eating disorders and the abuse of drugs and alcohol to anxiety, depression and suicide. These mental health statistics will overlap social statistics, as Rutherford (2019) argues. Thus, although 'symptoms of mental illness' among children are generally on the rise, poorer children are more likely to 'display symptoms of mental illness' (ibid.: 8) than richer ones. And, the 'dramatic rise in levels of chronic pain and in illnesses such as diabetes, depression and anxiety [and]…the rise of self-inflicted deaths caused by drugs, alcohol and suicide' (ibid.) are manifestations of the 'social disintegration' of poorer communities which 'has contributed to the rise of nationalist populism across capitalist democracies' (ibid.). I do not disagree. However, it is important, if my argument about the specificities of both levels, the psychological and the social, has merit that we not reduce one set of statistics to the other. There is much still to be learned of the relationship: between the mental health of individuals and the social characteristics of communities. For example, as I briefly noted at the end of Chapter 8, many of these issues are also manifestations of the crisis of masculinity.

Hall was, of course, right: working politically with psychoanalysis is difficult; but, then, so is attempting to construct an inclusive counter-hegemonic politics articulating relatively autonomous economic, political, and ideological issues and manifold differently interpellated constituencies. What I hope to have done is show something of the necessity of working politically with psychoanalysis and thus to have developed the paradox that Hall first noted but left undeveloped, namely, that it is only when psychoanalysis remains focused 'on its own object' that it can contribute to any cultural or political project. I don't know whether he would approve of my chosen journey, of 'taking his idea for a walk', to pinch a phrase from Phil Cohen; but it was conducted in his spirit, using a way of thinking that I owe to him.

References

Adorno, T., E. Frenkel-Brunswick, D. Levinson, and R.N. Sanford. 1950. *The Authoritarian Personality*. New York: Harper & Row.

Benjamin, J. 1998. *Shadow of the Other: Intersubjectivity and Gender in Psychoanalysis*. New York: Routledge.

Cavalletto, G. 2007. *Crossing the Psycho-Social Divide: Freud, Weber, Adorno and Elias*. Aldershot, Hants.: Ashgate.

Clarke, S. 2003. *Social Theory, Psychoanalysis and Racism*. Basingstoke: Palgrave Macmillan.

Clarke, J. 2010. Of crises and conjunctures: The problem of the present. *Journal of Communication Inquiry* 34 (4): 337–54.

Du Gay, P., J. Evans, and P. Redman (eds.). 2000. *Identity: A Reader*. London: Sage.

Fast, I. 1984. *Gender Identity*. Hillsdale, NJ: The Analytic Press.

Fast, I. 1990. Aspects of early gender development: Toward a reformulation. *Psychoanalytic Psychology* 7 (Supplement): 105–18.

Freud, S. 1929. *Civilization and Its Discontents*. London and New York.

Gadd, D., and B. Dixon. 2011. *Losing the Race: Thinking Psychosocially About Racially Motivated Crime*. London: Karnac.

Gadd, D., B. Dixon, and T. Jefferson. 2005. *Why Do They Do It? Racial Harassment in North Staffordshire: Key Findings*. Keele: Centre for Criminological Research, Keele University.

Hall, S. 2018. Psychoanalysis and cultural studies. *Cultural Studies* 32 (6): 889–96.

Hollway, W. 2006. *The Capacity to Care: Gender and Ethical Subjectivity*. London: Routledge.

Jefferson, T. 2002. Subordinating hegemonic masculinity. *Theoretical Criminology* 6 (1): 63–88.

Jefferson, T. 2013. Masculinity, sexuality and hate-motivated violence. *International Journal for Crime, Justice and Social Democracy* 2 (3): 1–12.

Jones, E. 1964. *The Life and Work of Sigmund Freud*, ed. and abridged in one volume by Lionel Trilling and Steven Marcus. Harmondsworth: Penguin.

Klein, M. 1946. Notes on some schizoid mechanisms. In Mitchell, ed. (1986: 177–200).

Klein, M. 1952. The origins of transference. In Mitchell, ed. (1986: 201–10).

Klein, M. 1956. A study of envy and gratitude. In Mitchell, ed. (1986: 211–29).

Lasch, C. 1979. *The Culture of Narcissism: American Life in an Age of Diminishing Expectations*. London and New York: Norton.

Menzies Lyth, I. 1960/2000. Social systems as a defense against anxiety. In Du Gay et al., eds. (2000: 163–82).

Mitchell, J. (ed.). 1986. *The Selected Melanie Klein*. New York: The Free Press.

Richards, B. 2019. Beyond the angers of populism: A psychosocial inquiry. *Journal of Psychosocial Studies* 12 (1–2): 171–83.

Rustin, M. 2000. Psychoanalysis, racism and anti-racism. In Du Gay et al., eds. (2000: 183–201).

Rutherford, J. 2019. From Woodstock to Brexit: The tragedy of the liberal middle class. *New Statesman*, December 18. https://www.newstatesman.com/politics/brexit/2019/12/woodstock-brexit.

Index

absolutism 152
abstract 40, 41, 65, 66, 69, 72, 73, 129, 153, 202, 216, 238
Adorno, T. 70, 251, 255
affective 219, 239
Africans 86, 144, 233
Afro-Caribbeans 49, 144
aggressive 62, 68, 84, 85, 95, 181, 226, 234, 236, 243, 253, 254, 259, 260
Agozino, Biko 5
Akomfrah, John 1
Alexander, Claire 139, 140
alien/alienated/alienation 14, 78, 83–85, 94, 95, 97, 194, 240, 265
'All Lives Matter' 238, 240, 241
Althusser, Louis 10, 24, 28, 29, 50, 62, 112, 113, 115–117, 120–124, 130, 131, 134, 140, 145, 221
ambivalence 145, 199, 258
'America First' 229
anarchistic 60, 88, 91, 94, 96, 98, 234
anarchist(s) 8, 59, 88, 89, 93, 94, 96, 107
Anderson, Perry 164
anger/angry 10, 15, 49, 75, 95, 97, 102, 146, 158, 161, 162, 168, 172–174, 178, 198, 203, 207, 209, 211, 233, 234, 237, 249–252, 254–258, 260, 261, 264–266
anti-racist 13, 140, 144, 224, 264
Antonucci, P. 167–169, 190
anxiety 258, 259, 261, 265, 266
    persecutory 259, 260
    social 11, 43, 200

Index

'anywheres' 207, 211
articulation(s)/articulating 13, 120, 130–133, 143, 150, 199, 219–221, 230, 238, 240, 266
Ashcroft, Lord 166–170
Asians 144, 154, 168, 176, 178, 181, 232, 234
assimilation 13, 49, 147, 150
attentiveness 60, 89, 90
austerity 14, 172–174, 195, 197, 205
authoritarian
  personality 70
  populism 6, 14, 62, 63, 122, 210, 218–222, 226
  state 62, 220, 222, 226
  statism 220–222

B

Back, Les 157, 202
'Back to Basics' 194, 210
Bakhtin, Mikhail 12, 82, 99–101, 105
balance of forces 24, 50, 96–98, 129, 130, 230
Bangladeshis 201, 202
Bannonism 226, 227
Bannon, Steve 230
Barnett, S. 160, 174
Barrett, F.J. 178
Barry, M. 93, 162
Barthes, Roland 117, 125, 126
base 10, 14, 25, 27, 28, 34, 35, 44–46, 49, 50, 52, 59, 61, 64, 72, 75, 82, 84, 92, 98, 106, 114–116, 118, 120, 123, 124, 129–131, 152, 158, 167, 178–181, 190, 193, 195, 198, 199, 201–203, 207, 222, 223, 227, 231–235, 237, 252, 263
Bauman, Zygmunt 67, 68
Bean, P. 177
Becker, Howard 7
'belongingness' 132, 151
Benjamin, Jessica 15, 258, 262–264
Bennett, Tony 4
Bhambra, G.K. 173
Biden, Joe 230–232, 234, 236, 237, 242
binary model 99–101
biography/biographical 50, 74, 78, 90, 95, 97, 250, 254, 255, 257
Birk, J. 174
bisexual(ity) 262
black crime 47, 52
Black Lives Matter (BLM) 15, 231, 233, 234, 238–240, 242, 243, 264
Black Skins, White Masks 146
Blairism 226
Blair, Tony 192, 194, 195, 210, 224
Blunkett, David 205
boundaries 71, 73, 74, 100
Bourgois, Philippe 90
Brewster, Ben 24
Brexit 10, 13–15, 98, 122, 157–162, 167, 168, 172, 174, 177, 181, 182, 188, 192, 193, 201, 205–209, 211, 212, 216, 217, 237, 241, 244, 249–251, 254, 255
British National Party (BNP) 181, 193–195, 198
British(ness) 2, 13, 33, 34, 42, 45, 49, 123, 147, 153, 154, 168, 170, 177, 178, 187, 191–193,

196, 205, 207, 209, 222, 224, 226, 228, 229
Brown, Gordon 195, 205
Brown, Michael 233
Buchananesque 230
Buchanan, Pat 229
bulimia 72, 76
busking 87, 91, 93
Butcher, J. 167, 168

C

Cameron, David 173, 195–197, 205, 211
Campbell, Beatrix 181
Campbell, C. 68
The Capacity to Care 263
Capital 112, 116
capitalism/capitalist 27, 28, 52, 53, 61, 62, 68, 102, 112, 116, 118, 120, 121, 149, 150, 162, 193, 206, 211–223, 227, 228, 231, 232, 235, 236, 266
care 78, 129, 196, 263
Caribbean 140, 143
carnival 12, 81, 82, 88, 98–102, 104–107
Carrigan, M. 5
case-study 60, 175, 261
Cavalletto, George 251, 253, 255–257, 264
celebratory 99–101, 105, 106, 228
Centre for Contemporary Cultural Studies (CCCS) 2, 4, 5, 32, 40, 50, 64, 117, 175, 221
'chain of equivalences' 219, 225
character structure 118, 119
Chen, K-H. 1
China 193, 229, 235, 236

Christian 224, 228, 230, 231
evangelical 231
Right 228–231
City Limits 11, 57, 64, 65, 74, 78
Civilization and its Discontents 254
civil society 122, 123
Clarke, John 6, 33, 36, 175, 188, 190, 205, 206, 210, 258
Clarke, Simon 261
class(es)
intermediate 167, 168
middle 2, 14, 34, 88, 92, 113, 121, 130, 140, 166–168, 170, 173, 175, 187–192, 196, 198, 200, 236–239, 241, 242, 251
problematic 34–36, 47
struggle 8, 9, 25, 49, 190
working 8, 13, 28, 33–36, 48, 52, 73, 75, 112, 117, 167, 168, 170, 173, 175, 176, 178, 180, 181, 188, 189, 191, 192, 203, 204, 206–208, 219, 223–225, 236–238, 241–243
climate 150, 165, 231, 232
Accord 232, 237
change 15, 231, 232, 234, 236, 243
Clinton, Bill 224
Clinton, Hillary 225, 242
coalition 173, 228–230
government 14, 192, 195
Cochrane, Alan 169, 190
code 84, 90, 125, 126
street 84
traditional 84
Coffield, Frank 176, 180, 182
Cohen, Phil 35, 36, 62, 192, 267
Cohen, Stan 7, 42, 45, 61
'Cold War' 13, 148, 227, 228

Coleman, Roy 6, 62, 210
colonisation/colonization/ colonised/colonized/ colonisers/colonizers 148, 149
commodity/commodification 63, 102–104
common 8, 25, 57, 66, 71, 91, 171, 188, 234, 264
   sense 8, 11, 13, 41, 43–45, 66, 122, 123, 160, 162–165, 188, 205, 206, 210, 223, 226, 229, 230
   will 219
commune 88, 98
   Paris 88, 98
complex(ity) 4, 7, 11, 13, 14, 31, 42, 58–60, 100–102, 106, 111–116, 119, 120, 122, 123, 126, 142, 144, 147, 190, 200, 201, 206, 218, 230, 242, 256, 257, 262, 264
concrete 11, 34, 41, 44–47, 65, 73, 75, 103, 131, 133, 134, 145, 177, 203, 216, 239, 244, 252
   in thought 157
conjunctural/conjuncture 4–7, 9–11, 13, 14, 24–27, 33, 34, 37, 47, 50, 51, 58, 78, 82, 97, 99–101, 103, 105, 107, 111–113, 122, 134, 135, 140, 147, 149, 157, 163, 205–207, 211, 216–222, 226–230, 243, 244, 249, 257, 258, 264
   analysis 4–7, 9–15, 27, 28, 30, 34, 40, 50, 51, 53, 60, 61, 65, 79, 81, 96–98, 103, 105–107, 111, 157, 205, 216–220, 223, 225, 226, 243, 249, 250

   global 141, 217, 231
Connell, R.W. 208, 209
connotation 42, 126, 131, 132, 202
consent 104, 121, 122, 124, 222
Conservative(s)/conservative 27, 159, 169, 171–174, 188, 189, 195–197, 205
   sense of Englishness 164, 191
consumer 65, 67, 68, 70, 71, 83, 88, 103, 206, 229
consumption 69, 73, 85, 87, 92, 95, 101, 102, 104, 149
contain(er) 260, 261
containment 101, 260
contingency/contingent 63, 77, 108, 132, 134, 201, 216, 230
contradiction(s) 24, 25, 34, 35, 62, 63, 73, 74, 94, 100–102, 112, 121, 150, 206, 218, 219, 223, 226, 230
convergence 45, 46, 115
Corbyn, Jeremy 64, 204
correspondence(s) 71, 119, 253
cosmopolitan(ism) 189, 207, 210, 211, 224, 241
counter
   culture 34
   hegemonic 266
   hegemony 223
COVID pandemic 230, 231
Cox, Jo 197
Cram, L. 161
crime
   expressive 72, 79, 81
   general theory of 11, 58, 65, 68, 78, 79
   individual theories of 65, 107
   instrumental 72

criminalisation 59, 61, 101, 103, 104, 106, 178, 209, 210, 243
criminology
  critical 8, 58
  cultural 6–9, 11, 12, 57–60, 64, 72, 77, 78, 81, 82, 89, 95, 98, 100, 106, 107, 111, 215, 216
  radical 8, 62, 63
critique/critiquing 11, 13, 33, 43, 61, 68, 82, 84, 99, 100, 105, 106, 111, 115, 119, 120, 129, 133, 160
cultural/culture
  criminology 6–9, 11, 12, 57–59, 64, 72, 77, 78, 82, 89, 95, 98, 100, 106, 107, 215, 216
  dominant 36, 99
  studies 2–5, 7, 9, 57, 59, 61, 82, 96, 106, 113, 117, 118, 124, 125, 215, 216, 252, 253
  turn 124
  wars 14, 189, 191, 210
Cultural Criminology and the Carnival of Crime 12, 82, 101
The Culture of Narcissism 256, 257

D

'Darren' 261–263
data 42, 43, 45, 47, 78, 89, 94, 96, 165, 167, 168
Davies, W. 165
Davis, Helen 1
Debord, Guy 62
debt 121, 172, 190, 229, 230
decoding 4, 5, 125
decolonisation/decolonization 13, 143, 148
defence(s) 30, 259, 261, 265
  mechanisms 259, 265
defer 146
'defund the police' 239, 242
de-industrialisation/de-industrialization 180, 224, 241
democracy/democratic 88, 153, 162, 193, 206, 222, 224–227, 230, 232, 234–237
democratisation/democratization 162
Democrats 231, 237
demographic/demography 13, 166, 232
Dench, Geoff 201, 202
denial 14, 231, 232, 234, 240, 259
denotation 126
depression 182, 198, 266
depressive position 260, 261
deprivation 52, 77, 78, 166, 167
  relative 67, 73–75
  spaces of 68
deregulation 193, 229, 235
Derrida, Jacques 146
Derridean 147, 199
desire 67–71, 76, 85, 90, 100, 103, 106, 107, 145, 171, 199, 204, 236, 242, 262, 266
determinacy 60, 114, 115, 121
determination(s)/determined 11, 24, 25, 30, 40–43, 45, 47, 60, 65, 71, 77, 78, 82, 96–98, 107, 108, 112, 114, 115, 121, 131, 133, 134, 150, 158, 170, 173, 174, 221
detoxify 260
dialogic(al)/dialoguing 64, 111, 116, 117, 119
diaspora/diasporic 141, 152, 199

differ/difference 9–11, 25, 26, 51, 57, 63, 76, 83, 89, 92, 105–107, 113, 114, 119, 123, 127, 128, 130, 133, 141, 144–147, 149–153, 169, 179, 181, 189, 199, 204, 205, 207, 211, 218, 220, 238, 239, 241, 243, 256, 261, 263
  living with 13, 14, 141
  politics of 13–15, 140, 146, 147, 152, 170, 176, 181, 182, 198, 199, 211, 216, 217, 243
différance 146, 151–153, 199
disarticulation 225, 238, 241
discourse 4, 5, 8, 9, 13, 51, 104, 114, 124, 127, 129–132, 141, 146, 205, 219, 225
discursive 114, 120, 124, 127, 129–134, 140, 198, 199, 204, 205, 219, 238, 240–242
'Disneyfication' 87, 91–93, 96
distribution 129, 223–226
Dixon, Bill 261
dominant/domination 34, 36, 98, 99, 120, 122, 123, 128, 149, 150, 160, 164, 168, 172, 175, 181, 193, 197, 207, 240, 241, 260
Dorling, Danny 166–169
drugs 67, 84, 90, 95, 102, 177, 178, 182, 188, 192, 198, 226, 243, 266
  crack cocaine 177
  heroin 177
Du Bois, W.E.B. 3, 113, 198

East End of London 35

eclecticism 12
economic/economism/economistic 25, 26, 33, 52, 62–64, 68, 71, 74, 78, 84–87, 95, 112, 115–119, 124, 132, 158, 159, 162, 165, 170–174, 179, 188–190, 193, 195, 197, 203, 204, 206, 210, 211, 219, 220, 223, 226, 232, 236, 242, 243, 264, 266
'edgework' 66, 67, 69
education 120, 123, 166, 169, 179, 180, 189, 197, 207, 208
effectivity(ies) 115, 120, 124, 126, 251, 255
egalitarian 225, 242
ego 259
The Eighteenth Brumaire 9, 26, 27, 29, 87, 115, 116
Eley, Geoff 2
Elias, Norbert 251
emotions 10, 66, 70, 102, 250, 266
  moral 70
'empathy bridges' 242
Empire 14, 151, 154, 188, 190, 191, 197
empiricism 27, 164
encoding 4, 5, 125
Engels, Frederick 115
English/Englishness 29, 40, 48, 88, 121, 146, 164, 168, 170, 191, 195, 198, 212
  conservative sense of 164, 191
  Defence League (EDL) 195
entitlement 201–205, 208
epoch 69, 258
equality 73, 74, 116, 153, 202, 205, 219, 238, 239, 243
essentialism 74

essentialist 13, 115, 151
ethnicity(ies)/ethnicised/ethnicized 3, 10, 13, 76, 140–142, 144, 147, 148, 152, 153, 168, 173, 176, 180, 198, 199, 204, 211, 241, 243
ethnographer 8, 82
ethnography(ies)
　direct 50, 83
　existential 82
　secondary 30, 49, 83, 97
ethnonational 224
Eurosceptic(ism) 13, 171–173
'exceptional' 84, 210, 221
　state 46, 50, 210, 222
excitement 67–70, 101–103
excluded 8, 68, 72–74, 76–78, 83, 100, 169, 180
exclusion(ary) 71–77, 85–87, 95, 100, 153, 154, 224, 225, 262
expertise 13, 40, 159, 161–164

F

Family and Kinship in East London 201
Fanon, Franz 51, 146, 239
Farage, Nigel 160, 193, 196
Fassin, E. 218
Fast, I. 262
femininity 175, 180, 208, 209, 263, 264
　emphasised 262
feminism/feminists 8, 59, 72, 77, 145, 163, 169, 170, 192, 203, 224, 253
Fenton, N. 174
Ferrell, Jeff 8, 9, 12, 57–63, 82, 86–94, 96, 98, 107

Feyerabend, Paul 60
fight(ing) 75, 142, 172, 204, 208
finance 193, 232, 235
financial 149, 167, 172, 173, 190, 193, 195, 205, 206, 228, 229, 235–237
　crash 173, 205, 229, 236
FitzGerald, Mike 6–8
FitzGibbon, John 163
'Flint Lives Matter' 240
Floyd, George 210, 233, 234
'folk devils' 75
formal 59, 84, 126, 129, 153, 203
For Marx 24, 121
Fornäs, J. 3
Foucault, Michel 104, 127–131
Frankfurt school 119, 255
Fraser, Nancy 217–219, 223–227, 229, 230, 242, 243
Freedland, J. 208
Freedman, Des 161, 171
freedom 93, 116, 150, 171, 257
free-market 229
Freud, Sigmund 24, 115, 116, 145, 191, 251, 252, 254, 255, 262
Fukuyama, Francis 162

G

Gadd, Dave 200, 261
Gates, Jr, Henry Louis 3
Geddes, Andrew 174, 193, 197
gender 9, 14, 69, 72, 76, 144, 145, 151, 175, 176, 182, 188, 191, 202, 203, 207, 208, 262, 263
'general' whole 41, 47, 71
genetic-historical 31, 32
Gentleman, Amelia 196
gentrification 87, 91, 92, 96, 107

The German Ideology 114, 115
ghetto 31, 49, 51, 72, 73, 76–78
Gifford, C. 171
Gilroy, Paul 1, 190, 191
global(isation)/globalization 13, 14, 30, 44, 53, 62, 75, 141, 147–149, 151, 152, 169, 194, 206, 208, 210, 217, 218, 220, 226–228, 230, 231, 233, 234, 243
Goes, Eunice 171, 205
Goldman, Emma 88, 119
'good enough' 36, 260
Goodhart, David 207, 211
'good sense' 8, 165
Goodwin, M.J. 166, 168, 169
Gove, Michael 159, 197
graffiti 63, 82, 87, 91
Gramscian 4, 5, 10, 14, 27, 122, 123, 217, 219
Gramsci, Antonio 4, 5, 9, 10, 25–29, 33, 43, 50, 62, 112, 115, 121–124, 157, 163, 208, 218, 221, 223, 225, 243
Gray, Ann 28, 29
'The great moving right show' 28, 53
green deal 236
Green, J. 172
Grossberg, Larry 4, 252
Grundrisse 40
guilt 254, 260

Hage, Ghassan 239, 240
'hail'. *See* interpellate(s)
Hallian 205, 222

Hall, Stuart 1–4, 5–7, 9, 10, 12–15, 25–34, 36, 40, 42, 47, 50, 51, 53, 61, 62, 82, 97, 100, 107, 111–135, 139–154, 157, 158, 160, 164, 178, 182, 187–189, 191–193, 198–200, 202, 205–207, 209–212, 215–222, 228, 238, 239, 243, 244, 250, 252–255, 258, 264, 266, 267. *See also* Stuart Hall Foundation
Handsworth 40, 43, 44, 47, 164
Harmer, E. 160
Hart, Gillian 14, 217–220, 222, 225–227, 229, 230, 238
hate 74, 196, 198, 199, 204, 209, 260, 262
  crimes 74, 196, 198, 204, 209
  motivated violence 209, 262
hatred 102, 199, 203, 204, 207, 259, 261
  racial 199, 203
Hayward, Keith 8, 11, 12, 57, 64–66, 68–72, 74, 77, 78, 107
Heath, O. 166, 168, 169
hegemonic 123, 211, 223–226
  masculinity 208, 209
hegemonising/hegemonizing 149
hegemony 9, 98, 122, 124, 163
  crisis of 11, 43–46, 50, 53, 58, 62, 97, 189, 206, 211, 223, 228
Hegemony and Socialist Strategy 132, 133
Henderson, L. 4
Henn, M. 169
Henriques, Julian 1
Hewitt, R. 202
hidden 35, 47, 107, 116, 147, 170, 198, 251

high/low relations 99
hippies 5, 10, 30–34, 50, 62, 204
historical
  genetic. *See* genetic-historical materialism 115, 117, 133
  moments 26, 33, 102, 107, 111, 264
  particularities 11, 58, 106
historically 5, 13, 34, 35, 41, 51, 58, 63, 78, 97, 103, 105, 108, 111, 114, 115, 118, 127, 129, 141, 158, 172, 175, 178, 199, 221, 228, 241, 255
  idealist 13, 111
  materialist 13, 111, 113–115
historicism 121
historicity 41
Hobbes, Thomas 254
Hochschild, Arlie 231, 242
Hoggart, Richard 32, 117, 124
Hollway, Wendy 263
Home Office 195
homicide 83, 85, 95
homogenising/homogenizing 92, 149, 189
homophobic 224, 225, 264
'hostile environment' 195, 205
hostility 162, 163, 176, 199, 201, 203, 207, 222
Hudson, Barbara 7
humiliation 70, 74–77, 85
'hustling' 49
hybridisation/hybridization 99
hybridising/hybridizing 152
hybridity 150
hyper
  masculinity 76
  reactionary 225

idealisation/idealization 259
idealism 113
  left 8, 64
ideal type/ideal typical 118, 225
identification/identificatory 13, 68, 97, 143–145, 151, 199, 259, 261–263
identity(ies) 2, 3, 8–10, 49, 67, 69, 74, 76, 78, 87, 100, 120, 130, 139, 141, 142, 146, 147, 152, 153, 203, 211, 242, 252
Ideological State Apparatuses (ISAs) 120–122, 124, 130
ideology/ideological/ideologistic 7, 25, 26, 42, 43, 46, 51–53, 64, 74, 88, 98, 115–124, 126–132, 140, 160, 164, 175, 196, 206, 207, 209–211, 222, 226, 229, 230, 236–238, 242, 264, 266
imaginary 71, 78, 100, 131
immigrant(s)/immigration 10, 13, 14, 48, 144, 147, 150, 158, 160, 161, 165, 169–171, 173–176, 182, 192–205, 207, 209, 211, 212, 232, 261, 265
impoverished 204
incarceration 62, 63, 83, 226
included/inclusion(ary) 13, 33, 47, 51, 52, 59, 61, 72–76, 78, 88, 95, 120, 123, 124, 142, 168, 173, 174, 198, 201, 237, 243, 261, 264
India 146, 148, 193, 222, 227, 228
inequality 74, 116, 173, 174, 179, 182, 229
informal 49, 84
insecurity 66, 69, 78, 203

instincts 255, 259, 260
instinctual 254
Institute of Contemporary Arts 141
institutional racism 192, 209
international 14, 141, 147, 177, 217, 237
interpellate(s)/interpellation 131, 133, 140, 145, 240, 266
  mis- 239, 240
  non- 240
interpretation/interpretative/interpretive 70, 158, 162, 164, 165
introjection 259
Islam(ism)/Islamic/Islamification 192, 193, 203, 204, 209
Islamophobia 209, 229

Jackson, Daniel 158
Jacques, Martin 4
Jefferson, Tony 5, 36, 59, 199, 210, 261, 263
Jenks, Chris 76
Jessop, Bob 53
Jhally, S. 5
Johnson, Boris 64, 159, 160, 197
Jones, Ernest 254
Jump, Robert Calvert 167
justice 74, 85, 90, 100, 105, 153, 202, 207, 219, 223, 228, 243
  social 207, 219

Katz, Jack 9, 11, 58, 64–67, 70, 71, 76, 77
Keith, Michael 202

Klein, Melanie 15, 253, 254, 258–262, 264
knowledge 3, 15, 73, 82, 117, 126–130, 149, 162, 163
Kureshi, Hanif 143

Labour
  heartlands 159, 169, 173, 194
  new 14, 154, 171, 179, 180, 192, 193, 205, 206, 210, 224, 226
  voters 159, 169, 170, 173, 195, 198
Lacanian(ism) 140, 253, 258
Lacan, Jacques 131, 253, 258
Laclau, Ernesto 113, 130–134, 153, 219–221, 238, 239
laddish 188
'lads' 175, 176, 180, 182, 206
Laing, R.D. 66
language 48, 73, 120, 121, 124–127, 130, 132, 133, 145, 147, 153, 160, 161, 163, 176, 232, 249, 253
Lasch, Christopher 256
late modern 9, 63, 65–69, 71, 74, 75, 77, 78, 107
Latino 232, 234
law and order 42, 86, 97, 189, 210, 234, 236, 239
Lawrence Inquiry 3
Lea, John 64
Learning to Labour 175, 178
leavers 48, 159, 160, 167, 169, 170, 176, 178, 207, 211
Leave Vote 13, 14, 166, 167, 171–174, 190. *See also* Vote Leave

Leavis, F.R. 117, 158
Leavisite 61
Lee, Murray 6
Lefebvre, Henri 31, 32, 50
left
   populism 14, 218, 219, 227
   realism 8, 58, 64
'left-behinds' 83, 102, 168, 173, 207, 208, 235
legitimacy/legitimate 46, 73, 129, 160, 200, 233, 234, 237
levels 36, 51, 52, 84, 95, 115, 117, 120, 134, 166, 169, 175, 178, 206, 227, 250, 251, 255, 256, 264–266
Levy, D. 161
Lilleker, D.G. 174
linguistic 125, 126, 146
   turn 125
Llewellyn, C. 161
local 13, 35, 40, 43, 73, 92, 94, 141, 149, 174, 177, 193, 196, 198, 202, 231
London bombings 193, 209
loops/looping 63
Lowery, W. 233
Lynch, P. 172, 173
Lyng, Stephen 66, 68

M

Macpherson, W. 192
The Manufacture of News 61
marginality 92, 101, 102, 121, 141, 144, 150, 168, 182
Martin, T. 173, 233
Marxism 8, 9, 24, 27, 29, 63, 64, 112, 114, 116, 121, 124, 125, 127, 128, 134, 252

Marxism Today (MT) 2, 3, 8, 53
Marx, Karl 9, 11, 26, 27, 29, 33, 40–42, 44, 50, 51, 65, 87, 107, 112–117, 121, 122, 125, 131, 134, 157, 220, 221
masculinist 144, 204, 209, 238
masculinity(ies) 174–176, 178, 180, 188, 198, 202, 203, 207–209, 211, 262, 263, 266
Massey, Doreen 205, 206
McDowell, Linda 178–180, 182, 188, 198, 207
McLaughlin, E. 6
meaning(s) 9, 10, 30, 32, 33, 47, 51–53, 63, 88, 93, 117, 118, 124–127, 130, 144, 146, 147, 150, 198, 199, 242, 251, 263
media 11, 13, 33, 41–45, 47, 50, 59–61, 73, 78, 87, 93, 102, 114, 123, 158–162, 164, 165, 189, 249, 265
   social 159, 161, 162, 164, 165, 249, 265
mediations 30, 31, 34–36, 42, 47–50, 78, 96, 97, 126
Meeks, B. 1
melancholia 191
   post-imperial 190, 191, 251
mendacious/mendacity 160, 161
Menzies Lyth, Isabel 265
merit(ocracy)/meritocratic 74, 175, 207, 258, 266
Merton, Robert 8, 11, 57, 64, 67, 71, 73, 76
'Merton with energy: Katz with structure' 71, 76
methodology(ies)/methodological 5–7, 10–13, 25, 27–30, 33, 34, 40, 41, 44, 53, 57, 58, 65,

72, 81, 89, 96, 105, 106, 118, 119, 126, 157, 158, 167, 221, 243, 244
middle
  class(es). *See* class(es)
  period 113, 121, 130, 140
migration(s) 148, 151, 196, 197
'misfit' outsiders 88, 107
misogynistic/misogyny 15, 225, 263
Mitchell, Jo 167
modern(isation)/modernization 2, 41, 69, 73, 102, 125, 145, 148, 149, 151, 175, 189, 195, 196, 210
  regressive 189, 210
'moments' 14, 24, 26, 32, 43, 44, 77, 82, 90, 105, 119, 120, 142, 181, 194, 209, 220, 225, 227, 228
moral panic 11, 42, 44–46, 62, 164, 220
Morley, David 1, 220, 238
Mouffe, Chantal 130, 132–135, 219, 225, 227
The Muck of Ages 103
'muggers'/'mugging' 33, 40–42, 44–47, 49–53, 58, 59, 62, 65, 68, 83, 142, 160, 164, 234
Mullen, A. 161
multicultural(ism)/multiculturalising/multiculturalizing 3, 13, 140, 144, 147, 148, 150–154, 169, 170, 182, 187, 192, 193, 198, 199, 203, 212, 226, 238, 239, 243
Murdock, Graham 5
Muslims 150, 168, 203, 207, 209, 211
My Beautiful Launderette 143, 144

Mythologies 125

narcissism/narcissistic 68, 237, 255–257, 261
  complex 256
National Deviancy Conference (NDC) 7, 61
nation(alism)/nationalistic 62, 141, 143, 145, 148, 149, 151–153, 188, 198, 207
nativism 230
neo-liberal(ism) 174, 175, 193, 197, 203, 206, 227
new criminologist 7
new criminology 5
The New Criminology (TNC) 47, 59, 62
The New East End 201, 202
The New Heroin Users 177
New Left 2, 27, 28, 53, 165, 171, 172
New Left Review (NLR) 2
'new times' 8, 58, 64
Nicolaus, Martin 41
Nightingale, Carl 12, 68, 72, 75, 78, 82–86, 90, 94–97
9/11 13, 14, 154, 157, 181, 187, 188, 196–200, 204, 209, 226, 229
1968 9, 26, 28–31, 87, 98, 116, 176, 196

Obama, Barack 224, 229, 230, 233, 234, 237, 242

Index

object 8, 30, 36, 42, 68, 90, 100, 106, 125, 130, 132, 217, 252, 259, 264, 265, 267
   love 260
   relations 258, 259
Oedipal 262
   pre- 262
Oedipus complex 262
The Old is Dying and the New Cannot be Born 223
omnipotence/omnipotent 259
On the Edge 12, 72, 75, 82, 83
ontological insecurity 66, 71, 74
Open University (OU) 2, 7, 126
organic 10, 25–27
O'Shea, Alan 164
'Other'/'othered'/othering' 74, 76, 198, 199, 261, 264
over
   controlled 66, 69, 70
   determination 24, 115, 121
   inclusive 262
   reaction 11

pain 78, 84, 86, 95, 104, 177, 200, 266
pandemic 15, 210, 217, 234–236
paradigm(s) 100, 251, 254
paranoid-schizoid 259–261, 264, 265
Parekh, Bikhu 3, 154, 192
parent culture 35, 36
participant 30, 36, 88, 94, 200
   observation 94
   observer 94
particular(istic)/particularities 6, 11, 12, 25, 29, 33, 35, 36, 41, 42, 44, 45, 47, 50, 58, 61, 62, 64–66, 69–72, 77, 81, 84, 92, 96, 97, 99, 103, 105–107, 111, 112, 118, 125, 127, 131–134, 144, 149, 150, 153, 160, 164, 165, 173, 188, 191, 202, 217, 227, 238–241, 249, 255–257, 263–265
patriarchal 77, 104, 192, 224
Patterson, Chauntey 84
Paul, Annie 3
Pearson, Geoffrey 177
Perry, Grayson 241
persecution 259
phantasy(ies) 257, 259, 264, 265
phenomenal forms 116, 117, 131
phenomenological/phenomenology 9, 11, 30, 31, 34, 36, 42, 51, 64, 71, 76, 77, 97
Pilkington, Hilary 204, 208
pluralistic 12, 59, 60, 63, 64, 111, 153
Policing the Crisis (PTC) 4–7, 10, 13, 14, 25, 27, 30, 32–34, 37, 40, 41, 47, 50, 58, 59, 61, 62, 64, 97, 112, 122, 140, 142, 157, 160, 164, 175, 189, 191, 200, 205–207, 210, 211, 215–217, 220–222, 228, 234, 238, 243, 244
Politics and Ideology in Marxist Theory 131, 132
The Politics and Poetics of Transgression 12, 82, 99
Polonski, V. 161
population 40, 65, 166, 168
populism 44, 99, 122, 198, 210, 217–226, 229, 230, 249, 257, 266

left 14, 218, 219, 227
progressive 218, 224, 225, 242
populist 14, 63, 160, 193, 195, 199, 205, 206, 208, 210, 211, 217, 218, 222–229, 236, 238, 242, 255, 258
positionalities/positions 32, 48, 58, 68, 71, 114, 128, 131–134, 144, 146, 147, 159, 167, 229, 242, 259–261, 263
post
 crash 172, 174, 194, 195, 197, 204
 Marxist 8, 9, 12, 111, 134, 219
 modernism 8, 58, 64, 66, 69, 102, 103, 162
Poulantzas, Nicos 62, 121, 220–222
poverty 76, 85, 91, 168, 173, 174, 177–179, 181, 182, 188, 194, 197, 243
Powell, Enoch 171, 176, 196
practice(s) 49, 51, 57, 87, 94, 104, 105, 108, 114, 115, 120, 123, 127, 130, 132, 133, 143, 151, 153, 192, 207–209, 221, 225, 232, 239, 266. *See also* levels
 discursive 127, 130
precarity 74
precariousness 74, 76, 205, 221
Presdee, Mike 8, 12, 82, 100–107
Prison Notebooks 121, 123
The Problem of Method (TPOM) 29, 31
Procter, J. 1
progressive
 neo-liberalism 174, 227
 populism. *See* populism
projection 259, 260, 265

The Protestant Ethic and the Spirit of Capitalism 118
protestors 234
'Proud Boys' 237, 241
psyche 251, 253, 255, 257
psychoanalysis/psychoanalytic 10, 15, 131, 140, 145, 165, 249, 250, 252–254, 258, 261, 262, 264, 266, 267
psychosocial(ly) 15, 250–252, 254–257, 264, 266

race/racism 9, 10, 13–15, 42, 48, 49, 52, 53, 74, 76, 95, 139, 141, 144, 145, 150, 173, 174, 180, 182, 188, 191, 192, 198, 200, 201, 204, 205, 207, 209–211, 218, 220, 221, 223, 234, 238, 240, 261, 264
racial/racialized 47, 86, 140, 147, 151, 153, 154, 181, 199, 203, 227, 233, 239, 241, 243
 hatred 203
 prejudice 199, 203
Rae, E. 167
rage 102, 256, 257, 260
reactionary 198, 210, 223–227, 229, 230, 232, 236
Reading Capital 121
Reaganism 211, 226, 228
Reagan, Ronald 228, 229
real relations 116, 117, 131
rearticulation. *See* articulation(s)
recognition 111, 121, 131, 151, 153, 215, 223–226
 mis 75, 240
redistribution 224, 225, 242

reductionism/reductive(ness) 9, 27, 42, 43, 61, 69–71, 75, 77, 96, 98, 101, 106, 107, 111, 115, 118, 123, 127, 132, 133, 251, 253, 255, 264
Redundant Masculinities? 178
Referendum 13–15, 157–159, 167, 170–174, 176, 177, 181, 182, 195, 197, 211, 264
  UK 13, 157
refugee crisis 15, 231, 232
regime of truth 127
regressive 31, 44, 45, 48, 51, 140, 150, 152, 189, 210, 224, 225, 232. See also reactionary
modernization 189, 210
relative autonomy 13, 116, 119, 120, 130
Remainers 158, 161, 169, 170, 211
renunciation 255, 262, 263
representation(s) 124, 125, 127, 243
repression 258
reproduction 111, 113, 120, 121, 131, 140, 251
  social 120, 123, 130
Republican 29, 224, 231–234, 236, 237
repudiation 262–264
resistance 31, 49, 50, 63, 71, 87, 88, 91, 93, 96, 98, 128–130, 144, 206
Resistance through Rituals (RTR) 5–7, 10, 28–30, 32, 33, 36, 47, 112, 126, 192
Richards, Barry 255, 256
rioting/riots 42, 142, 181, 212
The Rise of the Meritocracy 207
'rising crime rate' equation 41, 160
risk-taking 67, 68

Rivington Place 3
Roach, Colin 3
Rojek, Chris 1
Rustin, Michael 261, 264
Rutherford, Jonathan 188–190, 266

S

sadomasochistic (S&M) 102–104
The Sage Dictionary of Criminology 6
Sandbrook, Dominic 176
Sanders, Bernie 224, 225
Sanders, Clinton 57–60, 89
Sartre, Jean-Paul 10, 29–31, 33, 35, 42, 44, 48, 116
Saussure, Ferdinand de 125, 145
Sayer, Derek 173, 212
Scannell, P. 5
scapegoat(s)/scapegoating 75, 203, 209
scholarship 2, 189, 207
  boys 189, 207
  girls 189, 207
Scott, David 1
Seabrook, Jeremy 199, 200
Seductions of Crime 65
semiology 50, 125
Sennett, Richard 237
service-type jobs 180
sexism/sexist 74, 76, 264
sexual difference 253, 262
Shamsie, Kamila 192, 196
Sharpe, D. 169
'shit jobs' 176, 179
sign(s) 100, 125, 126, 177
signification 29, 36, 46, 51, 126, 147, 198, 199
spirals 45

signified 11, 45, 46, 51, 58, 125, 126, 175
signifier(s) 125, 199
  sliding 147, 198
Sim, Joe 5
Slimani, L. 172
Snyder, Greg 91
social
  control 84, 85
  democratic 193, 206, 226
  forces 9, 64, 111, 132, 143, 148, 219, 223, 238, 242
  formation 31, 46, 51, 52, 97, 100, 115, 120, 126, 129, 189, 217
  mobility 189, 207
  relations 13, 53, 58, 69, 77, 97, 111, 116, 119, 120, 132, 144, 147, 149, 202, 206
socio-cultural 254
'somewheres' 207, 211
Soundings 3
South Africa 140, 222, 227, 228, 238
Southall 3
sovereignty 62, 158, 165, 170, 174, 255
spatiohistorical 222
specificity(ies) 12, 44, 51, 58, 81, 82, 98, 99, 105, 106, 112, 115, 120, 123, 126, 128, 132, 148, 158, 165, 211, 222, 238, 241, 256–258, 264–266
speculative 11, 43, 65, 78, 102, 173
spiralling 63
splitting 145, 259–261, 263, 265
Stallybrass, Peter 12, 82, 99, 101, 105

state 6, 8, 9, 14, 24, 27, 33, 42, 43, 45, 46, 50, 52, 58, 61, 62, 67, 76, 77, 88, 98, 99, 104–106, 120, 122, 123, 127, 128, 140, 144, 149–151, 153, 166, 173, 179, 188, 192, 199, 201, 202, 208, 210, 216–219, 222, 226–230, 235, 236, 238, 254, 260
State, Power, Socialism (SPS) 221, 222
Stoke-on-Trent 200, 261
strain 67, 73, 77
  theory 67, 73
structural(ism) 27, 35, 44, 45, 48, 51, 61, 62, 64–66, 71–73, 76, 77, 199
structure(s) 9, 11, 25, 26, 30, 31, 47–50, 58–60, 71, 73, 76, 77, 79, 101, 113, 115–118, 119, 129, 172, 178, 217, 221, 223
Stuart Hall Foundation 1
'style' 32–36, 49, 78, 104, 126, 176, 178, 180
subaltern 149
subconscious 84
subcultures 5, 10, 32–36, 87, 91, 189, 192
  youth 5, 10, 33–36, 126, 189, 192
subject(ivity) 26, 32, 34, 46, 47, 49, 67, 69, 70, 72, 77, 78, 85, 87–89, 95, 96, 100, 107, 114, 125, 131, 133, 140, 141, 143, 145, 157, 158, 172, 180, 192, 201, 239, 253, 264
subordination 49, 107, 144, 199, 240

superstructures 13, 25, 114–118, 120, 122–124, 130
supremacists/supremacy white 233, 234, 238, 240, 241
surplus value 112, 116
symbol(ic)/symbolism 8, 50, 51, 59, 87, 99–101, 106, 234, 236
symptomatic 9, 50, 53, 98, 165, 207, 222, 250
synthesise/synthesize/synthesising/synthesizing 58, 78, 144

'Take Back Control' 162, 163, 165, 175, 198, 211
Taylor, Ian 7, 47, 59
Tea Party 231, 233, 242
Tearing Down the Streets 12, 82, 86, 96
terrorism 71, 188, 205
terrorists 165, 188, 193, 198, 204, 209, 211, 238
Thatcherism 8, 13, 26–28, 53, 58, 62, 140, 141, 158, 164, 178, 188, 189, 211, 216, 218–220, 222, 226, 228, 229
theory(ies) 5–7, 9–15, 26, 29, 33–35, 41–48, 51, 57–60, 62–65, 67–72, 75–78, 81, 82, 85, 89, 94–96, 100, 102, 106–108, 111–126, 128, 130–135, 140, 144–146, 150, 182, 199, 202, 207, 216–218, 221, 222, 225, 243, 244, 250, 252–256, 258, 259, 262, 263, 266
driven 58, 65, 72, 140, 141, 216

theoretical/theorising 6, 7, 10–15, 23, 26, 33–35, 41–46, 48, 51, 57, 58, 60, 62–65, 67–72, 78, 95, 96, 102, 106, 107, 111–117, 119, 121, 124–126, 128, 131, 134, 140, 144, 145, 182, 202, 207, 217, 218, 221, 243, 250, 252, 253, 255, 258, 262
Thompson, L. 172
thresholds 45, 46
Tomlinson, Sally 166–169
Tory 159, 170, 188, 189, 196
voters 159. *See also* Conservative(s)
traditional(ism)/tradition(s) 7–9, 12, 14, 29, 63, 82, 84–86, 89, 96, 102, 104, 124, 130, 145, 149–151, 159, 163–165, 173, 176, 180, 188–194, 196, 208, 210, 241, 242, 255
transcendence/transcending 65, 67
transgression 58, 63, 66, 67, 69–71, 75, 76, 98, 99, 101, 104, 105, 107
transnational(ism) 149
triangulation 94
true/truth 26, 28, 32, 37, 40, 44, 53, 62, 68, 96, 102, 107, 108, 112, 118, 126–129, 142, 145, 160, 162–164, 198, 222, 225, 237, 251, 254
Trump, Donald 10, 14, 15, 208, 211, 212, 217, 218, 222–226, 229–238, 241–243, 265
Trumpism 218, 223, 228–230, 237, 244
trust 90, 158, 197, 257
20 years 40

type(s) 46, 66, 70, 127, 199, 226, 251

U

unconscious 95, 199, 200, 203, 204, 250, 251, 253, 264
underclass 51, 72, 73, 76, 83
unemployment 48, 85, 142, 176–178, 181, 182, 200, 235, 236
UNESCO 32, 140, 220
United Kingdom Independence Party (UKIP) 169, 173, 193, 196, 198
United States (US) 87, 222, 223, 227, 230, 235, 243
unity 24, 129, 132, 233
universalism/universalistic 149–151, 240, 255
Universities Left Review 2
The Uses of Literacy 117, 124

V

Varoufakis, Yanis 172
Vasilopoulou, Sofia 170, 211
vernacular modernities 149, 150
vindictiveness 58, 71, 75, 76, 107
violence/violent 15, 46, 63, 65, 71–75, 83–86, 95, 97, 102, 104, 119, 176, 198, 208–210, 239, 253, 262, 263
Vote Leave 159, 168, 169, 172, 190, 197, 208, 249

W

'war on terror' 62, 154, 187, 204, 226

Weber, Max 117–119, 158, 251
West Indian(s) 49, 176
West, the 145, 148, 206, 210
Whannel, Gary 141
Whannel, Paddy 2
white
  supremacists/supremacy 233, 234, 238, 240, 241
  working class 52, 203, 204, 208
White, Allon 12, 82, 99, 101, 105
Whitehead, S.M. 178
whiteness 181, 240
Willmott, Peter 201
Willis, Paul 175, 176, 178, 180, 182, 206
Windrush 192, 196, 209
  generation 192, 209
Winlow, Steve 202, 207
Wobblies, the 88, 91, 98

X

xenophobia/xenophobic 14, 160, 173, 198, 204, 209, 225, 242

Y

YouGov poll 170, 174, 196, 197
Younge, Gary 196
Young, Jock 7, 8, 11, 47, 57, 61, 62, 64, 66, 68, 71, 72, 75–78, 95, 107
Young, Michael 201, 207

Z

Zhang, L. 3